AF496655

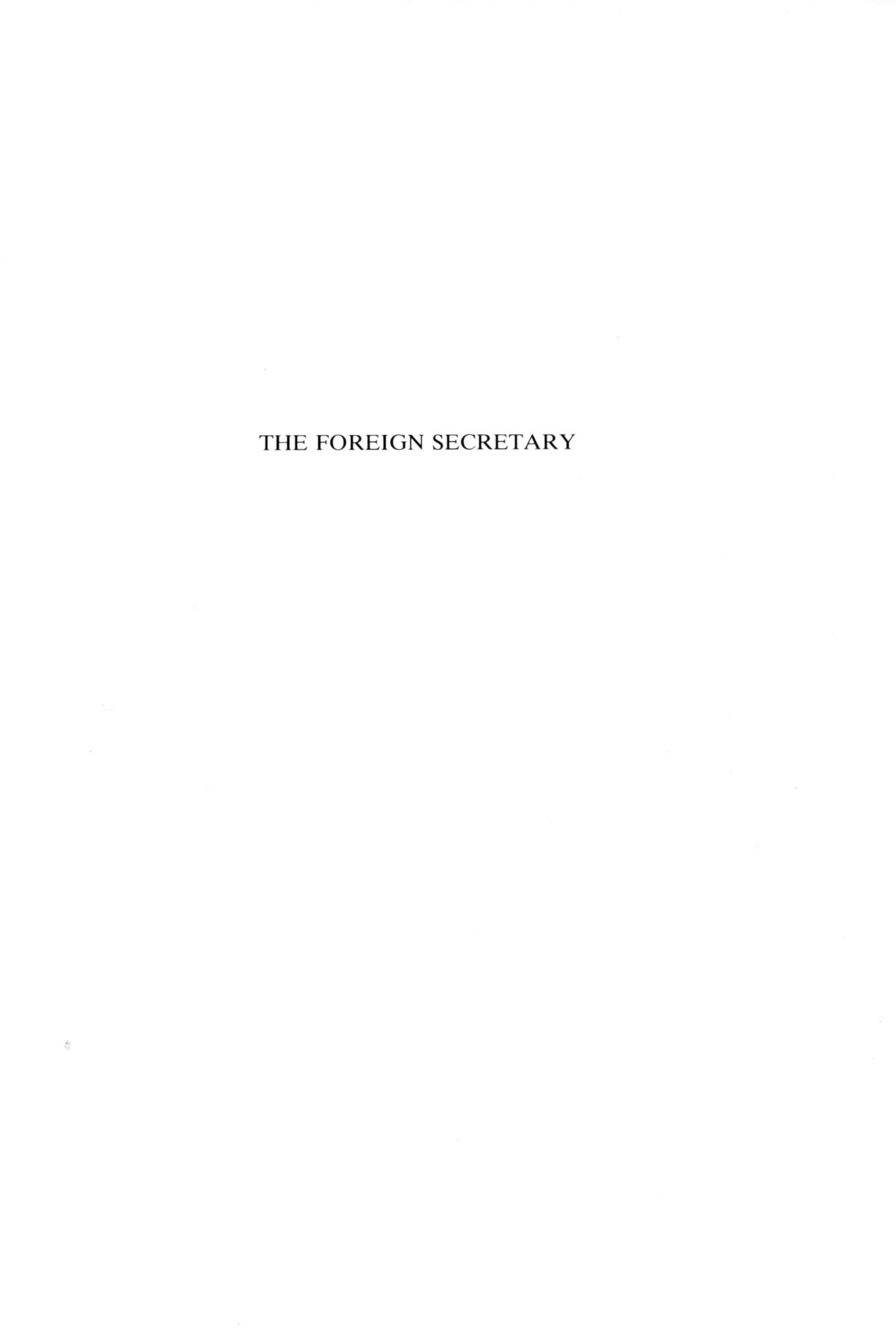

# THE FOREIGN SECRETARY

# THE FOREIGN SECRETARY

by

## NEIL HART

★ ★ ★ ★ ★ ★ ★ ★ ★ ★

## Offices of State
Series Editor: M. M. Reese

★ ★ ★ ★ ★ ★ ★ ★ ★ ★

TERENCE DALTON LIMITED
LAVENHAM . SUFFOLK
1987

Published by
TERENCE  DALTON  LIMITED

ISBN 0 86138 051 7

*Text photoset in 10/13pt Times*

*Printed in Great Britain at*
*The Lavenham Press Limited, Lavenham, Suffolk*

# Contents

# Index of Illustrations

# DEDICATION

for Pamela

# Acknowledgements

This volume does not pretend to be a work of original historical research and is based on no unpublished materials. The debt therefore owed to a large number of scholars will be apparent in the pages that follow. More widely, my especial gratitude is due to my wife and three daughters not only for their encouragement but for their patience during my periods of self-imposed exile from them. Mr Max Reese, the General Editor of this series, brought me to the work and, as an exacting yet entirely sympathetic taskmaster, saw to its completion. I owe a considerable debt to the Master and Fellows of Corpus Christi College, Cambridge, for their generous hospitality while I was working in Cambridge, and especially to the Senior Tutor, Dr Christopher Andrew. From the Librarian and staff of the Cambridge University Library I received unfailing help. In a fruitful reversal of roles my manuscript was read and corrected by my ex-pupil, Dr David Stevenson, of the London School of Economics. His many suggestions on matters of style and interpretation did much to improve my own efforts. I am grateful too for valuable conversations with Mrs Zara Steiner, Dr C. R. Middleton, Mr Kelvin White of the Foreign Office and my colleague Mr Clive Barnett. My thanks are also due to Mrs Thelma Wolfenden who so painstakingly typed large parts of the manuscript. Needless to say, any remaining errors are mine alone.

# Perspective

OF all the great offices of state, the Premiership alone excepted, the Foreign Secretaryship has been the most demanding and the most desirable. The great Lord Salisbury believed that of all the offices in the British Empire only these two were beyond the powers of men of good average ability. For some the Foreign Office has represented the summit of political careers and ambitions. In recent times Lord Carrington has affirmed that "it is the one job I have wanted all my life". For many statesmen the position has been a step to the Premiership: Grenville, Liverpool, Earl Grey, Russell, Aberdeen, Eden, Macmillan, Home and Callaghan were all Foreign Secretaries. Yet for some of those who reached the top of the greasy pole, such as Canning, Palmerston, Salisbury and Rosebery, the Foreign Office was to be preferred. Others, like Castlereagh, held the ascendancy in Cabinet by virtue of being Foreign Secretary, and could scarcely have been more influential even as Prime Minister. Canning is celebrated not as Prime Minister but as Foreign Secretary.

A. J. Balfour maintained that "the Foreign Office is the only departmental position really compatible with the dignity of an ex-Prime Minister". Wellington and Russell, as well as Balfour, were Foreign Secretaries after being Prime Minister. In our own time Sir Alec Douglas-Home was prepared to go back to the Foreign Office, while in 1979 it was widely expected that Edward Heath would accept the Foreign Secretaryship. Three Prime Ministers have combined the Foreign Office and the Premiership: Wellington; Salisbury, on no fewer than three occasions; and Ramsay MacDonald. During the Second World War Churchill considered doing the same thing.

The aristocracy dominated the office of Foreign Secretary from its inception. From 1782 until 1924 all its holders, with the exception of Canning, Grey and Balfour, were peers or the sons of peers. In recent times both Home and Carrington were Secretary of State for Foreign Affairs while members of the House of Lords. Given the heavy work load of the Foreign Office, membership of the Upper House is something of an advantage since the Commons has always made greater demands on time and energy. As holders of Irish peerages, however, Castlereagh and Palmerston sat in the Commons. Palmerston's robust physique carried him through but Castlereagh's double burden (he was also Leader of the House) brought him to breaking-point. Eden faced exactly the same problem during the Second World War. In 1906 Sir Edward Grey, newly arrived in the Foreign Office, had immediately to fight a general election campaign whilst at the sime time dealing with a major international crisis and bearing a deep personal tragedy. Each in his turn (including some of the very ablest of our Foreign Secretaries), Castlereagh, Canning, Palmerston, Salisbury, Grey, Curzon and Eden has testified to the almost intolerable strain of the office. Sir John Simon believed that this was due in large part to the complexity and variety of the problems to be tackled. What historians neatly categorize under headings and sub-headings in semi-watertight compartments all buzz around in the head of a Foreign Secretary at the same time.

Moreover, compared with the foreign ministry staffs of the great European powers, the British Foreign Office establishment was small, especially during the nineteenth century. In 1821 the Office handled just over 6,000 despatches. As British power and influence grew, this number rose to 30,000 by 1849, 51,000 by 1869, 102,000 by 1898 and 111,000 by 1905. Meanwhile the staff increased from 14 in 1796 to 23 in 1832. By 1861 there were still only 37 Foreign Office officials and 52 on the eve of the Great War. Throughout the nineteenth century the Secretary of State drafted all major despatches himself. Even today all telegrams bear his signature. Progress in communications technology has been a blessing and a curse. Typewriters and reprographic systems have, no doubt, saved time and facilitated the wider distribution of information, but the weight of paper is almost beyond control. The electric telegraph, the railway train and steamship, the telephone, aeroplane and telex have provided statesmen and officials with up-to-date intelligence and speedy travel. Nevertheless the strain on Foreign Secretaries has thereby been increased. There is less time to consider a decision. Travelling by horse-drawn coach to the Congress of Vienna gave more time for reflection than journeying by train to the Congress of Berlin, and infinitely more than flying across the Atlantic by Concorde.

Many factors have influenced the development of the office of Foreign Secretary. Two are of paramount importance: the personality, abilities and backgrounds of the incumbents; and the problems with which they had to deal in the context of Britain as a European, imperial and world power. This volume seeks to place these two sets of issues at the centre of the discussion.

There can be no doubt that individual Foreign Secretaries have caused fundamental shifts. Castlereagh's acceptance of the seals in 1812 was crucial to the development of the office itself as well as to British diplomacy. The same might be said of Palmerston's arrival at the Foreign Office in 1830 or Salisbury's in 1878. Scarcely less important was Attlee's decision in 1945 to appoint Bevin as Foreign Secretary rather than Chancellor of the Exchequer.

More than any other office of state, the Foreign Secretaryship has been characterised by continuity. The aims of British diplomacy were, certainly in the nineteenth century, remarkably constant. Foreign policy went across party lines and, for the most part, incoming administrations took on the obligations and commitments of their predecessors. At a very early stage retiring Foreign Secretaries made their experience and papers freely available to their successors who, in office, maintained a two-way exchange. In the nineteenth century personality was probably more important than party; it has been suggested that "the true line of division is not between Whig and Tory, but between activists like Canning, Palmerston, Russell and Rosebery and passivists like Aberdeen, Malmesbury, Granville and the younger Stanley".[1] On the theme of continuity it is especially relevant that men frequently returned for second or more terms as Foreign Secretary. Salisbury held the office on four occasions; Palmerston, Clarendon and Granville three times; Canning, Aberdeen, Russell, Malmesbury, Stanley (Derby) and Rosebery twice. Length of tenure was also important. Castlereagh and Sir Edward Grey were each at the Foreign Office for more than ten years continuously. Palmerston, in his first spell, with only a short break, held the portfolio for a similar period. Altogether Palmerston was Foreign Secretary for sixteen years, Salisbury for almost thirteen and Eden, in his three periods of office, for more than ten. In the forty years from 1812 to 1852 four men, Castlereagh, Canning, Aberdeen and Palmerston, between them occupied the Foreign Office for all but two years. With the exception of the short tenures of Iddesleigh and Kimberley there were only three Foreign Secretaries between 1878 and 1900: Salisbury, Granville and Rosebery. During the whole of the nineteenth century only twenty-three different men held the office. By contrast, in the thirty-four years since the resignation of Bevin in March, 1951, there have been fifteen Foreign Secretaries and only two, Home and Stewart, have enjoyed second terms.

As has been noted, physical and mental resilience are essential qualities for a successful Foreign Secretary. So, rather obviously, is negotiating ability. In the case of Bevin, however, before his appointment in 1945, this skill had been shown in fields other than foreign diplomacy. Among other qualifications are weight and standing in the party: Russell, Derby and Rosebery all provide good illustrations as, resoundingly, does Bevin. Relevant experience in other office is important: as Parliamentary Under Secretary (Eden and Grey); in another major department—the India Office (Salisbury), the War Office (Castlereagh, Palmerston and Lansdowne); or, say, as Viceroy of India (Curzon and Halifax). Travel and a facility with languages have helped to produce Foreign Secretaries with wide perspectives. Great oratory does not seem to have been an essential gift, although Canning was a glowing exception. Needless to say, until after the Second World War the Foreign Secretaryship and the Foreign Office were virtually monopolised by men from the two older universities and a handful of famous schools. In particular Eton and Christ Church, Oxford, seem to have provided an outstandingly large number of them.

In spite of his great power and wide responsibilities no Foreign Secretary has ever enjoyed an entirely free hand. First, and rather obviously, he has been constrained by the nature of Britain's international standing at any given time, by the finite nature of military and naval power (which provide the ultimate backing for diplomacy) and, in turn, by natural resources, population size and finance. In addition, there were significant periods in the nineteenth century when foreign policy took second place to domestic considerations such as Ireland or parliamentary reform. In the parliamentary democracy of Britain Foreign Ministers could never ignore public opinion and, in their different ways, men such as Canning, Palmerston, Salisbury and Austen Chamberlain sought both to shape and to follow it.

Sir Edward Grey believed that in war diplomacy was subordinated to military strategy. Although Eden maintained that "in wartime diplomacy is strategy's twin",[2] Grey's judgement was probably more correct.

A constant theme in the work of any Foreign Secretary is his relationships with his colleagues, particularly the Prime Minister. "The relationship of the Premier with his Foreign Secretary remained one of the most important factors in the changing patterns of British diplomacy."[3] Balfour considered it to be "the rarest thing when the Prime Minister and the Foreign Secretary don't clash . . . But you can't expect the P.M. *not* to interfere with Foreign Office business. It's only when you get a combination of two men who see absolutely eye to eye and work in perfect harmony that you can avoid it . . . The fact is that the Foreign Office cannot be a watertight compartment".[4] Relationships between Prime Ministers and Foreign Secretaries follow four major patterns: harmony, where there is close agreement on aims and methods; a strong Foreign Secretary who is given a free hand either because his chief entirely trusts him or is not sufficiently interested or expert to interfere; a strong Prime Minister whose foreign minister is simply a subordinate; clashes between two strong personalities which arise out of improper interference on the part of the Premier or undue independence by the Foreign Secretary. These basic patterns can be illustrated as follows. Halifax and Chamberlain were in close harmony, although here the Foreign Secretary tended to play a subordinate role. Baldwin gave a free hand to Austen Chamberlain, as did Asquith to Grey and Attlee to Bevin. The early Foreign Secretaries under Pitt were for the most part his ciphers. By contrast Lord Rosebery, with the support of the Queen, was able to safeguard his position under Gladstone. On the other hand, Lloyd George treated Curzon shamefully, at times conducting what amounted to a foreign policy of his own, and almost any other Foreign Secretary would have resigned. Eden did resign. He left Chamberlain's government in 1938 on the ground that he could not work with a Prime Minister who, exceptionally interested and active in foreign affairs, had so blatantly interfered in his sphere.

In Cabinet the Foreign Secretary is regarded as being responsible for the day-to-day running of foreign policy, with the obligation of consulting and informing his colleagues. Nevertheless there have been times when the Cabinet as a whole has been deliberately kept in ignorance. A notable example is the matter of early twentieth-century Anglo-French relations, when Edward Grey consulted and informed only the Prime Minister and one or two other close colleagues. To a large extent, of course, Cabinet members have been bound to give Foreign Secretaries considerable latitude since they lacked the necessary detailed and expert knowledge. Even so when Eden joined the Cabinet, Baldwin, the Prime Minister, thought it worth pointing out that of Eden's twenty colleagues there was probably only one who thought that he should be Minister of Labour and nineteen who thought they should be Foreign Secretary. As further encouragement for the newcomer, Baldwin recalled having seen Curzon burst into tears when the Cabinet saw fit to amend his despatches. Foreign Secretaries have been placed in some considerable difficulty when Cabinets have contained colleagues who have previously held their office. When Clarendon took over in 1853, he had four ex-Foreign Secretaries to deal with: Aberdeen, Russell, Granville and Palmerston. In certain aspects of their work Foreign Secretaries have found other Departments of State to possess a strong interest and reason to interfere; the War Office, the Admiralty, the Colonial and Indian Offices provide obvious examples.

An additional influence, and indeed interference, was that of the Crown. The sovereign's interest in the business of the Foreign Office persisted longer than in any other department. All the nineteenth-century monarchs felt that they had an important role to play in foreign policy. After all, diplomacy was concerned with relations with fellow-monarchs and other heads of state. Had it not been for the fall of the European dynasties as a result of the Great War, royal influence might have been maintained even longer.

Finally, what of the influence of the Foreign Office itself? For the most part nineteenth-century Foreign Secretaries made policy quite independently of their officials. The great watershed was at the beginning of the twentieth century during the tenures of Lansdowne and Grey. From that period a group of ambitious, able and far-sighted officials set out to make their department a policy-making institution. On the eve of the First World War the Office reached its peak of influence and power. Although it came under considerable attack after 1918 for its part in drawing Britain into the war, and for its aristocratic and exclusive membership and structure, its senior officials continued to hold great influence with their political chiefs. In the pre- and inter-war years the holders of the Permanent Under-Secretaryship, men such as Charles Hardinge, Eyre Crowe and Robert Vansittart, were especially formidable. Their role in formulating and conducting foreign policy was highly significant. Nevertheless it is the overwhelming impression that even in the twentieth century the Foreign Secretaries were still in ultimate control. Not everyone would share Under-Secretary Cadogan's view of his political masters that "they embody everything that my training has taught me to eschew—ambition, prejudice, dishonesty, self-seeking light-hearted irresponsibility, black-hearted mendacity".

**NOTES TO PERSPECTIVE**

1  Donald Southgate. *The Passing of the Whigs* (London, 1962), p. 266.
2  Earl of Avon. *The Eden Memoirs: The Reckoning* (London, 1965), p. 183.
3  Zara Steiner. *The Foreign Office and Foreign Policy* (Cambridge, 1969), p. 3.
4  B. E. C. Dugdale. *Arthur James Balfour*, Vol. II pp 292–293. Quoted by John P. Mackintosh. *The British Cabinet* (London, 3rd Edition, 1976), p. 460.

8

**CHAPTER ONE**

SECRETARIES OF STATE

| | |
|---|---|
| Charles James Fox | March 1782–July 1782 |
| Thomas Robinson, second Baron Grantham | July 1782–April 1783 |
| Charles James Fox | April 1783–December 1783 |
| George Nugent-Temple-Grenville, second Earl Temple | December 1783 |
| Francis Godolphin Osborne, Marquess of Carmarthen, fifth Duke of Leeds | December 1783–April 1791 |
| William Wyndham Grenville, first Baron Grenville | April 1791–February 1801 |
| Robert Banks Jenkinson, Baron Hawkesbury, afterwards second Earl of Liverpool | February 1801–May 1804 |
| Dudley Ryder, Baron Harrowby, afterwards first Earl of Harrowby | May 1804–January 1805 |
| Henry Phipps, Baron Mulgrave, afterwards first Earl of Mulgrave | January 1805–February 1806 |
| Charles James Fox | February 1806–September 1806 |
| Charles Grey, Viscount Howick, afterwards second Earl Grey | September 1806–March 1807 |
| George Canning | March 1807–October 1809 |
| Henry Bathurst, third Earl Bathurst | October 1809–December 1809 |
| Richard Colley Wellesley, first Marquess of Wellesley | December 1809–March 1812 |
| Robert Stewart, Viscount Castlereagh, afterwards second Marquess of Londonderry | March 1812–August 1822 |

# "Mr. Fox's Office"

## Foundations

THE creation of the Foreign Secretaryship in March, 1782, took place in the unpropitious circumstances of British defeat in the American War of Independence. Not until 1812, when Castlereagh accepted the seals, was the full potential of the office to be realised. Then, tenure by a man of remarkable powers coincided with a period of British pre-eminence. The Foreign Secretaryship became one of the truly great offices of state and its special importance was secured. In the years ahead the history of the office and of foreign policy itself was to be the history of the Foreign Secretaries.

Charles James Fox was the first Secretary of State for Foreign Affairs. His appointment to undertake "the sole Direction of the Department of Foreign Affairs" began the modern division between the Home and Foreign Offices which replaced the older Northern and Southern Departments. Before 1782 neither of these departments had had sole responsibility for foreign policy; there had been a theoretical geographical division but the two secretaries had intrigued against each other and trespassed shamelessly. There were occasions when both secretaries had accredited representatives at the same foreign courts. The new Home Office confined itself to domestic and colonial affairs, although until the mid-nineteenth century it also dealt with Algiers, Morocco, Tripoli and Tunis. As the sole minister responsible for foreign relations the Foreign Secretary gained special prestige which grew with Britain's own rise as a great power. Not surprisingly, the establishment of the Foreign Office has been judged "the most important administrative change in the sphere of foreign policy during the eighteenth century".[1]

Before 1782, not only had foreign policy been subject to divided ministerial responsibility but it had been much influenced by the Crown as well as by Parliament and public opinion. While George III retained his mental powers he was remarkably influential and very well informed. His immediate successors were less effective but the Crown continued to play an important role in foreign affairs throughout the nineteenth century and beyond. During the eighteenth century, foreign policy had been conducted as a result of discussions between the sovereign and his chosen advisers; relations with other states had for long been a jealously guarded aspect of the royal prerogative. Nevertheless, the constitutional changes of the late seventeenth century, and parliament's control of the commanding heights of finance, brought the legislature strongly into the field of foreign policy. Eighteenth-century governments were at pains to avoid parliamentary opposition to their foreign policies, but scarcely a session went by without a major debate on external relations. In some respects such open debates put Britain at a disadvantage compared to foreign despotisms. Moreover, foreigners were surprised at the degree of influence wielded by the eighteenth-century press and other expressions of opinion, such as lobbying by the great merchant companies and the City of London. British statesmen lamented that the country's cards were played too far from the chest, as when *The Times* printed details of the movements of the French and Spanish Fleets before the Battle of Trafalgar, thus giving prior warning that their manoeuvres were equally well known to the Admiralty.

By 1782 certain central aims of British foreign policy were clearly recognized. Although the loss of the American colonies made for some new departures, these objectives were generally maintained. They played their part in the conduct of the French Revolutionary and Napoleonic Wars and, with some modifications, continued through the nineteenth century and into the twentieth. It was axiomatic, for example, that Britain should act to preserve the European balance of power. Such a strategy did not involve the permanent acquisition of continental territories. Instead the Low Countries were to be kept in friendly or neutral hands. Action was also taken to prevent any dramatic change in the European state systems. To the same end it was already considered desirable to maintain what was later called the two-power naval standard; Britain aimed to outrank the combined fleets of the next two greatest maritime powers. The use of naval blockade, so effective in future wars, had been developed too.

For strategic as well as commercial reasons, a strong presence was necessary in the Mediterranean; Gibraltar had been taken from Spain in 1704 and, over the next century, Minorca, Malta and Sicily all came to be used as naval bases. The Baltic supplied naval stores and raw material for industry and these considerations did much to determine relations with

Russia. Further afield, in the Caribbean, Canada and the American colonies, in Africa and India, commercial motives were paramount. Such interests had led Britain into a wide-ranging colonial war with France and Spain between 1756 and 1763.


## Foreign Policy 1782–1815

At the end of the Seven Years War, in 1763, Britain's very success and her spectacular colonial gains left her isolated in Europe. The Bourbon rulers of France and Spain awaited their opportunity for revenge; Prussia and Russia were unwilling to aid the maintenance of British supremacy. When the American colonies rebelled the Bourbons seized their chance while Russia and the Scandinavians stood aside in an armed neutrality. The result was a humiliating reverse for Britain, the independence of the American colonies, and the loss of substantial imperial territories. Even so, a naval recovery at the end of the war, together with British diplomacy, achieved a remarkable salvage operation at the Treaty of Versailles in 1783.

William Pitt became Prime Minister in the aftermath of defeat; the ink was scarcely dry on the peace treaties when he took office. Not only did he achieve reconstruction at home, probably the best-known aspect of his work, but he also aimed to restore British influence abroad and to bring her out of isolation. His responsibility for the new directions in foreign policy was very considerable; "his influence was personal and direct, for his first Foreign Secretary (Carmarthen) was a mere clerk in his hands".[2] Pitt directed the negotiations of his envoys abroad, of whom the most remarkable were William Eden, Sir James Harris and William Grenville, and wrote despatches himself.

There was limited success in making commercial treaties, although negotiations were opened with a range of countries. Relations with the new United States remained troubled, and clashing trading and shipping interests were a major stumbling-block. The one major success in this field was the commercial treaty of 1786 negotiated with France by Eden.

Much more was achieved in the field of political diplomacy. In 1785 France made an alliance with the States-General of Holland. Traditionally, Holland and its leading family, the House of Orange, had been a friend of Britain. Now the States-General had overthrown the predominance of the

Prince of Orange while moving into the orbit of France. The dangers of a strong French presence in the Low Countries aroused all the old feelings of British Francophobia as well as fears for the European balance of power. As a result Britain drew closer to Prussia whose King, Frederick William II, was the brother-in-law of the Prince of Orange. In the late summer of 1787 Prussia, with powerful British diplomatic support, made a military intervention in Holland to restore Orangist authority. France, hamstrung by a grave financial crisis and a rising crescendo of political discontent, failed to act. A further triumph followed in 1788 when Prussia and the Dutch joined Britain in a Triple Alliance.

Outside Europe, but almost as important for the restoration of British prestige, was a dispute with Spain in North America. In 1790 a small British settlement at Nootka Sound, in what is now Vancouver Island, was overthrown by Spaniards. With the support of public opinion parliament voted large sums in preparation for war and a fleet was made ready. With the support of the Triple Alliance, firm diplomacy and the threat of force, Britain prevailed upon Spain to grant compensation. France, once again, stood aside.

By contrast, Pitt's attempt in 1791 to check a Russian advance at the expense of Turkey failed to gain public support. On this occasion Britain was compelled to back down. To gain a base on the Black Sea, Russia had taken the city of Oczakov from Turkey, and Pitt presented an ultimatum to the Empress Catherine II for its return. In spite of Pitt's fears about a changing balance of power in South-eastern Europe, and the beginnings of a realization that Russia might in time constitute a threat to the British position in India, nothing could be done. Russia kept Oczakov. In the eighteenth century British public opinion was inclined to be Russophile; in the next century rabid Russophobia took its place.

The end of British isolation and the recovery of her international prestige came not a moment too soon. The great French Revolution of 1789 breathed fresh life and vigour into that country and the challenge which the new rulers offered to the ancien régime throughout Europe set the continent ablaze. However, for Britain, the issues in the war she entered in 1793 were far from ideological. She was concerned as always to prevent the overthrow of other states by French armies, and the domination of Europe by one great power. In addition, her colonial, commercial and naval interests had to be safeguarded. There was a powerful anti-French bias to British policy whoever ruled in Paris or Versailles.

The immediate cause of Britain going to war with the new French republic was its successful invasion of the Austrian Netherlands (modern Belgium) and the threat posed to Holland. Pitt's aims were limited to helping Austria, thus relieving the threat to the Netherlands while redressing the European balance of power; to safeguarding Britain's interests in the Mediterranean and Baltic; to taking any opportunity of stripping France of her colonial and commercial assets.

On land, Britain's efforts met with scant success. An expedition to the Low Countries under the Duke of York accomplished nothing, while interventions on the mainland of France, at Toulon in 1793 and Quiberon in 1795, were mere pinpricks. The policy of joining forces with expeditions to the West Indies drew severe criticism; Burke called it "a terrible roundabout road", and the casualties were disastrous. Nevertheless, substantial colonial gains were made in the Caribbean and Indian Ocean. At sea a string of naval victories, the Glorious First of June in 1794, Cape St Vincent and Camperdown in 1797 and the Nile in 1798, did much to save the government's reputation. Britain's maritime, commercial and colonial interests were upheld. As for diplomacy, Britain turned once more to her traditional policy of subsidising and otherwise supporting the enemies of France. In the first phase of the great French wars, between 1793 and 1802, Britain built up and sustained two coalitions. Unfortunately, they were never more than very loose-knit confederations and were brought down by French victories, internal divisions and other preoccupations outside Western Europe. Russia, for example, found much to engage her attention in Poland. On the Continent, therefore, revolutionary France went from strength to strength and there was a gaining realization that she represented a truly formidable menace of a new kind.

As early as 1793 Castlereagh had written: "The tranquillity of Europe is at stake and we contend with an opponent whose strength we have no means of measuring. It is the first time that all the population and all the wealth of a great kingdom has been concentrated in the field: what may be the result is beyond my perception".[3] An extra dimension was added when Napoleon Bonaparte seized power as First Consul of France in November, 1799.

Not surprisingly, during a long-drawn-out war of disappointing results, the British Government seriously considered a compromise peace. Diplomatic approaches began as early as 1795 but talks broke down in 1796 and again in 1797. In 1801, however, a further opportunity presented itself with the final collapse of the Second Coalition. By this time Pitt had resigned, on issues unconnected with foreign policy and war, to bring Addington in as head of the ministry. The outcome was the Treaty of Amiens, signed in March, 1802. It proved disastrous for Britain. Bonaparte eventually conceded nothing while Britain gave up most of her gains, including Malta and the Cape. To make matters worse, Bonaparte was able to continue his policy of aggression and expansion under the cloak of peace. Within fourteen months Britain declared war.

The renewal of hostilities in May, 1803, was rather more than a second phase of the struggle which preceded Amiens. In some ways it was a different war altogether. First, George III's government was no longer dealing with a republic which threatened the Low Countries and disturbed the equilibrium of Europe, but an Emperor whose ambition it was completely to dominate the whole continent. Second, Britain's own survival was at risk. Invasion was a serious possibility in 1805 and this threat did not disappear with the victory at Trafalgar. Moreover, Napoleon's Continental System, launched by the Berlin Decrees in 1806, used Britain's own weapon of economic blockade and embargo against her. Britain's response, the Orders in Council, imposed a counter-blockade which damaged France but also placed serious restrictions on the freedom of neutrals to trade. A particularly important result was the further damage caused to Anglo-American relations, already uneasy as a result of the impressment of United States citizens in the Royal Navy. War with the Americans broke out in June, 1812, and did not end until the Treaty of Ghent in 1815.

With Britain at war again Pitt's return to office was not long delayed. As before, the major aim of diplomacy was to construct a coalition. This was done during the spring and summer of 1805 and drew Russia, Austria and Sweden together with Britain. Once again, however, internal disagreements and crushing defeats caused the alliance to collapse. In autumn, 1805, the Austrians were defeated at Ulm and before the year was out the Austro-Russian armies were routed at Austerlitz. This was a severe blow to Pitt, who died early the next year. Defeats followed for Prussia at Jena in October, 1806, and for Russia at Friedland in 1807. Napoleon, now the master of Europe, made the Treaty of Tilsit with Tsar Alexander I. Britain was isolated. The conduct of British foreign policy suffered gravely from Pitt's death and the gap was not properly filled until June, 1812, when Castlereagh, Pitt's disciple and political protégé, became Foreign Secretary.

A new departure for Britain in the struggle against Napoleon was the sending of substantial forces to the continental mainland, not just as an expedition but as a long-standing commitment. The first such operation was in the Iberian Peninsula. Napolean had initially allied with Spain, then tried to annex it to his empire. The Spaniards resisted. British troops landed in 1808 under the future Duke of Wellington, Sir Arthur Wellesley. At first, the position of this army was perilous and an anxious section of public opinion clamoured for its recall. However, Wellesley made sure of his foothold. In 1811 he was able to expel the French from Portugal and step by step and victory by victory he drove his way across Spain, crossed the Pyrenees and defeated the enemy on their own soil at Toulouse in April, 1814.

On the other side of Europe, in 1812 Napoleon embarked on his fatal invasion of Russia. His disastrous retreat encouraged the Tsar to push forward into Polish territory and brought Russia and Prussia together in an alliance. The foundations of a fourth coalition were laid; Austria joined after failing to gain terms for a negotiated peace and Britain entered in her familiar role of paymaster. Although Napoleon was decisively defeated at Leipzig, the Battle of the Nations, in October, 1813, he was by no means finished. There was the possibility that he might once again break the coalition apart. It was the personal intervention of Castlereagh, who met the allied rulers as they marched on the French frontiers, that pulled the alliance firmly together. In so doing he played "a part in settling Europe never equalled by any British statesman".[4] By the Treaty of Chaumont in March, 1814, the allied powers agreed to unite for the complete overthrow of Napoleon and the preservation of European peace. Britain agreed to divide a subsidy of £5 million between her allies and to contribute 150,000 men. As a result of this unity and determination Napoleon was forced into exile on Elba. Europe was still not safe, however. Napoleon's defeat at Waterloo in the summer of 1815, after his escape from Elba, was by no means a foregone conclusion. That his defeat was accomplished was in no small part a result of the self-same considerations that had prevailed at

Chaumont: British diplomacy and gold and her commitment of large-scale land forces. In 1815 Britain stood on a pinnacle of power and influence greater than she had ever known.

## The Early Foreign Office and the First Foreign Secretaries

The office of Foreign Secretary took time to acquire the prestige and weight that it enjoyed in the nineteenth century. Castlereagh's appointment was the great turning-point in its development. Much depended upon the personalities and abilities of the men who held the position. Apart from Fox and Grenville the early Foreign Secretaries were political lightweights like Carmarthen; lacking in experience like Hawkesbury; indolent in the case of Wellesley, or in some other way men of little account and virtual ciphers of the Prime Minister. For almost the whole of the first twenty-five years of the Foreign Secretaryship Pitt himself was the first minister. His interest and activity in the field of foreign policy were direct and powerful. Moreover, during the twenty-year struggle with France diplomacy generally took second place to war. After 1815 diplomacy had more scope since the main objective of external relations was the maintenance of peace.

"Mr Fox's Office" took over the staff and premises of the old Northern Department in Cleveland Row. In 1786 it moved to a house in Whitehall belonging to the Duke of Dorset and seven years later to Lord Sheffield's house in Downing Street. As work and staff expanded, houses were acquired on either side but the old Foreign Office was always cramped and inconvenient. Sir Horace Rumbold described the buildings as "dingy and shabby to a degree, made up of dark floors and labyrinthine passages—four houses at least tumbled into one, with floors at uneven levels and wearying corkscrew stairs that were cursed as they climbed—a thorough picture of disorder, penury and meanness".[5] In 1861 the demolition of the old buildings was begun, to make way for the splendid edifice designed by Scott which houses the present-day Foreign and Commonwealth Office. During the work the department operated from Pembroke House and Malmesbury House in Whitehall Gardens. The final move took place in 1868.

The staff of the Office was small in 1782, consisting of two Under-Secretaries and eight clerks. By 1796 the salaries ranged from £1,500 for the Under-Secretaries to £80 for the most junior clerk, with £650 for a senior clerk. These were substantial sums. The first chief clerk was Jeremy

Sneyd, who had joined the Northern Department in 1750. In 1785 he described the work of the Office as "conducting correspondence with all Foreign Courts, negotiating with the Ambassadors or Ministers of all the Foreign Courts in Europe, as well as of the United States of America, and receiving and making representations and applications to and from the same, and in corresponding with the other principal Departments of State thereupon".[6] Most clerks started their careers in their teens, and for many their place of work became their home. Certainly after the Office moved to Downing Street the attics were occupied by young clerks who brought in a piano, boxing-gloves and other amusements. Their quarters were dubbed "the Nursery".

The work of the clerks was routine with no responsibility for formulating policy or even giving advice. They prepared correspondence and copied despatches as well as recording these items in the registers. Ciphering and deciphering fell to the more senior men. The chief clerks distributed their duties. At first the work seems to have been light, and regular attendance was required only from eleven in the morning to four in the afternoon. As the Office got into its stride, however, its business rapidly expanded and when Carmarthen was Foreign Secretary there were complaints to him of overwork. Although there seems to have been no security clearance of the clerks they were remarkably trustworthy; at the Congress of Vienna, for example, only the British delegation succeeded in keeping confidential material out of the hands of the Austrian secret police. The clerks were not always so dependable when it came to supplying opposition leaders with information.

At the head of the Office and directly responsible to the Secretary of State were the Under-Secretaries. For most of the early period there were two. Even they had relatively little influence over policy, although no doubt they gave informal advice when asked. They allocated work, composed reports and drafted despatches. A crucial development in the history of the Office was the emergence of the position of Permanent Under-Secretary as the chief official in the department. In 1782 such a position did not exist: one at least of the Under-Secretaries was closely identified with the Secretary of State and almost invariably left office with him. The other Under-Secretary tended not to be replaced with each minister, and some had risen from clerkships. Although, generally speaking, after 1795 only one Under-Secretary was changed, the first official to refer to himself as Permanent Under-Secretary and to define his role was John Backhouse. He served Canning during his second term as Foreign Secretary and, although he had the closest political connections with Canning, he survived his chief's death in 1827 as well as the withdrawal of the Canningites from the Government in 1828.

As to social origins, the Under-Secretaries were drawn very largely from the upper class of peerage and gentry, with a sprinkling from the professions. A number were M.P.s, particularly before 1808, while some, like Dudley Ryder (later Earl of Harrowby) and George Canning, later obtained Cabinet rank and even the Foreign Secretaryship itself.

The aristocracy dominated the Cabinets of the late eighteenth and early nineteenth centuries. All the early Foreign Secretaries, with the exception of Canning, were peers or sons of peers; indeed this tradition was maintained until Sir Edward Grey came to office in 1905. Of the first twelve Foreign Secretaries four—Grenville, Canning, Hawkesbury (as Earl of Liverpool) and Howick (as Earl Grey)—subsequently served as Prime Minister, while a fifth (Harrowby) refused the post when offered. The importance of the office was reflected in the salary, £5,680 in 1782 plus fees and other revenues. Although the early development of the Foreign Secretaryship was retarded by Pitt's powerful influence over policy it nevertheless became highly sought after, especially with the growth of British power abroad. Since the administrative changes of 1782 had given sole responsibility for the conduct of foreign relations to one Secretary, it became more and more difficult for Cabinet colleagues to challenge his authority. Certainly the Cabinet had a part to play in formulating the broad lines of foreign policy but, except in a crisis, it did not interfere in the day-to-day running of the Foreign Office, nor did other ministers have the necessary knowledge and information to do so. Within the Foreign Office itself, although the smallness of the staff placed a great strain on him, the Secretary of State had a free hand. The department's regular and central activity was correspondence with British representatives abroad—a handful of ambassadors in the major capitals, envoys and consuls elsewhere. The Foreign Office received copious information, albeit often out of date, and sent instructions back. Few other ministers had the time or even the inclination to master the details of foreign policy and, generally speaking, only the Prime Minister and Foreign Secretary kept a close eye. When Prime Minister and Foreign Secretary disagreed, however, the foreign minister generally had the final say. On a good many issues the early Foreign Secretaries, like their successors, either acted independently or consulted a very small group of Cabinet colleagues, sometimes simply the Prime Minister. In the 1790s an inner Cabinet consisting of Pitt, Grenville (then Foreign Secretary) and Dundas[7] frequently met before full Cabinets to decide upon matters concerning the whole sweep of foreign and war policy.

As to the Crown, George III, immensely hard-working, attentive to detail and very experienced, showed a special interest in foreign policy. He exercised considerable influence and was within his constitutional rights to do so. On most issues he accepted the recommendations of his ministers but his agreement could never be taken for granted. George read despatches, often before ministers themselves, and even took the initiative by suggesting lines of policy. In exceptional cases George possessed the ultimate threat of replacing a minister. On some issues he stubbornly held out for his own view. During the 1790s, for example, he strongly opposed his ministers' proposals for a negotiated peace with France. For the most part, however, King and Cabinet were in close agreement.

The first Foreign Secretary, Charles James Fox, was one of the very ablest of the early period. His appointment on 25th March, 1782, in Rockingham's ministry was immensely popular, he was the people's idol, but his reputation in establishment circles was less secure. In 1774 George III had written: "That young man has so thoroughly cast off every principle of common honour and honesty that he must soon become as contemptible as he is odious".[8] At an early age he had been taken off to Paris by his father, where he had been encouraged to indulge himself. Thereafter, his foppishness, extravagance and heavy drinking and gambling were conducted on an impressive scale. At one stage his debts amounted to £140,000. Yet he had great talents: he was an entertaining and shrewd speaker in the House of Commons; a fluent linguist who had spent long periods abroad, especially in Italy and France; a good all-round sportsman; widely read. At his best he was warm-hearted and unselfish. He spoke in favour of parliamentary reform and relief for Catholics. As a minister he proved an indefatigable worker.

Having for years attacked the King's minister, Lord North, and the conduct of the American War it fell to Fox to negotiate for peace. Alas, a major obstacle lay within the Cabinet itself. The reorganization of the

Secretaryships had given Shelburne the home department together with the colonies. Whereas negotiations with France clearly belonged to Fox, Shelburne claimed to deal with America, which was technically not yet independent and thus fell within the colonial sphere. For obvious reasons Fox proposed that the independence of America be unconditionally recognized. He could then properly claim to negotiate the entire peace settlement. At first the Cabinet supported Fox's view although the King took Shelburne's side. Thus the two Secretaries regarded each other with suspicion and jealousy. Meanwhile, negotiations proceeded separately: Thomas Grenville, Fox's envoy to France, treated with Vergennes, the French foreign minister; Richard Oswald, Shelburne's representative in Paris, held conversations with the head of the American delegation, Benjamin Franklin. In the Cabinet, rivalry and intrigue reigned and, when a majority swung round to Shelburne, Fox made up his mind to resign. He delayed because of the critical illness of his chief, Rockingham. When he died on 1st July the King sent for Shelburne. Fox then immediately surrendered his seals. This decision has been regarded as the greatest error of Fox's political career; his resignation appeared petulant and partisan.

Within less than a year, however, Fox was back in the Foreign Office. Shelburne fell for two reasons; the unpopularity of the peace treaties he had made and an unholy alliance between Fox and North. The first task was the formal completion of the treaties with France, Spain, Holland and the Americans, and Fox was unable to improve upon Shelburne's terms. His main plan thereafter was to work for a continental alliance to balance France and Spain. Prussia would have been a desirable ally but the ministry was too short-lived for any worthwhile achievement: it was brought down in December, 1783, by royal manoeuvrings and its own inherent divisions.

Fox's third term as Foreign Secretary began in January, 1806, in the "Ministry of All the Talents" headed by Grenville and brought to office by the death of Pitt. Europe had utterly changed since Fox had last held office. In 1789 he had welcomed the French Revolution with the words: "How much the greatest event it is that ever happened in the world! And how much the best." As revolutionary violence increased, and Britain went to war, he lost more and more support even though he condemned the September Massacres in 1792 and the execution of Louis XVI in 1793. Fox approved the Treaty of Amiens and in 1802 went on a tour of the Low Countries and France, meeting with Bonaparte himself. Fox was not impressed: "a young man considerably intoxicated with success"[9] was his opinion. In 1804 Pitt had wished to bring Fox into his ministry but the King had objected.

This last spell at the Foreign Office was "disillusioning and disheartening".[10] He longed for peace but circumstances prevented him from achieving a negotiated settlement. Napoleon was bent on conquest. Nevertheless, when Fox was approached by a disaffected Frenchman named Gervillière, with a plan for the assassination of Napoleon as a way of bringing peace to Europe, he had the man arrested and informed Talleyrand, the French foreign minister. Negotiations with France were begun but broke down when Fox became convinced that the Emperor was playing him false. By the summer of 1806 Fox's health was seriously impaired, he gave up attending the House and died of dropsy in September. He was buried in Westminster Abbey close to his lifetime rival, Pitt.

Fox's undistinguished successor in July, 1782, and the second Foreign Secretary, was Thomas Robinson, second Baron Grantham. Shelburne called upon his assistance in negotiating the Treaty of Versailles, which Grantham believed to be "as good a one as, considering our situation, we could possibly have". He resigned with the fall of the ministry early in 1783 with a pension of £2,000 per annum. When offered the seals again in Pitt's first ministry in December, 1783, he declined. Instead, Pitt's first Foreign Secretary was Earl Temple, who lasted just four days. Temple's successor, Francis Osborne, Marquess of Carmarthen and later Duke of Leeds, presided rather longer, until April, 1791, but "brought to the Government more of polish than weight".[11] At least he did not complain when others, such as Dundas, Grenville and Hawkesbury, undertook matters, like commercial negotiations, which properly belonged to his department. In any case, Pitt ran foreign policy as a whole and Leeds was no real loss when he resigned over the Oczakov incident. His staff, however, clearly had some affection for him and presented his wife with a portrait of him.

Pitt's other long-serving Foreign Secretary, and certainly his ablest, was William Wyndham Grenville, first Baron Grenville. Not only was he Pitt's cousin but also his trusted friend and confidant. He resigned with Pitt in 1801. Grenville had already served in a number of ministerial offices under Pitt, including Home Secretary, as well as being employed on diplomatic missions to the Hague and Paris. His command of French was excellent, "probably better than that of any British Foreign Secretary before or since",[12] and he paid close attention to the day-to-day business of his department. He was a patrician and an outstanding patriot; able, energetic and courageous, yet haughty, cold and unbending. Once the war had started he proved an unrelenting enemy of revolutionary France. It was he who expelled the French ambassador, Chauvelin, with the message: "His Majesty has thought fit that you should retire from this Kingdom within the term of eight days".[13]

His views were well summed up when he wrote to his brother in September, 1794, "it is a perfect blindness not to see that in the establishment of the French republic is included the overthrow of all the other governments of Europe".[14] When peace negotiations were mooted Grenville always stood at the head of the war party.

Robert Banks Jenkinson, Baron Hawkesbury, was appointed Foreign Secretary when Addington came in as Prime Minister in February, 1801. He was aged thirty. After his first government appointment, soon after the outbreak of war, he was scarcely out of office for the rest of his life. As the Earl of Liverpool he was Prime Minister from 1812 to 1827. Yet his period at the Foreign Office was disappointing.

By far his most important task was the negotiation of the Peace of Amiens and the defence of its provisions in the House of Commons. The talks opened four days after he came in and were largely completed by the following autumn. The terms aroused howls of protest as Britain threw away most of the advantages she had won. In Hawkesbury's defence it should be said that the war had reached a stalemate; there was anti-war fever in Britain, Bonaparte's aide-de-camp, General Lauriston, was dragged in triumph through the streets of London; Hawkesbury was young and very inexperienced and his Prime Minister was second rate. But fail he did and it was as much for the shortcomings of his character as for those of his policies that Pitt dropped him when he returned to the premiership in 1804. Hawkesbury was not only very nervous, being referred to by Huskisson as the "great figitatus",[15] but was heartily disliked by foreign representatives in London. George III regarded him as utterly unfit for his office and said that Hawkesbury "always approached him with a vacant kind of grin, and had hardly anything business-like to say".[16] For the future development of the Foreign Secretaryship, however, one aspect of Hawkesbury's tenure was of considerable importance. On relinquishing

Charles James Fox, seen in an engraving from the *European Magazine*.
*The Mansell Collection*

William Wyndham Grenville, first Baron Grenville, by John Hoppner.

the Secretaryship Grenville had offered Hawkesbury any aid or knowledge he might require. Once in office Hawkesbury sent draft despatches to his predecessor for comment and criticism. This fruitful interchange set a precedent.

In his second administration Pitt was served by two Foreign Secretaries: Dudley Ryder, first Earl of Harrowby, until 1805 and Henry Phipps, first Earl of Mulgrave. Both were loyal supporters of Pitt but undistinguished Secretaries of State. At the end of 1804 Harrowby had the misfortune to fall on his head in the Foreign Office itself. Malmesbury recorded in his diary that Harrowby thereupon resigned since he was rendered "totally disqualified for so laborious a post".[17]

Mulgrave was a soldier who had served in the American war and later reached the rank of general. The common opinion was that the Foreign Secretaryship was beyond his powers; Thomas Grenville in writing to the Marquess of Buckingham suggested that he had been "put in *ad interim* until Lord Wellesley's arrival who is expected in June".[18] Nevertheless, he proved satisfactory in debate and certainly kept a close eye on the details of running his department. For example, he instructed that clerks should not leave the premises without first gaining the consent of an Under-Secretary. Such pernicketiness did not make for popularity.

Fox's successor in the Ministry of All the Talents was Charles Grey, Viscount Howick. Previously First Lord of the Admiralty in the same ministry, he now combined the Foreign Secretaryship with leading the Government in the Commons. Although he continued Fox's negotiations with Napoleon he had no success and his period of office was too short for any real judgement to be made of his capacity. He resigned with the rest of the ministry in March, 1807. When he next came to office, more than twenty years later, it was as Earl Grey, the Prime Minister who passed the Great Reform Bill.

Canning's fame rests upon his second period as Foreign Secretary from 1822 to 1827. Nevertheless, his first spell (under Portland, March 1807, to October, 1809) was eventful and controversial. The Marquess of Wellesley had been the Prime Minister's first choice, but when he declined, Canning was swiftly transferred from the Admiralty. Canning's policies were risky and aroused great criticism but times were desperate, perhaps the critical period of the whole war, and bold measures were required. "As Foreign Secretary, at a time of grave and deepening crisis in the struggle against

Napoleon, Canning was more stretched, with more work and responsibility, than ever before. It was the kind of situation in which he throve and which brought out the best in him."[19] He saw himself as rather more than a Foreign Secretary; as a minister who might draw the whole war effort into his hands. From the start he was convinced that acceptable peace terms could not be negotiated with Napoleon. He was therefore at pains to convince the European powers of Britain's determination. Prussia, for example, began to receive subsidies immediately Canning came into office.

Canning's main concern in the summer of 1807 was the negotiations between Napoleon and Tsar Alexander I at Tilsit. He feared a secret engagement whereby Emperor and Tsar might, for example, dismember Turkey. Even more perilous was that they had agreed to bring the Danish fleet into the war against Britain and deny British ships entry to the Baltic. The Cabinet was united in its determination to prevent this. It has been held that the details of the Tilsit conference were provided for Canning by a spy concealed on the raft moored on the River Niemen on which Alexander and Napoleon met. This dramatic explanation now seems unlikely, although Canning may well have been in possession of secret intelligence of some sort. In any event, this explanation was used to justify the action later taken.

The Cabinet prepared a formidable expeditionary force to back up a diplomatic mission to Copenhagen led by Francis Jackson. Jackson was unable to persuade Denmark to join a British alliance and, as Canning had feared from the outset, force had to be used. Copenhagen was subjected to a naval bombardment and after the city's capitulation the British Fleet made away with eighteen Danish ships of the line and fifteen other vessels. Britain's safety had been at stake but Denmark's neutrality had been violated and the Government had to ride out a storm of protest and opposition at home. However, when Russia declared war on Britain in December, 1807, Canning wrote, "The Peace of Tilsit you see is come out. We did not want any more *case* for Copenhagen; but if we had this gives it us".[20]

To tighten his Continental System Napoleon needed to deny Lisbon to British shipping. While a French army was despatched to carry this out Canning anxiously negotiated with the Portuguese lest their fleet should fall into Napoleon's hands. After frustrating delay, and only when French troops were on the outskirts of Lisbon itself, the Portuguese fleet was escorted out into the Atlantic by a British squadron. It carried the Portuguese royal family bound for Brazil. The Copenhagen solution was avoided.

Napoleon's intervention against Portugal drew him into the wrangles of the Spanish court. Finally, the King of Spain was virtually deposed and replaced by Napoleon's own brother, Joseph. This, and the passage of French troops, stirred Spanish resistance and in June, 1808, two envoys representing this movement arrived in London. Britain was thus provided with the opportunity of intervention and the means of checking Napoleon. Having left a dinner in honour of the Spanish envoys, Canning arrived in the House of Commons to announce his policy. "We shall proceed on the principle that any section of Europe that stands up with the determination to oppose a Power [France] which, whether professing insidious peace or declaring open war, is the common enemy of all nations, whatever may be the existing political relations of that nation with Great Britain, becomes instantly our essential ally."[21]

A force was sent out to Portugal under the command of Sir Arthur Wellesley. It met with early success but, although the Peninsular Campaign in the end proved an effective theatre of war, there were, in Canning's time, more disappointments than successes. Wrangles over the command, a damaging armistice with the French in Portugal and misgivings about Spanish reliability all caused domestic political discord.

By late summer, 1809, the Portland ministry was beginning to break up. Apart from criticisms of the war effort, two of the leading members of the government, Castlereagh, the Secretary of War, and Canning himself, were on a collision course. Unbeknown to Castlereagh, Canning had been working for months for his dismissal from the War Office. The Foreign Secretary was critical of the way his colleague ran his department and became more impatient as bad news poured in from the Peninsula and from the expedition to Walcheren in the Low Countries. There was also a strong element of personal ambition; Canning wanted full control over the conduct of the war, seeing foreign policy and war as one. Both ministers resigned and when Castlereagh discovered Canning's campaign against him he challenged the Foreign Secretary to a duel. At the encounter, as Canning's second handed him his pistol he remarked to Castlereagh's second, "I must cock it for him for I cannot trust him to do it for himself. He has never fired a pistol in his life".[22] Both men missed at the first attempt; at the second Canning was shot through the thigh. Honour was satisfied, but the scandal of two leading ministers fighting a duel precipitated the final collapse of the shaky government.

War does not provide the best circumstances in which to judge a Foreign Secretary and Canning's first term was relatively short. However, he certainly set out to be master of his department and of its staff at home and abroad. Erskine, the British Minister in Washington, was recalled for exceeding his instructions. The practical result was the loss of an excellent representative and a deterioration in Anglo-American relations which, hitherto, Erskine had handled with understanding. Nevertheless, Canning was determined to make his point. For the Foreign Office itself Canning's term marked an important point in self-identity. It was Canning who began the practice of putting "Foreign Office" instead of "Downing Street" at the head of his department's despatches and papers.

After Canning's resignation Henry Bathurst, third Earl of Bathurst, was Foreign Secretary from October to December, 1809. An able man, he nevertheless held the post only as a temporary arrangement until the Marquess of Wellesley could return from Spain.

Wellesley (Foreign Secretary from December, 1809, to March, 1812), the elder brother of Wellington, had been a highly successful Governor-General of India between 1797 and 1805. His experience of war, administration and diplomacy in India was wide. As for European interests, he had been sent to Seville in 1809 as ambassador-extraordinary to the Spanish Junta. Yet he made a poor Foreign Secretary. At a time when the whole war was in the balance, with the country isolated and in peril, Britain deserved better. Perhaps as a result of his autocratic role in India he communicated little with his ministerial colleagues and throughout 1811 scarcely attended a Cabinet. In spite of considerable oratorical powers he rarely made speeches. He knew very little French. More seriously, the running of his department suffered from Wellesley's sheer laziness. The Prime Minister complained about delays in the preparation of despatches, the diplomatic corps seldom received instructions. John Wilson Croker called him "the most brilliant incapacity in England".[23] Even his own brother could write, "I wish that Wellesley was castrated; or that he would like other people attend to his business and perform to".[24] At last he resigned to make way for a man who would transform the office of Foreign Secretary, Viscount Castlereagh.

**NOTES TO CHAPTER ONE**

1   D. B. Horn. *The British Diplomatic Service 1689–1789* (Oxford, 1961), p. 1.

2   H. M. V. Temperley and L. M. Penson, eds. *Foundations of British Foreign Policy from Pitt to Salisbury* (Cambridge, 1938), p. 1.

3   Sir C. Webster. *The Foreign Policy of Castlereagh, 1815–22* (London, 1934), Vol. I, p. 7.

4   J. Steven Watson. *The Reign of George III 1760–1815* (Oxford, 1960), p. 560.

5   Ray Jones. *The Nineteenth-century Foreign Office* (Weidenfeld and Nicolson, 1971), p. 11.

6   Quoted by Valerie Cromwell. *The Foreign and Commonwealth Office* in Zara Steiner (ed.) *Times Survey of Foreign Ministries of the World* (Times Books, 1983), pp. 544–545.

7   Henry Dundas, first Viscount Melville. Home Secretary 1791–94, Secretary at War 1794–1801.

8   *Dictionary of National Biography.*

9   *D.N.B.*

10   J. W. Derry. *Charles James Fox* (London, 1972), p. 424.

11   Quoted by C. R. Middleton, *The Administration of British Foreign Policy 1782–1846* (Duke University Press, 1977), p. 100.

12   Middleton, p. 101.

13   *D.N.B.*

14   *D.N.B.*

15   Middleton, p. 104.

16   Middleton, p. 105.

17   *D.N.B.*

18   *D.N.B.*

19   Wendy Hinde. *George Canning* (London, 1973), p. 159.

20   Quoted by Hinde, p. 227.

21   Quoted by P. V. J. Rolo, *George Canning* (London, 1965), p. 196.

22   Quoted by Hinde, p. 227.

23   Quoted by Middleton, p. 106.

24   Quoted by Paul Langford, *Modern British Foreign Policy: The Eighteenth Century 1688–1815* (London, 1976), p. 6.

**CHAPTER TWO**

SECRETARIES OF STATE

| | |
|---|---|
| Castlereagh | March 1812–August 1822 |
| George Canning | September 1822–April 1827 |
| John William Ward, fourth Viscount Dudley and Ward, afterwards first Earl Dudley | April 1827–June 1828 |
| George Hamilton Gordon, fourth Earl of Aberdeen | June 1828–November 1830 |

# Castlereagh and Canning

## Foreign Policy 1815–1830

IN 1815 Britain stood in a position of unrivalled power and prestige. Of all the countries opposed to France she alone had remained steadfast throughout the twenty-year struggle. Her fleet outclassed that of any other power and almost any combination of powers, her gold had subsidised continental coalitions and her diplomacy had kept the allies together in the final phases of Napoleon's overthrow. Such had been Britain's familiar role. Less characteristically she had sent considerable land forces overseas, notably to the Peninsular and Waterloo campaigns. In 1819, in time of peace, her army still numbered 123,000. Outside Europe, Britain had a clear predominance and had already "acquired the greatest commercial empire the world had ever seen".[1]

Britain's achievement in the war and the position she had won were paramount in determining her objectives at the peace settlement as well as her longer-term aims. Although Britain's relative position was altered in the course of the nineteenth century, when she lost her earlier and complete industrial dominance while new powers such as the German Empire and the United States arose, her aims in foreign policy remained remarkably constant.

The first objective of Britain's leaders was the maintenance of national security. To this end the fleet had to be kept up to at least the necessary two-power standard. This was largely a matter of domestic arrangements, the finding of men and money, but Britain could not rely on her fleet alone. It was also necessary to maintain a balance of power in Europe. No one great power could be permitted to dominate the continent; no hostile combination of countries could be allowed to array itself against Britain. This meant the exercise of diplomacy, the threat and use of sea power and, as a last resort, military intervention. It was not within even Britain's means to pay for a great army as well as for naval supremacy. Garrisons had to be maintained all over the globe and the creation of a large army for use in Europe was unthinkable, although, exceptionally, it could be done. By the end of the Crimean War the British army was in excess of half a million.

Britain therefore had important interests in Europe but no territorial ambitions. Her aim above all was peace, since this provided the best conditions for her trade. Britain's ideal would have been the possession of an "informal empire" where she enjoyed the benefits of commerce and prime influence without the responsibility of colonial administration. Such a policy was followed in South America and China. But inevitably, in order to safeguard trade, it became necessary to exert closer political control, to acquire and defend strategic zones, to bring gunboat diplomacy to bear, to keep rivals at bay, to protect the rights of British subjects abroad.

In due course "the Chinese walls" of reluctant trading partners were battered down by naval artillery. A world-wide *Pax Britannica* was established. It is hardly surprising that Britain also developed her policy of Free Trade. With her naval supremacy, long industrial lead and cheap mass-produced articles such a policy gave Britain great advantages. But Britain's leaders also firmly believed that a flourishing international trade benefited the whole world: Britons, Europeans and non-Europeans alike. Furthermore, Britain's world-wide power enabled her to play the leading part in the suppression of the slave trade.

Although Britain had no interest in European conquest, there were certain areas whose stability she would intervene to secure. Holland and Belgium, Britain's "vestibule to the trade of Europe and the potential base for the invasion of England",[2] were especially important. Greece also attracted particular interest, as did Spain and Portugal.

It would be inaccurate then to see Britain simply as an isolationist power sheltering behind her fleet. The European powers were not only potential commercial and colonial rivals but their activities affected the continental balance that Britain was concerned to maintain. In one sense, however, Britain was isolated in that she made no commitments to a permanent ally. An ally might be relied upon to uphold Britain's interests in Europe, as Prussia had in the Seven Years War, but, conversely, Britain could be drawn into damaging continental entanglements. In any case there was no guarantee that Britain would be able to fulfil commitments to an ally: Parliament acted as an important check and there was a constitutional obligation to publish the texts of treaties. Moreover, public opinion could be relied upon to oppose engagements entered into with a despotic power. These obstacles in the way of fixed alliances were considerable, and British Foreign Secretaries remained hesitant and sceptical about such arrangements right up to the eve of the First World War.

Britain's crucial role in the overthrow of Napoleon was mirrored in the influence she brought to bear in the treaty settlements. The Treaty of Chaumont, signed by Britain, Austria, Prussia and Russia in 1814, bound the allies together not only for the duration of the conflict but, in order that peace might be made to last, for twenty years afterwards. With Napoleon's first exile, the relatively lenient First Treaty of Paris was made in 1814. The Bourbons were restored, France was given her borders of 1792, no reparations or indemnities were imposed. In the following autumn the Congress of Vienna was summoned to deal with the wider issues of territorial settlement. The British Foreign Secretary, Castlereagh, while anxious to control France's future ambitions, was nevertheless concerned to pacify France and involve her in maintaining a European balance. The former enemy therefore attended the Congress.

Important divisions arose, and there was even a chance of a realignment of the powers in a fresh war. Prussia's designs on Saxony offended Austria and the Tsar's claims in Poland raised British fears of an overmighty Russia. Napoleon's escape from Elba in March, 1815, reunited the allies but some divisions were re-opened after his defeat. The Second Treaty of Paris, signed in 1815, was harder on France. Her boundaries were to be those of 1790, she was to pay an indemnity and suffer an army of occupation. Significantly this was to be commanded by Wellington. More widely, the deliberations in Vienna re-drew the map of Europe. France was to be contained as follows: to the north-east the former Austrian Netherlands (Belgium) and Holland were combined; to the east Prussia was given most of the Rhineland; in Italy, Sardinia-Piedmont was enlarged and Austria was given Lombardy and Venetia while enjoying further influence in other smaller Italian states. The formation of the new German Confederation was designed to prevent French intrigues with the smaller German states. In the end, Russia took the lion's share of Poland as well as the whole of Finland. Britain's pickings were limited but carefully chosen and strongly reflected her commercial and strategic interests: the Cape of Good Hope; Malta and a protectorate over the Ionian Islands; Trinidad, St Lucia and Tobago; Mauritius; Heligoland. Britain's aims, Castlereagh's legacy from Pitt, were largely achieved: a redistribution of territory to check French ambition and a concert of the Powers to guarantee the settlement as well as future international stability. "What the master first sketched in 1792 and formulated in 1805, the pupil brought into practice at the Congress of Vienna."[3]

The defeat of Napoleon brought the long period of conflict between Britain and France to a close. At Vienna Castlereagh was concerned not to treat France harshly, although public opinion demanded a Carthaginian peace. The new relationship was quickly recognised by the restored Bourbons as well as by British statesmen. As early as December, 1814, Lord Liverpool was able to write to Wellington: "The more I hear and see of the different Courts of Europe, the more convinced I am that the King of France is (amongst the great powers) the only Sovereign in whom we can have any real confidence".[4] There were some uneasy moments ahead, such as the French intervention in Spain in 1823, but for the most part Britain and France acted more as allies than adversaries during the nineteenth century.

The Vienna settlement was far from perfect. Moreover, it came to be seen as a set of ultra-conservative arrangements which stood in the way of the rising forces of nationalism and liberalism. But it provided stability and there was no general rearrangement of European territories until the treaties following the First World War. For Britain world-wide power was confirmed and pre-eminence established.

When the victorious allies signed the Treaty of Paris they also concluded the Quadruple Alliance. Its immediate objective was to prevent the return of Napoleon but it expressed the wider aim of holding regular conferences for the maintenance of peace. This arrangement came to be called the Congress System.

A further proposal was the treaty of the Holy Alliance. It was the brainchild of Tsar Alexander, then in a period of religious fervour, and bound its signatories to act according to Christian principles. Its very vagueness was its chief weakness and Castlereagh described it as "a piece of sublime mysticism and nonsense". In due course it was signed by all European rulers except the Pope, the Sultan and George III. It was, in effect, an inner alliance of Russia, Prussia and Austria and was later used by Metternich, the Austrian Chancellor, as an anti-liberal agency. As such it played its part in the eventual failure of the Congress System proper.

The first Congress was called to Aix-la-Chapelle in 1818. The Allies agreed to withdraw Wellington's army of occupation and then invited France to join them. However, differences between the Powers were already emerging. There was disagreement, for example, on the issue of intervention in states affected by revolution. When a circular from the Tsar suggested suppression of revolution by concerted action Castlereagh condemned it, and during 1819 Britain began to distance herself from her allies. In 1820 revolts broke out in Spain, Naples and Portugal and, in alarm, the Tsar called for a Congress. This met at Troppau in October. Significantly, Britain sent an observer only and, when Austria, Russia and Prussia claimed the right to intervene, Castlereagh strongly protested. When the Congress moved to Laibach in January, 1821, Austria, with her special interests in Italy, was authorised to put down the Neapolitan revolt. Troppau and Laibach ended the period of post-war co-operation. At Verona in 1822 no agreement could be reached over Spain or the Greek revolution which had broken out in 1821. After this the Congress System virtually collapsed; Britain had stood out for non-intervention and after 1822 began to follow more pragmatic and unilateralist policies. This new emphasis coincided with Canning's acceptance of the Foreign Secretary-ship, following Castlereagh's death by suicide.

The occasion for Britain's change of direction was the revolts in Spain and Portugal and the independence movements in Spain's colonies. Differing approaches to these events showed how Britain's interests were at variance with those of the other Powers. Britain had a special interest in the Iberian Peninsula following her intervention in 1808. Moreover, serious instability there or intervention by another power would affect Britain's Mediterranean strategy. Portugal was a trading partner of long standing. A flourishing, though strictly speaking illegal, trade had been developed with the Latin American colonies, where Spain claimed a monopoly, albeit unenforceable. However, with Britain's wartime support for the Spanish cause this trade was able to expand and did much to save Britain from the worst effects of the Continental System. Spain's struggle with Napoleon had also presented the Latin Americans with the opportunity to throw off colonial rule.

In January, 1820, after a military revolt in Cadiz, King Ferdinand VII of Spain was forced to agree to a democratic constitution. Although Ferdinand appealed to his fellow-rulers to intervene, Britain at this stage successfully opposed such interference. Three years later, however, a French army crossed the Pyrenees to restore Ferdinand's power. Although Britain was anxious not to see the revival of the close co-operation between the Bourbon rulers which had threatened her in the eighteenth century, she was unable to prevent French action. But Britain made it clear that she would act to prevent France aiding Spain to recover her colonies and, of course, possessed the sea power to put the warning into effect.

The independence of Spain's former colonies suited British commercial interests but the Cabinet was understandably cautious in giving recognition to rebel governments. A complication was that the United States, whose relations with Britain were far from easy, had given recognition. Furthermore, in December, 1823, President Monroe issued his famous declaration that the American continents were "henceforth not to be considered as future subjects for colonization by any European power".[5] These were fine words, but the only power which could uphold this doctrine was the British fleet. It was a considerable triumph for British foreign policy that after successful negotiations with France she was able, in 1824, to grant recognition to the colonies. Within a very short space of time British influence and commercial interests were dominant in Latin America.

Britain was forced to go rather further in upholding the independence and stability of Portugal. King John VI's position was threatened by revolts in 1823 and 1824 and a British squadron was sent to cruise off Lisbon. Further upheavals in 1826, following the death of John, and encouraged by Madrid, led the Portuguese to make a direct approach to Britain. By the end of that year British ships and troops were sailing up the Tagus itself. British influence also had a major part to play in the negotiated independence of Brazil from Portugal in 1825.

In 1821 it was the turn of the Greeks to break into full-scale revolution. The Greek struggle against the Turks won passionate support in Britain where the mood of philhellenism was strong. It was raised to fever-pitch by Byron's journey to Greece in 1823. But the Greek revolution drew attention to much wider issues than Greek independence and these crucially affected British foreign policy for the rest of the nineteenth century. These issues may conveniently be placed under the heading "the Eastern Question". In the nineteenth century the Ottoman Empire came to be regarded as the "sick man of Europe". Stratford Canning,[6] Britain's ambassador in Constantinople between 1824 and 1829, believed that "the state of Turkey itself was anything but satisfactory in view of those powers who did not wish the Porte to become a prey either of Russia or France . . . morally and materially this empire bordered on decrepitude". As well as internal weaknesses the Turks suffered from attempts by their subjects in Greece and the Balkans to set themselves free, and from the designs of the Powers for influence over these peoples or for more direct control over Ottoman territory.

During the eighteenth century Austria and Russia had co-operated in order to profit from Ottoman weakness. Russia had been particularly successful. By the Treaty of Kutchuk Kainardji in 1774 she had made important gains on the Black Sea and imprecise, but therefore extremely useful, rights of protection over the Sultan's Christian subjects. Pitt had been made aware of the dangers of Russian expansion at the time of the Oczakov crisis but public opinion had been less perceptive. In the eighteenth century, for the most part, Britain had been concerned to maintain friendly relations with Russia. By 1815 attitudes were changing. Russia's ambitions to drive south towards Constantinople and the Straits were now plain and these clashed with Britain's growing economic penetration of the Levant. Russia's presence in the Mediterranean would represent a direct challenge to Britain's naval power. Domination of the Balkans by the Tsar would conflict with Britain's scheme of a European balance of power. Above all, perhaps, Russian expansion would threaten vital lines of communication, especially to India; Napoleon had described Constantinople as the 'key to India'. Thus Britain adopted the policy of sustaining the crumbling Ottoman Empire and checking Russia.

It is perhaps surprising that Britain fought only one war against Russia in the nineteenth century, the Crimean. The despotic Tsarist regime came to be heartily disliked by public opinion and suspected by the politicians of holding vast designs to wrest India away. Indeed, it was the swaggering dislike of Russia, the great enemy, that later gave birth to the term "Jingoism". The difficulty with upholding Turkey, however, was that her bloodstained reputation was even worse than Russia's. Her savagery in suppressing rebellion made it embarrassing to support her and, again, public opinion expressed strong sentiments. Nevertheless, as Castlereagh remarked, "barbarous as it is, Turkey forms in the system of Europe a necessary evil".[8]

The Greeks were at first successful in their rebellion but the Sultan invoked the aid of Mehemet Ali, Pasha of Egypt. His forces, under his son Ibrahim, landed in the Morea in February, 1825, and quickly carried all before them. Britain's solution to the risk of Russian intervention, and response to the pressures of philhellenic opinion at home, was to work with Russia. The death of Alexander I in December, 1825, provided such an opportunity and Wellington was despatched to St Petersburg. He was able to negotiate a protocol which provided for a large measure of Greek independence under nominal Turkish suzerainty. France was eager not to be left out of these arrangements and joined with Russia and Britain. The three powers confirmed the terms in the Treaty of London in July, 1827. To enforce the settlement a combined fleet was despatched and, when the Turks and Egyptians failed to give satisfaction, their fleets were sent to the bottom of Navarino Bay.

This naval action created fresh problems. It was feared that Russia could now more easily exploit Turkish weakness. Moreover, within six months of Navarino a Russo-Turkish war had broken out over another issue, the failure of the Turks to fulfil their obligations to the Russians over the government of the Danubian Principalities of Moldavia and Wallachia. Initial Turkish resistance collapsed and the Russians reached Adrianople, where they were able to gain a favourable peace treaty in September, 1829. Meanwhile, in the Morea, now stripped of Turkish troops, the Egyptian forces were driven out by the French. In these circumstances Britain could not sensibly maintain a pro-Turkish policy. Greek independence had rapidly to be granted. In February, 1830, in London, the Greek state was recognised and guaranteed by Britain, France and Russia. For the time being its size was deliberately restricted since Britain believed, mistakenly, that it would fall under Russia's influence.

**The Foreign Secretaries 1812–1830**
For fifteen years the Foreign Secretaryship was held in succession by Castlereagh and Canning. Both were disciples of Pitt and were Tories but, even as Cabinet colleagues, they were deadly rivals. Although Canning gained the supreme office of Prime Minister he, like Castlereagh, is chiefly remembered as a Foreign Secretary. As men they were strikingly different. While Canning was more obviously brilliant, eloquent and clever, Castlereagh was shy, awkward and, as a public speaker, dull. Unlike

Canning, he was not the master of the striking phrase and, partly as a result, his policies found less resonance with contemporary opinion and later generations. Even so it was said that "Castlereagh never made a speech without making a friend, nor Canning without making an enemy".[9] Castlereagh was influential at Court and on close terms with foreign statesmen, who admired him, but was hated in the country. Canning was enormously popular at home but was distrusted by his colleagues. Foreign statesmen were suspicious of him; Metternich, the Austrian Chancellor, regarded him as the devil incarnate and a supporter of revolution. Castlereagh has been cast as the classical reactionary, Canning as the archetypal liberal. Their foreign policies have been sharply contrasted. But Castlereagh was never as reactionary as he seems nor Canning as liberal, and their policies differed more in method and approach than in aims.

Robert Stewart, second Marquess of Londonderry, better known by his courtesy title of Viscount Castlereagh, was born in the same year as Wellington and Napoleon, 1769. He was an Ulsterman whose father was wealthy enough to provide him with £60,000 to fight his first election campaign. Brought up a Presbyterian, he conformed as an Anglican on going up to St John's College, Cambridge. Castlereagh's Irish experience was of the utmost importance. He first sat in the Irish Parliament and as Acting- and then Chief Secretary of Ireland he experienced the bitter revolution of 1798 and its aftermath. At first hand he learned much of the forces of revolution and nationalism which were already playing their part on the broader European stage and which helped shape his policies at the War and Foreign Offices. A little later he was almost entirely responsible for steering the Act of Union through the Irish Parliament. With the end of the Irish Parliament he more completely shifted his political ambitions to Westminster, although he resigned office in 1801 when Catholic emancipation, so closely linked for him with the issue of Union, was prevented by George III.

Castlereagh's experience of office was widened later by a spell as President of the Board of Control with responsibility for the Government's relations with the Governor-General of India and the East India Company. From the Board of Control he went to the War Office. His activities there went far beyond military matters. He was drawn into the power politics of Europe and as Foreign Secretary he owed much to this experience. "Castlereagh had certainly proved himself an abler Secretary of State for

War than any of his predecessors."[10] After his duel with Canning in September, 1809, he was out of office until he became Foreign Secretary and Leader of the House of Commons in February, 1812.

During his lifetime, and for long after, Castlereagh and his policies were a subject of execration. As the architect of the Act of Union he was branded as the betrayer of his country. In the period of post-war economic distress and political agitation he was the cold-hearted advocate of repression. Abroad he was the ally of despotism and the tool of Metternich. At the height of his unpopularity, while walking in Parliament Street with Sidmouth, the Home Secretary, he suffered the attentions of a jeering crowd. "Here we go, the two most popular men in England", remarked Sidmouth. "Yes, through a grateful and admiring multitude", replied Castlereagh.[11] He was handled with particular savagery by poets and radical writers. Shelley in the *Masque of Anarchy* wrote:

> "I met murder on the way —
> He had a mask like Castlereagh."

On Castlereagh's death Byron rejoiced:

> "So he has cut his throat at last! He? Who?
> The man who cut his country's long ago."

As Leader of the House Castlereagh was the chief spokesman for the Government's unpopular domestic policies. It was largely for this reason that he was hated and his dignity and self-control were easily mistaken for an icy disdain. But he made little attempt to explain his foreign policy to the public and it is not surprising that his objectives were misunderstood and confused with those of the Holy Alliance.

To many observers Castlereagh was indeed "like Mont Blanc . . . a splendid summit of bright and polished frost".[12] To his friends, however, he was warm, generous and kind and his marriage to Lady Emily Hobart, though childless, was very happy. He was most at ease at his home at North Cray with his flowers and country pursuits. After signing the Quadruple Alliance he told his companion, "I am going Thursday to Cray and the Merinos, thank God that I am once more *unsaddled* and may roll on the grass".[13] This side of him is certainly at odds with the heartless reactionary, the duellist who insisted upon a second shot at Canning, the forger of Britain and Europe's post-war fetters. To outward appearances Castle-

Robert Stewart, Viscount Castlereagh.                    *The Mansell Collection*

George Canning, by Sir Thomas Lawrence.                    *The Mansell Collection*

reagh was the typical aristocrat, handsome, tall and dignified; but shyness was taken for aloofness and restraint for cold indifference. Even when he was at the height of his powers the wife of the Russian ambassador, Princess Lieven, remarked, "It is strange how timid he is of society, as if he were just beginning".[14]

As an exponent of personal diplomacy he was supreme, and much of his success resulted from the close relationships he had developed with the ministers and monarchs of the European powers. The Earl of Ripon, who had been at Castlereagh's side during his continental mission of 1814, paid tribute to these qualities: "The suavity and dignity of his manners, his habitual patience and self command, his considerate tolerance of difference of opinion in others, all fitted him for such a task; whilst his firmness, when he knew he was right, in no degree detracted from the influence of his conciliatory demeanour."[15] When Castlereagh returned from the Paris negotiations Ripon remembered that "the whole body of the Commons of England rose from their seats on his appearance, and greeted him with cordial acclamations".[16] But Castlereagh's friend Wellington spotted his principal shortcoming: "he could do everything but speak in Parliament, that he could not do".[17]

The Foreign Office which Castlereagh took over in 1812 was in poor shape, to a large extent the result of Wellesley's neglect. Even in 1821 the staff numbered only twenty-eight.[18] There was a Turkish interpreter but no recognized expert in the French language. The British delegation at the Congress of Vienna was likewise small: Lord Charles Stewart, Castlereagh's half-brother and ambassador to Vienna; the Earl of Clancarty; Edward Cooke, one of the Under-Secretaries, who fell ill during the negotiations; Joseph Planta, Castlereagh's private secretary; and ten others, mainly young men. As for the diplomatic service, Britain had six full ambassadors, at St Petersburg, Paris, Vienna, Constantinople, Madrid and The Hague. Elsewhere the representatives were Ministers Plenipotentiary or other envoys of lesser rank. Castlereagh himself worked prodigiously hard, generally twelve to fourteen hours per day while Parliament sat, and the leadership of the House involved extra strain. He kept a close eye on his staff, spending five to six hours per day in the office, he delegated little of importance and wrote much of the correspondence of the department in his own hand. During the momentous period of the final campaigns against Napoleon and the peace negotiations he spent sixteen months out of two years on the Continent. He was indeed "the most European Foreign Minister in [British] history".[16] For the conferences at Vienna and Aix-la-Chapelle Castlereagh prepared himself with meticulous care and wove the threads of diplomacy himself.

In his relations with Crown, Cabinet and Prime Minister, Castlereagh was fortunate. His mastery of detail and confidence in himself gave him a dominating position. The rest of the Cabinet, except for Castlereagh's friend Wellington, generally kept out of foreign affairs; even Canning interfered very little. Liverpool, the Prime Minister, assured the Foreign Secretary of his whole-hearted trust. As for the Prince Regent, Castlereagh established such an ascendancy that there was little serious interference from the Court.

On coming to the Foreign Office Castlereagh was faced with a formidable array of problems: the necessity of creating a new coalition against France, of holding it together and bringing about Napoleon's overthrow; the reconciliation of the conflict of interests between the Allies, notably Austria and Russia; the safeguarding of Britain's own interests, especially in the colonial sphere; tension between Britain and the United States; how to restore and guarantee peace and the balance of power in Europe; the protection of a defeated France from a too-revengeful peace settlement.

The Foreign Secretary's chief guide in these matters was his mentor Pitt, who in 1805 had drawn up a Memorandum on the future of Europe. "First, to rescue from the Dominion of France those countries which it has subjugated since the beginning of the Revolution, and to reduce France within its former limits, as they stood before that time. Secondly, to make such an arrangement with respect to the territories recovered from France, as may provide for their Security and Happiness, and may at the same time constitute a more effectual barrier in future against Encroachment on the part of France. Thirdly, to form, at the Restoration of Peace, a general Agreement and Guarantee for the mutual protection and Security of different Powers, and for re-establishing a general System of Public Law in Europe."[20] Here, in brief, were the aims pursued in the closing stages of the war, at the peace negotiations, and afterwards in the new diplomacy of the Congress System.

Castlereagh was the chief architect of the allied victory. By personal diplomacy of the highest order he won the confidence of foreign rulers and ministers, and strengthened their resolution for the complete overthrow of Napoleon. He told his allies: "We have now the bull close pinioned between us, and if either of us lets go our hold till we render him harmless, we shall deserve to suffer for it".[21] At the outset of his mission to the allies' headquarters he was well aware of the longer-term obstacles to European security. On his way to Basle early in 1814 he confided to Lord Ripon that "one of the great difficulties which he expected to encounter in the approaching negotiations would arise from the want of an habitual confidential and free intercourse between the Ministers of the Great Powers as a body".[22] As the allied armies drove Napoleon back inside his own frontiers, Castlereagh continued to argue the twin themes of unity and resolution. At Chaumont in March, 1814, he was able to complete the grand alliance for which he had striven for the past six months. As well as making the financial and military dispositions necessary for final victory, the Allies bound themselves together for a further twenty years as a guarantee of European stability.

In the two Paris peace treaties and the wider discussions at the Congress of Vienna, Castlereagh's aims remained constant: to achieve peace and stability; to create sufficient bulwarks against future French expansion without storing up future resentment by imposing over-harsh terms. Thus he worked for a stronger Holland and, in spite of Napoleon's escape and Waterloo, lenient terms for France. He saw the restoration of the Bourbons to be essential, preferably as a constitutional monarchy enjoying good relations with Britain. The Vienna settlement certainly achieved stability but the charge has been levelled that it made Europe safe only for monarchy and aristocracy. "The dynamic forces of the age—liberalism and nationalism—too often found themselves thwarted or repressed and therefore sought fulfilment in more violent ways."[23] Yet the settlement itself was moderate, especially in view of the length of the war.

By way of completing the treaties the victorious powers bound themselves together in the Quadruple Alliance. Signed in 1815, it aimed to defend Europe against new French aggression, to prevent the restoration of the Bonaparte dynasty and to define the circumstances in which the Powers might intervene against a new French Revolution. In the celebrated Clause VI of the treaty, drafted by Castlereagh himself, a new principle was established. "To facilitate and to secure the execution of the present Treaty, and to consolidate the connections which at the present moment so closely unite the 4 Sovereigns" the Powers "agreed to renew their meetings at fixed periods".[24] Diplomacy by conference, the Congress System, was Castlereagh's special contribution to the international diplomacy of the post-Napoleonic period.

In contrast to Tsar Alexander's Holy Alliance, Castlereagh was concerned with practicalities. He knew how easily alliances had disintegrated during the war and regarded the Congress System as the best way of holding the allies together. In turn, such unity provided for the future peace and stability of Europe. Though pragmatic, his policy was new and adventurous. Unfortunately his European allies, Metternich and the Tsar in particular, saw the Congress System as a means of international intervention in revolutionary disturbances in other countries. Castlereagh saw the danger of revolution but did not allow this to dominate his policy. Only when revolution threatened the equilibrium of Europe as a whole was international intervention justified. Where the interests of a particular power were seriously affected by revolution, as Austria's might be in Italy, then the right of intervention by that power might be permitted. Moreover, Castlereagh knew full well that the structure created at Vienna could not last for ever and that the Congress System might provide the machinery for change and adjustment. It was simply not in Britain's interests to be drawn into a concerted campaign to maintain legitimacy or an ossified *status quo*. When Castlereagh saw the structure he had created being used for purposes he had not intended, he drew away from his partners. After Vienna he attended only one Congress, at Aix-la-Chapelle in 1818. At Troppau in 1820 and Laibach in 1821 Britain was represented by an observer, Lord Charles Stewart. Although the Foreign Secretary was preparing to travel to Verona in 1822, his death intervened.

. At Aix-la-Chapelle the differences between the allies seemed slight. Castlereagh and Wellington favoured an early withdrawal of the army of occupation from France and joined in extending an invitation to France to join the Concert of the Powers. Castlereagh wrote, "all are gone home in good humour and vowing eternal peace and friendship so that we shall be enabled to make our [arms] reductions with a good conscience".[25] By 1820, however, against a rising tide of disorder in Spain, Portugal and Italy, the relationships between the Powers had drastically changed. The response of the continental powers to the rising in Spain led Castlereagh to denounce the doctrine of international intervention. In his State Paper of May, 1820, he pointed out that the Alliance was never "intended as a Union for the Government of the World, or for the superintendence of the internal Affairs of other States".[26] As for Britain, "we shall be found in our place when actual Danger menaces the System of Europe, but this Country cannot and will not act upon abstract and speculative Principles of Precaution".[27] However, the continental Powers believed that Castlereagh was in favour of repression and that he only expressed the views he did to satisfy Parliament and public opinion. Esterhazy, the Austrian ambassador in London, said that Castlereagh was "like a great lover of music who is at Church; he wishes to applaud but he dare not".[28] Castlereagh was thus between Scylla and Charybdis, for his international approach was misrepresented and attacked at home, especially by the radical journalists. In the Cabinet his policies were supported because he himself was trusted rather than because his ideas were fully understood.

Although joint intervention did not take place in Italy or the Iberian peninsula, Castlereagh's warnings in the State Paper of 1820 and his Circular of 1821 fell on deaf ears and, without him, the Powers enunciated a general principle of intervention. Already by the end of 1820 Castlereagh could see that the Alliance was falling apart. In the end the Congress System failed because the interests of the allies were irreconcilable. Austria, for example, because of the nature of her multinational empire, believed that the very theory of revolution constituted a threat. Although Castlereagh had shown that Britain had a role in Europe, she could not surrender her freedom of action. Specifically, she could not stand by while the Powers intervened in Spain and Portugal or their Latin American colonies. The Congress System scarcely outlived its chief author. It was, nevertheless, an experiment worth trying and provided the model for the later Concert of Europe.

Although European affairs absorbed most of Castlereagh's time and energy, he did not neglect the wider world. Above all, he was concerned to improve the disastrous state of Anglo-American relations. No British statesman of the period was as prepared to accept the full implications of American independence. On pragmatic grounds alone, not least mutual economic interests, it was important that relations should be improved. Castlereagh therefore sought every opportunity to gain American goodwill and to smooth over controversial issues. His representatives in Washington, Charles Bagot and Stratford Canning, were chosen with special care.

In London the American minister, Richard Rush, was Castlereagh's unashamed admirer. Once again in Castlereagh's policies personal diplomacy played its part. Whilst continuing to uphold British interests in the matter of the rebellious Latin American colonies, Castlereagh was careful not to arouse the suspicions or anxieties of the United States. His preference would have been for monarchical governments for the colonies, as a check on American republicanism, and he looked to the Congress of 1822 as an opportunity of securing European recognition of their independence. Such a solution was ruled out by his death.

In many ways Castlereagh's Secretaryship directed the Foreign Office towards the non-European business which was to occupy so much of its time in the later nineteenth century. The improved relations with the United States have been regarded as the most successful aspect of his foreign policy and he anticipated Canning's concern with promoting British interests in Latin America. His effort for the suppression of the international slave trade gained the approbation of Wilberforce himself. Britain as a world power was pursuing world-wide policies.

During the summer of 1822 those closest to Castlereagh noticed a deterioration in him. The burden of work and the strain of long hours in the Commons was crippling. In the Foreign Office alone he had to contend with three issues at once: the Greek revolution; the Spanish question; and recognition of the Latin American colonies. His stature in the government made him Prime Minister in all but name. Planta "thought him during the latter part of the Spring very much worn by the session, and though not ill as to his bodily health much oppressed by the weight of business".[29] By August, however, he was depressed, dejected and melancholy. His handwriting was almost illegible. In an interview with George IV he broke down. "I am mad. I know I am mad. I have known it for some time, but no one has any idea of it."[30] Although a close surveillance was maintained and pistols and razors were kept from him he committed suicide at North Cray on 12th August. He cut his throat expertly and quickly with a small knife. There is a possibility that he feared blackmail in connection with accusations, probably groundless, of homosexual activities. More likely, however, is that he was suffering from a brain tumour which would account for his failing handwriting and a reported incapacity of his left side.[31] What is beyond doubt is the strain and overwork inflicted upon him by the office of Foreign Secretary.

Castlereagh's death was of profound importance for British foreign policy and European politics. In a very real sense he was irreplaceable since the success of his schemes depended upon the personal relationships and vast experience he had built up. His novel policies were highly personal and could only be implemented because of his own standing in the Cabinet. "Sir!" he announced in his last audience with the King, "it is necessary to say good-bye to Europe; you and I alone know it and have said it; no one after me understands the affairs of the Continent".[32] There was bound to be a change whoever succeeded him.

He was buried in Westminster Abbey, not far from Pitt. A good many notices were as cruel as Byron's but Brougham, no friend, could write, "Put all their other men together in one scale, and poor Castlereagh in the other—single he plainly weighed them down".[33]

Canning's second term at the Foreign Office gave every appearance of a dramatic change in policy. However, the difference was one of style and method rather than of aims. Castlereagh had already begun a process of disengagement from the Quadruple Alliance; Canning had fully endorsed the famous State Paper of 1820; and Castlereagh's instructions for the Congress of Verona pointed out fresh directions which Canning could follow. Nevertheless, Canning gave an exciting and more obviously patriotic flavour to policy and in some ways different methods led to different results.

Canning has been described as "perhaps the cleverest of all the men who have served as foreign secretary".[34] His enemies, and some of his friends, would have said he was too clever by half and he was a man who made enemies rather too easily. He was suspected for his ambition and self-seeking, his impetuosity, hot temper and trickery. Foreign statesmen hated him. Yet, equally, he had his friends and admirers. Liverpool, who knew him at Christ Church, Oxford, had respect and liking for him. In the last five years of Liverpool's premiership they were on intimate terms. Among the diplomats and professionals Charles Bagot,[35] Granville Leveson-Gower,[36] Joseph Planta (Under-Secretary between 1817 and 1827), and Stratford Canning regarded him with affection and esteem. Of the younger politicians, Palmerston and the future Lord Melbourne were enthusiastic admirers. All his contemporaries were struck by his insatiable appetite for work. Liverpool lamented that he had "not the strength and nerves to bear Mr Canning's perpetual notes. He sends me a dozen a day".[37] A holiday for Canning was the freedom to work without interruption; when at his country house he rose just after eight, had his despatches ready before breakfast and continued writing until six. His industry was all the more remarkable since his health was never good. Like other Foreign Secretaries before and after him, he worked himself almost to death. In the last five years of his life, his great period at the Foreign Office, he suffered an almost endless round of fevers, chills and gout.

In the House of Commons and the public platform he was a thrilling, passionate speaker. For important occasions he rehearsed both word and gesture but excelled in cut-and-thrust debate as well as the set pieces. His mind was remarkable in its capacity, range and lucidity. The Greville Diary records, "Such was the clearness of his head that he could address himself almost at the same time to different subjects with perfect precision and without the least embarrassment. He wrote very fast but not fast enough for his mind, composing much quicker than he could commit his ideas to paper. He could not bear to dictate because nobody could write fast enough for him".[38] Canning was known to dictate on two completely different subjects to two clerks at the same time. Virtually all the vast number of despatches to representatives abroad were dictated or written by him.

Considering his later distinction, Canning's background was somewhat bizarre and there were some who threw it in his face. Grey opposed him in later years because "he regarded the son of an actress as being *de facto* incapacitated from being premier of England".[39] Canning came from a good family on his father's side but after his father had failed in a number of ventures, including the law and the wine trade, he died when George was an infant. It was at this point that his mother took to the provincial stage. He was rescued from what might have been a raffish career by his uncle, who settled money on him and sent him to Eton in 1782. From there he went to Oxford, where he proved a good classicist and showed considerable literary talent. As a protégé of Pitt, he was elected to the Commons in 1794. A string of offices followed, including Under-Secretary of State at the Foreign Office between 1796 and 1799, Paymaster-General and Treasurer of the Navy. His reputation was secured by his first tenure of the Foreign Office between 1807 and 1809. In 1812 he was faced with the most momentous decision of his career and made his most serious misjudgement. Liverpool, anxious to strengthen his ministry by bringing Canning in, offered him the Foreign Office, which Castlereagh was prepared to surrender. Canning referred to Castlereagh's offer as "perhaps the handsomest that was ever made to an individual"[40] but, nevertheless, refused because he was not given the Leadership of the Commons too. "Had Canning acted with more discrimination he might have occupied the Foreign Office during the momentous years between 1812 and 1815."[41]

It was in 1812 also that he was elected as M.P. for Liverpool, a seat he was to hold until 1822. In representing Liverpool, he was in close touch with the capitalist class and was made more keenly aware of the commercial and material interests which help to shape foreign policy. Also of importance was his ambassadorship to Lisbon from 1814 to 1816. This widened his experience still further, although he regarded his acceptance of the post as "a great political mistake".[42]

When Canning's chance came again in 1822, he had already accepted the Governor-Generalship of India. Some three weeks elapsed between Castlereagh's suicide and Canning's acceptance of the seals. During the anxious time of waiting Canning's ship lay moored and ready in the Thames while he held out for the "whole heritage" of Castlereagh, the Foreign Office and Leadership of the Commons. At last, Liverpool's offer came. When Countess Lieven heard Wellington say that Canning was to enter the ministry she no doubt spoke for others too: "In Heaven's name, don't have him; that man will cheat you! This is my private belief. Canning has the most brilliant talents but no stability in his principles. He is excessively ambitious."[43]

Although Canning's relations with Lord Liverpool were excellent he met considerable opposition from his Cabinet colleagues, especially Wellington, who took issue with the Foreign Secretary on Britain's role in European affairs in general and on policies towards Portugal and Greece in particular. In addition Canning had to win over the King. Canning had been a friend of George IV's estranged wife, Queen Caroline, before her departure abroad in 1814. On her return, and amidst the scandal which gathered around her, Canning resigned from the Government in 1821. George saw this as a hostile action. Quite apart from personal issues there were important matters of principle. George regarded himself as an expert on foreign affairs; as King of Hanover he received information from his German Minister which he was under no obligation to pass on to the British Foreign Secretary; he was the last British monarch to give private audiences to foreign envoys. Canning discovered an atmosphere of intrigue and later wrote that "the system which I found established of personal communications between the Sovereign and Foreign Minister was one under which no English Minister could do his duty".[44] Esterhazy, the Austrian ambassador, the French ambassador, Polignac, and the Lievens all attempted to influence the King directly. George denounced his own ministers in the presence of foreign representatives; he once remarked to Countess Lieven that Canning was "No more capable of conducting foreign policy than your baby".[45]

Above all, George was concerned about the policy of severing the European connections forged by Castlereagh and in January, 1825, wrote to Liverpool requiring the individual views of the Cabinet. This demand was refused. Later in the year Canning learned that the King intended to invite Metternich for a private meeting at Windsor. Since Metternich was at this time in Paris, Canning wrote to Granville, the British ambassador there, instructing him to apprise Metternich of British constitutional practice. Private conversations between foreign ministers and the British monarch were contrary to the British constitution and it was the duty of the Foreign Secretary to be present. Metternich did not make the visit.

It was about this time that the King's attitude to Canning changed, partly because the Foreign Secretary stood firm and his resignation would have led to a public revelation of the King's actions. But Canning was also determined to cultivate the King, and once good relations were established he was shown every mark of confidence, including knowledge of the Hanoverian correspondence. Canning played the courtier and became a royal favourite.

Under Canning the work handled by the Foreign Office increased markedly. The number of despatches sent and received by the Office rose from 6,193 in 1821 to 12,402 in 1826. There was also an increase in staff and significant reorganization for the sake of greater efficiency. Canning was one of the very few Foreign Secretaries actually to live at the Foreign Office; he drove his staff hard but showed concern for their welfare. More than forty years later Edmund Hammond, in evidence before a Select Committee, averred that "Mr Canning was a great man, and a rule which he laid down was no doubt well-considered, and, on the whole, I should not be disposed to alter it".[46] His despatches were powerfully effective, although the following rhyming example to Sir Charles Bagot at the Hague was rather untypical:

Sir,
    In matters of commerce the fault of the Dutch
    Is offering too little and asking too much.
    The French are with equal advantage content
    So we clap on Dutch bottoms just 20 per cent.
        I have no other commands from
    His Majesty to convey to Your Excellency
    to-day.
        I am, with great truth and
    respect,
        Sir,
    Your Excellency's most obedient
    humble servant,
        George Canning.


It was entirely characteristic of Canning's style that he should publicize his policies. In the House of Commons, in the publication of despatches in the press and on the public platforms he set out to win popular support and to make a patriotic appeal. A speech he made at Plymouth in 1823 is justly famous. He compared England to a great ship of the line like one of those "mighty masses that float in the waters above your town". From its silent stillness, "upon any call of patriotism" like England herself, it may "quickly collect all its beauty and its bravery" and springing from inaction into a display of might "awaken its dormant thunder".[47]

It was, then, the "interest of England" that stood as the object of his contemplation. To this end he set out to destroy the Congress System, on the grounds that it was seriously disadvantageous to Britain, and to break up that alignment of Russia, Prussia and Austria known as the Neo-Holy Alliance. In 1824 he outlined his policies to his cousin Stratford Canning. "Great Britain maintains a policy of her own suited to her position and constitution."[48] He disavowed any general interference in the affairs of other states, except in special circumstances such as upholding a treaty. In trying to steer "a middle course between Jacobinism and Ultraism"[49] he preferred constitutional monarchy to despotism or republicanism. Above all "our foreign policy cannot be conducted against the will of the nation".[50]

How far were Canning's aims achieved? Verona was the last Congress of the old style and Canning's attitude had much to do with its failure. On the specific issue raised at Verona, of intervention in Spain, Canning was unable to prevent a French army crossing the Pyrenees but attained his foremost objective of preventing an extension of French activity across the Atlantic to Spain's colonies. He did this by extracting an undertaking from Polignac[51] that France would not take this step; by recognizing the independence of the colonies, and by working closely with the United States. Monroe pronounced the doctrine of no European intervention in the affairs of the New World, but it was due to Canning and the invocation of the British fleet that the doctrine was upheld. When the stability of Portugal was threatened by internal disorder and the family quarrels of the monarchy, it was Canning who sent ships to the Tagus to prevent the intervention of France and Spain. He was able to justify his action as a response to treaty obligations. "While Great Britain has an arm to raise, it must be raised against the efforts of any Power that should attempt forcibly to control the choice and fetter the independence of Portugal."[52] By his good offices Brazil was peacefully separated from Portugal and, alone among the newly independent colonies, preserved its monarchy. In 1826 Canning could justifiably claim that he had "called the New World into existence, to redress the balance of the Old".[53]

Canning was anxious not to become directly embroiled in the struggle for Greek independence but, given his views on public opinion, he could scarcely ignore the enthusiasm for the Greek cause in Britain. Neither could he neglect Britain's commercial and strategic interests in the Levant. His solution was to act with Russia and, by doing so, restrain her. Co-operation with Russia also provided him with the opportunity of breaking finally with the Holy Alliance. In September, 1826, he wrote to Stratford, "You have no reason to dread being shackled by the Holy Alliance. They no longer march *en corps*. I have resolved them into individuality".[54] His triumph was complete when France was made a party to his arrangements. Austria and Prussia were left out. The Greeks had good reason to be grateful to Britain, and Canning's policy of working with Russia promised a solution to the wider issues of the Eastern Question. Much blood and treasure could have been saved in the course of the nineteenth century had Canning's immediate successors not lost the advantages he had gained.

Canning achieved his ultimate political ambition when he succeeded

Liverpool in the premiership in April, 1827. He did not live long to enjoy it as he died in the following August. His fame rests on his Foreign Secretaryship.

Once Prime Minister, Canning appointed John William Ward, Viscount Dudley, to be his Foreign Secretary. Dudley was an intimate friend and Canning was well satisfied with the appointment. Nevertheless the new Prime Minister kept a close eye on his old department and Dudley was largely Canning's mouthpiece. Canning expected Dudley's appointment to be temporary and this suited the new Foreign Secretary, who wrote to Aberdeen, "In three months I cannot do *much* harm to the public, nor to myself".[55] As it happened, Dudley served three Prime Ministers. He was reappointed by Canning's successor, Goderich, and then served under Wellington for six months before resigning with the rest of Canning's followers in June, 1828.

Dudley was well educated, hard-working and deeply read. He knew Virgil almost by heart. But early doubts were expressed by the Duke of Bedford, who commented "You may appoint one of your stable boys to be your cook, and when your friends come to dinner with you, tell them the appointment is only provisional, but I believe they would be as little satisfied with it as the Foreign Courts and Ministers will be with the provisional appointment of Lord Dudley, with his unfitness for business and various wanderings and distractions".[56] Bedford's fears were all too fully realized: Dudley's tenure of the Foreign Office proved disastrous. Although diligent and perhaps able to do little real damage while Canning remained alive, he was indecisive, shy and highly eccentric. Increasingly he became the target for political jokes. His practice of rehearsing aloud what he intended to say in two voices, one high-pitched and the other gruff in order to simulate an exchange, led to the remark that "it is only Dudley talking to Ward".[57]

He proved unable to deal with the combination of the political uncertainty of Goderich's ministry and the storm over the battle of Navarino, and when Wellington came into the premiership he was totally dominated. His health had always been poor and this, combined with his lack of self-confidence and the strains of office, drove him into a mental collapse, and later, near-imbecility. One of Dudley's few admirers was Lieven, the Russian ambassador. Shortly after Navarino, in a moment of absent-mindedness, Dudley put a despatch for the French ambassador in an envelope addressed to Lieven. The document was returned, ostensibly unread, but Lieven took it for a diplomatic trap of surpassing cunning and subtlety.

After Canning's death Dudley was helpless in face of the political and diplomatic challenges presented by the Greek war. Navarino, in which the British commander Codrington operated with very unclear instructions, raised the possibility that Turkish defeat would actually increase the danger of Russian intervention. A large part of the Tory party was highly critical of the action and this played no small part in the eventual fall of Goderich's government. Wellington's intervention was vigorous but disastrous. His support for continued Turkish control in Greece rather than an independent state which might resist overwhelming Russian influence did serious damage to future British interests. In these events and decisions poor Dudley was a helpless cipher.

Dudley was succeeded by George Hamilton Gordon, fourth Earl of Aberdeen. As a member of Wellington's Cabinet, holding the office of Chancellor of the Duchy of Lancaster, he had been shadowing the work of the Foreign Secretary with, apparently, the right of succession.

Like so many politicians of the day, Aberdeen was deeply influenced by Pitt. Indeed, as a result of the death of both Aberdeen's parents, Pitt, together with Dundas, an old family friend, was appointed his guardian. Educated at Harrow, where Palmerston was one of his contemporaries, and St John's College, Cambridge, Aberdeen had spent a lengthy period travelling abroad, especially in Greece and Turkey. He became an active philhellene and founded the Athenian Society. Byron referred to him as "the travelled thane, Athenian Aberdeen".

Aberdeen was a modest and serious-minded Scot. His deep faith led him to apply Christian principles to the conduct of policy and he preferred the role of mediator to that of aggressor. Tact, charm and sensitivity were among his principal assets and in the Foreign Office he led by example and kindness rather than by cracking the whip in the style of his successor, Palmerston. Personal tragedies left their mark on him. His beloved first wife died in the early stages of his political career and this blow was compounded by the deaths of his infant son and young daughters. For the rest of his life he wore mourning.

His first important opportunity was his appointment in 1813 by Castlereagh as ambassador extraordinary to the Austrian court. Still under thirty, he was almost totally untried and had very scanty knowledge of French, the language of diplomacy. But a man of rank was required for a post of such vital importance. He was given wide instructions concerning the conduct of the war and the terms to be imposed on France, as well as on relations with Austria. Aberdeen was not unsuccessful but his inexperience was demonstrated by his belief that he could handle Metternich (in fact he fell under the Austrian Foreign Minister's spell) and the presumptuous advice he sent home to Castlereagh. Perhaps his strongest impression, as he followed the Austrian Emperor and the allied armies, was of the horror and barbarity of war. After the battle of Leipzig he wrote "How shall I describe the entrance to this town? For three or four miles the ground is covered with bodies of men and horses. Wretches wounded, unable to crawl, crying for water amidst heaps of putrefying bodies. Their screams are heard at an immense distance and still ring in my ears".[58] These feelings never left him.

In his first period as Foreign Secretary, from June, 1828, to November, 1830, Aberdeen was "little more than a sounding-board for Wellington's opinions"[59] and his reputation really depends on his return to the Foreign Office under Peel from 1841 to 1846 and his term as Prime Minister between 1852 and 1855. Like Dudley, he was mainly concerned with the Greek question and under him British interests were damaged further. Fundamental to the Wellington–Aberdeen approach was that an independent Greece would be a Russian client state. Thus they failed to exert pressure on the Turks to come to a reasonable settlement. At the same time they disavowed the substantial territorial additions allotted to Greece at the ambassadorial conference at Poros. The British ambassador to Constantinople, Stratford Canning, had played a crucial part at this conference and angrily defended his powers as a plenipotentiary in a letter to the Foreign Secretary. "I should really think myself unworthy . . . of any place whatever in the trust of my sovereign, if I were to shrink from the responsibility of modifying or suspending any part of my instructions, when happening to be in possession of information unknown at the time to H.M.'s Government and calculated in my opinion to affect materially their views of the question involved in those instructions."[60] In fact a large and truly independent Greece promised a far more effective bulwark against Russian ambitions than a truncated Greece under Turkish suzerainty. Resulting Greek frustration would have invited Russian interference.

Since Britain would not discourage Turkish resistance to the loss of Greece, Russia saw that her best chance was to act unilaterally. Accordingly she pressed ahead in the Danubian Principalities in her war against Turkey. Russian success and the resulting Treaty of Adrianople, which greatly enlarged the Tsar's influence within the Ottoman Empire as well as recognizing a large and independent Greece, represented a defeat for Aberdeen's policies. The Greeks now had every reason to be grateful to the Russians, the very outcome the British Cabinet had hoped to avoid. Now that it was almost too late, Aberdeen tried to salvage something from the wreck. By the time of his resignation he was prepared to accept the enlarged and independent Greece with a monarchy as some guarantee of stability. More widely, however, Aberdeen's earlier approach had committed his successors to the perilous and often embarrassing policy of sustaining Turkey as a buffer against Russian expansion. Nineteenth-century British foreign policy might otherwise have been very different.

**NOTES TO CHAPTER TWO**

1  Kenneth Bourne. *The Foreign Policy of Victorian England 1830–1902* (Oxford, 1970), p. 3.
2  Bourne, p. 11.
3  Temperley and Penson, p. 11. For a further discussion of Pitt's Memorandum of 1805, see below.
4  Quoted by Paul Hayes, *Modern British Foreign Policy: The Nineteenth Century 1814–1880* (London, 1975), p. 63.
5  Quoted by Hayes, p. 137.
6  Stratford Canning, first Viscount Stratford de Redcliffe (1786–1880). Cousin of George Canning. First in Constantinople in 1808, left in charge of the Embassy in 1810. To Switzerland, 1814, and Washington, 1820. Ambassador to Constantinople 1824–29 and 1842–58. Special envoy to Constantinople 1831–32. Britain's greatest nineteenth-century ambassador.
7  Quoted by Hayes, p. 233. The Sublime Porte was the Ottoman Court at Constantinople.
8  Quoted by R. W. Seton-Watson, *Britain in Europe, 1789–1914* (Cambridge, 1937), p. 61.
9  Algernon Cecil. *British Foreign Secretaries, 1807–1916* (Edinburgh, 1927), p. 57.
10  C. J. Bartlett. *Castlereagh* (London, 1966), p. 87.
11  Quoted by J. W. Derry. *Castlereagh* (London, 1976), p. 227.
12  Quoted by Middleton, p. 107.
13  Quoted by Wendy Hinde, *Castlereagh* (London, 1981), p. 234.
14  Quoted by Bartlett, p. 259.

15  Quoted by Webster, Vol. I, p. 200.

16  Quoted by Derry, p. 7.

17  Quoted by Derry, p. 7.

18  Establishment and salaries of the Foreign Office, 1821.
    Secretary of State—£6,000
    2 Under-Secretaries—£3,349
    Chief Clerk—£2,242
    3 Senior Clerks—£3,567 between them
    13 Junior Clerks—£5,555 between them
    Librarian—£700
    Sub-librarian
    Clerk—Chief Clerk's department
    Private Secretary
    Précis Writer
    Translator
    Turkish Interpretor
    Collector
    Transmitter of papers.

19  Webster, Vol. I, p. 3.

20  Quoted by Bourne, p. 197.

21  Quoted by Bartlett, p. 119.

22  Quoted by Webster, Vol. I, p. 199.

23  Bourne, pp. 11–12.

24  Quoted by Webster, Vol. II, p. 55.

25  Quoted by Bartlett, p. 212.

26  Quoted by Bourne, p. 200.

27  Quoted by Bourne, p. 207.

28  Quoted by Webster, Vol. II, p. 326.

29  Quoted by Webster, Vol. II, p. 484.

30  Quoted by Derry, p. 227.

31  See McAlpine and Hunter, Pathography of the Past, *Times Literary Supplement*, 15 March 1974 and Prof. I. R. Christie's review of Wendy Hinde, *Castlereagh* in *Books and Bookmen*, No. 315, December 1981, p. 39. (I am indebted to Prof. Christie for these references).

32  Quoted by Webster, Vol. II, p. 489.

33  Quoted by Webster, Vol. II, p. 487.

34  Middleton, p. 109.

35  Sir Charles Bagot (1781–1843). Parliamentary Under-Secretary for Foreign Affairs 1807; Minister-plenipotentiary to France 1814, and to United States 1815–20. Ambassador to St Petersburg 1820, and to the Hague 1824. Later Governor-General of Canada.

36  Granville Leveson-Gower, first Earl Granville (1773–1846). Canning's contemporary at Christ Church, Oxford. Ambassador-extraordinary at St Petersburg 1804–05. Ambassador at Paris 1824–41.

37  Quoted by Rolo, p. 47.

38  Quoted by Rolo, p. 47.

39  H. W. V. Temperley, *The Foreign Policy of Canning* (London, 2nd edition 1966), p. 39.

40  Quoted by Webster, Vol I, p. 25.

41  Bartlett, p. 267.

42  Rolo, p. 99.

43  Quoted by Rolo, p. 112.

44  Quoted in A. W. Ward and G. P. Gooch, eds. *The Cambridge History of Foreign Policy* (Cambridge, 1922), Vol II, p. 108.

45  Quoted by Rolo, p. 118.

46  Quoted by Sir John Tilley and Stephen Gaselee, *The Foreign Office* (London, 1933), p. 46.

47  Cecil, p. 72.

48  Quoted by Temperley, p. 458.

49  Quoted by Temperley, p. 458.

50  Quoted by Temperley, p. 471.

51  Auguste Jules Armand Marie, Prince de Polignac. An intimate of Charles X of France. Appointed French Ambassador in London, 1823. Later Charles X's last First Minister.

52  Quoted in *Cambridge History of Foreign Policy*, Vol II, p. 117.

53  Quoted by Bourne. p. 210

54  Quoted in *Cambridge History of Foreign Policy*, Vol II, p. 114

55  Quoted by Middleton, p. 113.

56  Quoted by Rolo, p. 156.

57  *D.N.B.*

58  Quoted by Cecil, p. 103.

59  Hayes, p. 92.

60  17 January 1829. Quoted by Hayes, p. 164.

**CHAPTER THREE**

SECRETARIES OF STATE

| | |
|---|---|
| Henry John Temple, third Viscount Palmerston | November 1830–November 1834 |
| Arthur Wellesley, first Duke of Wellington | November 1834–April 1835 |
| Palmerston | April 1835–September 1841 |
| Aberdeen | September 1841–July 1846 |
| Palmerston | July 1846–December 1851 |
| Granville George Leveson-Gower, second Earl Granville | December 1851–February 1852 |
| James Harris, third Earl of Malmesbury | February 1852–December 1852 |
| Lord John Russell, afterwards first Earl Russell | December 1852–February 1853 |
| George William Frederick Villiers, fourth Earl of Clarendon | February 1853–February 1858 |
| Malmesbury | February 1858–June 1859 |
| Russell | June 1859–October 1865 |
| Clarendon | October 1865–June 1866 |

# The Age of Palmerston

## Foreign Policy 1830–1865

THE middle years of the nineteenth century were the age of Palmerston. From his appointment to the Foreign Secretaryship in November, 1830, to his death in October, 1865, he was scarcely out of major office. He was Foreign Secretary from 1830 to 1841, except for a few months in 1834–35, and again between 1846 and 1851; Home Secretary from 1852 to 1855; Prime Minister from 1855 to 1858 and from 1859 to 1865. Throughout this period his voice was the most important single influence on British foreign policy.

In these years Britain reached her zenith as an industrial and commercial power. By the mid-century she produced some two-thirds of the world's coal, about half its iron and a staggering five-sevenths of its steel. It has been calculated that over 40% of the traded manufactured goods of the whole world was produced in Britain, that over 90% of Britain's imports were raw materials and foodstuffs while 85% of her visible exports were finished goods.[1] It is no wonder that Britain needed a great fleet to protect her interests and safeguard her food supplies or that she more and more assumed the stance of a world power.

Nevertheless, it was during this same mid-century that new challenges to Britain's economic and naval supremacy were arising. In Germany and the United States in particular, political and economic forces combined to reduce Britain's early industrial lead. Moreover, by the 1840s it was feared that the development of steam-powered ships had removed the obstacles of tide and wind to a potential French invasion fleet. At the end of the next decade fresh alarm was created with the construction of ironclad ships by the French. The British ironclad *Warrior*, launched in 1860, restored some confidence, although since the new ship could have fought and sunk every capital ship constructed before the Crimean War, the implications were serious. With the building of ironclads by other powers Britain's traditional supremacy was much reduced; in a sense Britain was starting from scratch.

The continent of Europe was, in this period, shaken by revolution and the associated forces of liberalism and nationalism. Britain's diplomacy could not but be affected. Upheaval threatened to upset the balance of power on which her interests depended. British public opinion had a part to play too. In general it favoured the movements which challenged despotism and furthered the growth of liberalism. It expected its governments to follow suit; in some cases governments did so, but such a course was not always practical or desirable. British foreign policy remained pragmatic and undoctrinaire.

In July, 1830, a revolution in Paris overthrew the restored Bourbon monarchy. As by a chain reaction successful uprisings occurred in Belgium and Switzerland. Revolts in Poland and Italy, however, were crushed by the reactionary powers, Russia and Austria. The revolutions of 1848 were more widespread and even more important. In France, the Orléanist King Louis Philippe was overthrown and a new republic proclaimed. Widespread disturbances followed in Germany, including a rising in Berlin; the Austrian Empire was seriously disturbed, especially by the movements in Vienna, Prague, Hungary and Lombardy; in the face of determined opposition and demonstrations Italian rulers were forced to grant constitutions and other concessions. Revolution failed everywhere except in France; the Russians were called in to assist in the subjugation of the Habsburg lands and the Austrians themselves restored their authority and influence in Italy.

The events of 1830 and 1848 seemed to divide Europe even more clearly into autocratic and constitutional states. On the whole Britain preferred to deal with constitutional states and the new French monarchy of 1830 was welcomed. The French Revolution of 1848, however, raised the spectre of a powerful and aggressive Republic as in the 1790s. Therefore, although Britain deplored Austria's methods in suppressing revolution in Hungary and Italy, and most certainly placed her among the despotic powers, she had a strong interest in seeing Austria's position as a Great Power maintained. The balance of power had to be preserved. Moreover, the revolutions of 1830 and 1848 threatened to undermine the Vienna Settlement which British diplomacy upheld as a prime guarantee of European stability.

By the time of Palmerston's death Europe was about to be transformed by the rapid rise of Prussia. Bismarck was already Minister-President in

Berlin. He had taken his first steps towards the achievement of greater German unity and within a short space both Austria and France were to be vanquished. Across the Atlantic the Union had triumphed in the American Civil War. The results of this victory were far-reaching, not only for the United States but for the balance of economic and political power throughout the world.

In Palmerston's time, although France was still regarded as Britain's chief rival, the two countries generally acted more as allies than enemies. Indeed, the period 1841 to 1846 has been referred to as the "first *entente cordiale*".[2] Queen Victoria's meeting with Louis Philippe in 1843 was the first visit to France of a reigning English sovereign since Henry VIII. There was a further exchange of visits in 1845. Yet in spite of close co-operation over Belgium, the Eastern Question and the Iberian peninsula, these self-same areas of common interest caused suspicion and prevented an even development of amicable relations. Even so, in the Crimean War, the only non-colonial conflict fought by Britain between 1815 and 1914, France and Britain stood as allies.

As part of the strategy of containing France, the Treaty of Vienna had joined Belgium with Holland under the rule of the House of Orange. In August, 1830, the Belgians rose to expel the Dutch. The Dutch King, William I, responded by preparing an army to re-establish control. A general European war was a serious possibility: the French were tempted to intervene on the side of Belgium, thereby extending their own influence; such an intervention would provoke Austria and Prussia on the side of the Dutch; any activity in the Low Countries by the Great Powers would involve Britain in a defence of what she saw as her vital interests. A conference of the Great Powers, together with Holland, was summoned in London under the chairmanship of Aberdeen. In a matter of weeks he was succeeded as Foreign Secretary by Palmerston, to whom it fell to see the Belgian crisis through. Apart from the issues of French intervention and Dutch withdrawal, the principal difficulties consisted in finding a ruler for the newly independent Belgium, settling its frontiers and determining the future of Luxembourg. The summer of 1831 was particularly tense when a French army came to the aid of the Belgians after a Dutch invasion. A British fleet maintained a watching brief off the Belgian coast lest the French should decide not to withdraw once their task had been completed. The solution was for Britain and France to act jointly against the Dutch, and a cessation of hostilities was then speedily achieved. However, a final settlement was not reached until the Treaty of London in 1839 when Belgian neutrality was guaranteed by all the Great Powers.

In the Iberian peninsula the problems of Spain and Portugal showed striking similarities to each other. The young Queen of Spain, Isabella, and her regent mother, supported by Liberal elements, were opposed by Isabella's uncle, Don Carlos. He enjoyed the support of the absolutists. Meanwhile, the constitutionalist Queen Maria of Portugal was opposed by her absolutist uncle Don Miguel. Portugal's difficulties were more easily solved than Spain's. Maria's position was secured by a combination of the French fleet, with British agreement, and unofficial British action in the form of volunteers. Although Britain's interests were not directly threatened by events in Spain and Portugal, Palmerston still feared the consequences of French intervention. Once more the solution was to work with France and in April, 1834, a Quadruple Alliance was signed between Britain, France and the Queens of Portugal and Spain. The wicked uncles were to be expelled, the aid of the British fleet was enlisted and the French undertook to prevent assistance to Carlos.

Fresh difficulties over Spain arose when the marriages of Isabella and her sister were discussed at the meetings between the French and British monarchs in 1843 and 1845. Louis Philippe had hoped to gain Isabella's hand for one of his sons. This was opposed by the British who would have preferred a member of the house of Saxe-Coburg. However, by 1845, the Foreign Secretary, Aberdeen, was prepared to accept that Isabella should marry her cousin, the Duke of Cadiz, while her sister should marry Louis Philippe's youngest son, the Duke of Montpensier, but not before Isabella had produced heirs. On his return to the Foreign Office in 1846, and in an atmosphere of mutual suspicion, Palmerston brought matters speedily to a head. As a result of a provocative set of instructions to the British ambassador in Madrid, an offended Louis Philippe announced the betrothal of Isabella to Cadiz and of her sister to Montpensier. The marriages were to take place simultaneously. A major breach was thus created between France and Britain, but within two years Louis Philippe had been swept from his throne.

The accession to power of Louis Napoleon Bonaparte (after a *coup d'état* in 1851), first as President and then in 1852 as Napoleon III, Emperor of the French, caused some alarm in Britain. A Bonapartist

France might easily be committed to wholesale revision of the Vienna settlement and thus plunge Europe into war. Another view, held by Palmerston, was that such a régime was preferable to a Republic or to an Orléanist restoration.

Nevertheless, Britain's attitude to France under the Second Empire was always ambivalent. At the peace negotiations in Paris after the Crimean War, France gave strong support to the former enemy, Russia. Britain, France's ally in the war, was displeased. There was further suspicion concerning Napoleon's intervention in the cause of Italian unification. In 1858 France agreed to join with the independent state of Piedmont to drive Austria from Northern Italy. The British government favoured the Italian cause but although Palmerston regarded the Austrian presence in Italy as a "public nuisance" he was anxious that it should not be replaced by French influence. When France took Savoy and Nice, as her reward for helping to defeat the Austrians, Palmerston was offended by Napoleon's lack of consultation with Britain. However, this did not prevent a Franco-British free trade treaty in 1860. When southern Italy was liberated from despotic rule Britain turned a blind eye. Having freed Sicily, the Italian nationalist Garibaldi invaded the mainland while a British fleet looked on. Although Britain's role in the unification of Italy was largely passive, Palmerston gained a reputation for championing Italian nationalism.

The failure of Britain and France to act together in the 1860s proved significant in the advance of Prussia. Russia's ruthless suppression of the Polish Rebellion in 1863 was strongly condemned on both sides of the Channel. Yet the British and French governments failed to co-operate. The result was the complete breakdown of the entente: France refused to aid Britain in checking Prussian aggression against Denmark in 1864; the defeat of Austria in 1866 and France in 1870, both at the hands of Prussia, were made the more easy.

In Anglo-Russian relations the Eastern Question remained as the chief issue. Superficially at least, Russia and Britain were in agreement in claiming to believe that the Ottoman Empire should be preserved. But while Britain advocated the strengthening of the Empire by internal reform the Russians could not accept the prospect of its revitalisation. Privately, the Tsar looked forward to the eventual collapse of the Sultan's rule in the Balkans. This is not to say that Britain and Russia did not attempt to work together. In June, 1844, for example, Nicholas I, on a state visit to Britain, believed that he had come to an agreement with Peel and Aberdeen that they should co-operate in maintaining the Ottoman Empire. In the event of its collapse they would concert their policy. For the Tsar this meant partition; for British governments the agreement was not regarded as binding. This misunderstanding had disastrous consequences in 1853 as the Powers moved towards war. Britain's deep-seated suspicions about Russian ambitions were intensified by Tsarist advances in Persia which seemed to threaten communications with India.

At the beginning of Palmerston's first term at the Foreign Office it was Mehemet Ali of Egypt who once again opened the Eastern Question in a critical form. In 1831 his son Ibrahim invaded Syria. He was so successful that by the end of 1832 he was able to advance towards the Bosphorus. Aid for the Turks came from an unexpected source; the Sultan appealed to the Tsar and a Russian fleet appeared in the Bosphorus. Ibrahim retreated. Tsar and Sultan concluded the treaty of Unkiar Skelessi by which the Turks agreed to close the Dardanelles to all foreign warships at Russia's request. So matters remained until 1839 when the Turks invaded Syria, which Ibrahim had retained, and met with humiliating defeat. Constantinople was once again endangered.

Britain's response was to co-operate with France and a joint fleet was sent to the Dardanelles. Palmerston's next move was to call an international conference of the five Great Powers, but at this point a serious split opened between France and Britain. France had important interests in Egypt and gave stronger support to Mehemet Ali than Palmerston considered wise or desirable. Palmerston therefore concluded an agreement with Russia, Prussia and Austria, leaving out France. Mehemet Ali was coerced into accepting the terms laid down by the Powers and was confined to Egypt. More widely, by the Straits Convention of 1841 the Powers, including France, reversed the terms of Unkiar Skelessi. The Straits were to be closed to all foreign warships while the Ottoman Empire remained at peace. Turkey was saved, but once again Anglo-French co-operation had broken down in the face of mutual suspicion and clash of interests.

After the Tsar's visit to England in 1844 relations deteriorated and finally broke down completely with the outbreak of the Crimean War in 1854. Russophobia was stoked up by the Tsar's part in the suppressions of the 1848 revolutions and Nicholas was seen as the policeman of Europe.

The issues in the crisis which led to the Crimean War appear to have trivial origins. Nevertheless they raised important questions about the right of the Powers to interfere in the affairs of the Ottoman Empire. Above all the British and French were determined that its fate should not be decided by Russia alone. Soon after his accession Napoleon III, in order to assert French interests in the Near East and to cultivate the Catholic party at home, pressed the Sultan to grant the French rights of protection over the Christian shrines in the Holy Land. His success provoked a response by Nicholas I early in 1853; the Tsar, believing the collapse of the Ottoman Empire to be imminent, decided to advance Russia's own interests. Nicholas was optimistic about Britain's likely attitude since Aberdeen, with whom he had had important conversations in 1844,[3] was now Prime Minister. Indications from the Foreign Secretary, Russell, were not discouraging and the Tsar was led to believe that Russia and Britain would co-operate. Alas, Nicholas had mistaken politeness for support and in demanding concessions at Constantinople encountered a Sultan stiffened into resistance by the British Ambassador, Stratford Canning.[4]

Russia's next move was to invade the Danubian principalities of Moldavia and Wallachia. In reply, in June, 1853, a British fleet supported by the French was sent to the Dardanelles. The following month the ambassadors of the Great Powers, in conference at Vienna, produced a conciliatory Note which was accepted by Russia. Despite Stratford Canning's advice the Turks refused to sign because they believed that Britain and France would never allow Constantinople to fall into Russian hands. Further emboldened, the Sultan declared war on Russia in October. When a Turkish flotilla was sunk by the Russians at Sinope Bay British opinion was enraged. Early in 1854 the British and French fleets were sent into the Black Sea, an ultimatum was delivered to Russia and by the end of March the Western Powers, as allies of the Turks, were at war with the Tsar. After initial confusion about the objectives of the war the Allies planned to seize Sebastopol, the Russian naval base in the Crimea. Thus Britain "drifted" into the Crimean War.[5]

After a bloody and badly managed series of campaigns Sebastopol fell and peace was negotiated at Paris in March, 1856. Russia was damaged but got off more lightly than she might have expected. The most important international consequence was that the treaty neutralized the Black Sea by excluding warships from it. But the treaty provided no permanent settlement of the Eastern Question. For the time being Russia remained quiet but waited for the moment when she could abrogate the Black Sea clauses of the treaty.

Beyond Europe Britain's relations with the United States remained clouded. In the 1840s, with the deterioration of Anglo-French relations, there were genuine fears of a Franco-American combination against Britain. Unresolved and long-standing boundary disputes were an important source of trouble. The Maine–New Brunswick frontier was particularly crucial, especially in view of the Canadian rebellion of 1837, which had led to border incidents, and the deeply held view in the United States that Canada should be "liberated" from Britain. After years of dispute the frontier was agreed by the Webster–Ashburton treaty of 1842. On the western side of North America the Oregon frontier question came into prominence with the growth of the "Manifest Destiny" movement in the United States. Thousands of Americans took the Oregon trail in the 1840s. Agreement was reached in 1846 when the 49th parallel, with a deviation enabling Vancouver Island to remain in British hands, was fixed as the frontier. Other matters causing anxiety were British attempts to stamp out the slave trade. This led to an unresolved dispute over the rights of search at sea and, in addition, tension over the position of Texas. The Lone Star Republic was in an ambiguous situation in the period between its break with Mexico in 1835 and its admission to the United States in 1845. Britain saw an independent Texas as a possible counterpoise to the United States; as a commercial opportunity to breach the American tariff walls; and as open to persuasion in abandoning slavery. The government of the United States was understandably suspicious.

America's expansion westwards and southwards (the admission of Texas to the Union and the discovery of gold in California with its acquisition, in 1848, after war with Mexico) made her anxious about Central America and sea communications between her east and west coasts. In this area Britain had island bases in the Caribbean and a number of footholds, including British Honduras, in Central America. A clash might have occurred but for Palmerston's recognition that America's uneasiness might be used to gain a useful compromise. In 1850, therefore, in the Clayton–Bulwer treaty it was agreed that neither power would seek further colonization in Central America and would work for the construction of a neutral canal.

From 1850 until the outbreak of the American Civil War in 1861 relations remained relatively quiet. But the Civil War raised innumerable problems for Britain and divided public opinion. First and foremost was the matter of Britain's neutrality, how it was to be maintained and safeguarded. However, the mere proclamation of Britain's neutrality gave recognition to the belligerent status of the Southern States and was therefore resented by the North. Had the Northern States begun the war with an unequivocal anti-slavery stance then British opinion would have been overwhelmingly in their favour, but as it was there was considerable sympathy for the South's right to secede. Of crucial importance was the Northern naval blockade of the South. As a result of this American supplies of cotton to Britain had almost ceased by the end of 1861. This caused considerable distress since some 20% of Britain's population depended directly or indirectly upon the cotton industry. Eighty per cent of Britain's raw cotton came from the United States.

Relations with the North were seriously jeopardised by the celebrated *Trent* and *Alabama* affairs. In 1861 two Southern envoys, Mason and Slidell, embarked on a British steamer, the *Trent*, at Havana. Once at sea the *Trent* was intercepted by a Northern warship and the two envoys arrested. For a while excitement ran at fever-pitch on both sides of the Atlantic. The son of Charles Francis Adams, the American minister in London, believed that had it not been for the recently laid Atlantic cable war would have broken out. Good sense and diplomacy prevailed. Mason and Slidell were released but received a cool reception in London. The Foreign Secretary, Russell, refused to see their credentials.

The *Alabama* affair, a British blunder, was more complicated and took longer to settle. British law prohibited the provision of ships of war for conflicts in which Britain was neutral. Nevertheless, the South placed orders in British yards. One vessel, the *Florida*, was completed and did conspicuous damage to Northern shipping. Charles Adams protested to the British government but owing to administrative confusion a second ship, the *Alabama*, was able to slip out of Liverpool. She also caused great damage.

The North demanded compensation, which was not conceded until 1872, but for the rest of the Civil War Palmerston's government took determined measures to prevent further breaches of its own neutrality laws. It was as well that there was no irreconcilable breach between the Northern States and Britain. In the early stages the Civil War seemed to hang in the balance but by the end of 1864 the advantage had turned in favour of the Union.

The age of Palmerston has been seen as an age of gunboat diplomacy and nowhere was it used more blatantly than in China. In the Far East the interests of British and other European merchants in opening up a lucrative trade clashed with the Chinese Empire's policy of restricting contacts with the West. Up to 1833 the East India Company held a monopoly of Britain's trade with China. The ending of the Company's monopoly brought Chinese officials face to face with representatives of the British government attempting to uphold the interests of its nationals. This situation was complicated by the trade in opium developed by the company. Opium trading was forbidden by the Chinese government in Peking but, since the bulk of the trade was in distant Canton, large-scale smuggling continued. A Chinese attempt in 1839 to suppress the trade led to a clash. A war followed in which Canton was bombarded. By the Treaty of Nanking in 1842 the Chinese opened Canton, Shanghai and three other ports to Britain and other European nations. Britain also gained the island of Hong Kong.

Peace proved fragile; the merchants worked for further privileges, the Chinese government looked to reduce those already granted. In 1856 Chinese officials boarded the *Arrow*, technically a British ship, and arrested the crew. In retaliation a British naval force bombarded forts in the Canton river, and in 1860 Franco-British forces actually marched on Peking. As part of their policy of reprisal the Imperial Summer Palace was burned. The Chinese then granted a fresh set of concessions, including the opening of Tientsin.

In the 1860s there was a notable reverse for Palmerstonian foreign policy when British support for Denmark against Prussia was revealed as an empty bluff. The occasion of the débâcle was the longstanding and complicated dispute over the duchies of Schleswig and Holstein. In the longer term the more important issue was the opportunity it provided for Prussian aggrandizement.

The Treaty of Vienna had given Schleswig and Holstein to the King of Denmark, who ruled these duchies, as their Duke, separately from his kingdom. Northern Schleswig was largely Danish-speaking, the south and Holstein were German-speaking. As Duke of Holstein the King of Denmark was a member of the new German Confederation. A further complication was that although the Crown of Denmark could pass in the female line, in the duchies a Salic Law reserved the succession to the male line. When the childless Frederick III succeeded in 1848 he attempted a solution by which Schleswig was incorporated into Denmark while Holstein was given its own institutions with membership of the German Confederation. This arrangement was contested by the heir to the duchies, the Duke of Augustenburg. A short war ended in his defeat by Frederick. The Powers intervened and in 1852 imposed a settlement by which Christian of Glücksburg, Frederick's heir in the female line, was given the succession to the kingdom and the duchies on condition that the duchies were not incorporated into Denmark.

In 1863 Christian succeeded to the throne and attempted, as Frederick had before him, to divide the duchies. This prompted the revival of the Augustenburg claim. Bismarck saw an opportunity of gaining the duchies, together with the port of Kiel, for Prussia. He secured Austrian support for joint action against Denmark.

Palmerston and his Foreign Secretary, Russell, completely misjudged the situation and the growing strength of Prussia. In the House of Commons Palmerston had said "We are convinced, I am convinced at least, that if any violent attempt were made to overthrow [the rights] and to interfere with [the] independence of Denmark, those who made the attempt would find in the result that it would not be Denmark alone with which they would have to contend".[6] Bismarck was dismissed as "crazy". When it came to action Britain found herself isolated. Bismarck had Austria on his side. He had carefully cultivated Russia, especially over the Polish question, a matter which divided France and Britain. As Austria and Prussia moved against them the Danes appealed for British assistance. Public opinion, whipped up by Palmerston himself, clamoured for aid to be sent. But although the Cabinet authorized a fleet to be despatched to Copenhagen it was only by a majority of one. With such a sharp division between his colleagues Palmerston saw that decisive action was impossible. The Danes were left to their fate. Prussia was given Schleswig to administer and Austria Holstein. Bismark had won the first of the three wars which were to obtain hegemony in Germany for Prussia. In the House of Lords Derby cast Russell as Bottom the Weaver, who for all his roaring turned out to be "no lion at all". The government's foreign policy he summed up in two short, homely but expressive words—"meddle and muddle".[7]

## The Foreign Secretaries 1830–1866

In writing Palmerston's obituary the *Daily Telegraph* recognized him as "the most English minister that ever governed England".[8] Palmerston's outspokenness, his prejudices and patriotism, his fine bearing and love of sport appealed directly to popular opinion. He came to personify the John Bull qualities which Englishmen understood. In his middle years his lack of tact and abrasive language gained him the nickname "Lord Pumicestone". Bulwer,[9] his contemporary and biographer, remarked that "generally when Lord Palmerston talks of diplomacy, he talks also of ships of war".[10] He was apt to express contempt of foreigners and foreign ways, he saw Austria as "an old woman" and "a European China". The Turkish ambassador in London was dismissed as "a greasy, stupid old Turk", Mehemet Ali as "an ignorant barbarian". The dislike was mutual. German conservatives saw him as the friend of European revolution and circulated the lines "Hat der Teufel einen Sohn, so ist er sicher Palmerston". The Duchess de Dino, Talleyrand's niece, conceded that Palmerston "may have a gift for the despatch of business; he may speak and write French well; but he is a rude and presumptuous person, his behaviour is arrogant, and his character not upright".[11] In his later years Palmerston was a legendary figure and to Englishmen "good old Pam".

Henry John Temple, third Viscount Palmerston, was born at Westminster in 1784. His title, which he inherited aged seventeen, was in the Irish Peerage, so like his father and grandfather he was able to sit in the House of Commons. Although the family had extensive Irish lands, it also held estates in Yorkshire, Northamptonshire and Hampshire. The Temples hardly qualified as Irish and sought their social and political life in London.

The young Palmerston travelled widely in Europe with his family, especially in Italy and Germany, and was in Paris during the revolution of August, 1792. On his return he went to Harrow and in 1800 to the University of Edinburgh. While he was there his father died, in 1802. His guardian was an old friend of his father, the Earl of Malmesbury. Not only was he a very distinguished diplomat but he had important political connections too. In 1803 Palmerston left Edinburgh for St John's College, Cambridge, where in 1806, while still an undergraduate, he stood in a by-election as a candidate for the University seat. He failed at this first hurdle but was returned unopposed in 1807 for Newport, Isle of Wight. He had already been appointed Junior Lord of the Admiralty.

In 1809 Palmerston refused the Chancellorship of the Exchequer but accepted instead the Secretaryship at War. He held this portfolio under successive prime ministers for nearly twenty years, but it was not until 1827 that he was given Cabinet status, by Canning. It is a matter for some speculation why one of the greatest Foreign Secretaries should have laboured for so long in a relatively unambitious post. One suggestion is that he was too much concerned with his own pleasures; these were the years when he was called 'Lord Cupid'. More convincing is that it was largely a matter of chance and opportunity. His admission to the Cabinet caused a fundamental change. "It brought him access to Cabinet papers which transformed his whole outlook . . . at a time when foreign affairs were important and even dramatic. They made a strong appeal to him . . . Henceforward his main preoccupation was foreign affairs and the Foreign Office itself was his goal."[12]

The changing political situation, the death of Canning, the loosening of party ties and the growing split in the Tory party gave him his opportunity. When Grey formed his Whig ministry in 1830 Palmerston, a Tory, was offered the Foreign Secretaryship. Although he was in favour of only mild parliamentary reform he had spoken in favour of Catholic Emancipation. Above all, he had fiercely criticized the foreign policy of Wellington's government and was thus acceptable, if only just, to the Whigs. Even so his appointment was unexpected. Many Whigs remained jealous and suspicious of him but they could not do without him. His growing popularity in the country was of electoral value; in Parliament the Tories approved his patriotism and the Radicals his denunciation of European reactionaries.

Bulwer described the new Foreign Secretary as "a man in the full vigour of middle age, very well dressed, very good looking, with the large thick whiskers worn at that time. His air was more that of a man of the drawing-room than of the senate".[13] So far, perhaps, Palmerston's reputation had been more that of a dandy than a statesman. His love affairs were well known, for example, with Lady Cowper,[14] whom he later married, and Lady Jersey. Mrs Stanley, the wife of a Whig M.P., recorded that Palmerston had made love to her just after her marriage in 1826 "in his impudent brusque way, with a 'Ha, ha!' I see it all—beautiful woman neglected by her husband—allow me, etc.'"[15] To the end of his life he dressed in the height of fashion and at the age of eighty-eight was cited as a co-respondent in a divorce case.

Henry John Temple, third Viscount Palmerston, by J. Partridge.

*National Portrait Gallery, London*

Granville George Leveson-Gower, second Earl Granville.

*The Mansell Collection*

Once in the Foreign Office, however, he worked unremittingly. Although he still rode regularly, especially in the mornings, he had less time to spend on interests he had hitherto followed passionately, hunting, shooting and prize-fighting. He rarely left London, even in the Parliamentary recess. It was only with the completion of the railway line that he could visit his beloved estate at Broadlands with any frequency. Like Castlereagh, Palmerston shouldered the double burden of the Commons and the Foreign Office. That he survived was tribute to his magnificent physique and robust health. "The life I lead", he once said, "is like that of a man who on getting out of bed every morning, should be caught up by the end of one of the arms of a windmill and whirled round and round till he was again deposited at night to rest."[16]

Behind the bullying and bluster, the arrogance, the imperious style there was a remarkable professional. He was a very able linguist with a mastery of French, Spanish, Italian and, later, Portuguese. His tactlessness and impetuosity have been given more prominence than his qualities of patience, powers of concentration, shrewdness in negotiation, care, and even brilliance, in the drafting of despatches.

Above all a Foreign Secretary depends upon accurate, detailed and copious information. Later in his career Palmerston, with the development of railways, steamships and the electric telegraph, had the benefit of more rapid communications. In 1830 despatches from embassies in Western Europe took two or three days to arrive in London, from Southern and Eastern Europe up to a fortnight, from Constantinople and Washington a month, from Canton not less than five months. Inevitably considerable discretion remained in the hands of the man on the spot; most dramatically, the British ambassador in Constantinople was given the authority to summon a fleet to the Dardanelles. This power was used. Unlike modern Foreign Secretaries, Palmerston rarely went abroad to attend conferences and other meetings. He remained firmly ensconced in the Foreign Office where he was like "a general commanding a division of élite troops",[17] making all the decisions. Although British representatives abroad took considerable initiatives they did so only within the lines mapped out for them. On taking up their posts they received full and unequivocal statements of British policies. These were supplemented at appropriate intervals.

Palmerston drafted all important despatches himself and read every document of any significance which passed through his department. "In England", he once told Queen Victoria, "the Ministers who are at the head of the several departments of State, are liable any day and every day to defend themselves in Parliament; in order to do this, they must be minutely acquainted with all the details of the business of their offices and the only way of being constantly armed with such information is to control and direct these details themselves".[18] Such constitutional considerations and Palmerston's own temperament placed the Foreign Secretary and his department under an exacting régime. Palmerston spent about eight hours each day on Foreign Office business in addition to attending the House and Cabinet. He rose before seven and, after taking exercise riding or swimming, read some despatches before breakfast. Arriving at the Office at about ten, he worked through the morning until the late afternoon, unless there was a Cabinet. After dinner he attended the House and then would return home to work on his despatches, generally until one but sometimes as late as four in the morning. When keeping late hours he did not sit down but worked standing up at a specially designed desk for fear of falling asleep. Not only was his command of detail exceptional but he took great pains to have information at his finger-tips. Every important despatch he had written or received was copied for him into large books which he kept constantly to hand. This was at a time when the number of despatches received and sent by the Office increased from 11,546 in 1830 to 30,725 in 1849. In the same period the staff increased from 35 to 40.[19]

Palmerston was hated by his staff not only because he made them work hard, sometimes unreasonably so, but because of his high-handed treatment of them. On going to the Office on a Sunday morning with his wife Palmerston expressed irritation that the head of department was not there. Lady Palmerston interceded, "But you see, my dear, some people go to church on Sundays".[20] Granville,[21] as Under-Secretary, recorded in 1840 that "the clerks detest Palmerston, and have an absurd idea that he takes pleasure in bullying them".[22] Even the Under-Secretaries were confined to routine tasks. Sir George Shee[23] wrote to Backhouse:[24] "Lord Palmerston, you know, never consults an Under-Secretary. He merely sends out questions to be answered or papers to be copied when he is here in the evenings, and our only business is to obtain from the clerks the information that is wanted".[25] There were complaints that Palmerston's demands and the late hours affected seriously the domestic life and even the health of his staff. The clerks objected to being summoned by the Foreign Secretary by bell rather than by messenger; Palmerston's economies cut back on perquisites and allowances for coal and candles. He also forbade smoking in office hours.

In the pre-typewriter age clear handwriting was essential, especially since Palmerston suffered from dazzling and eye-strain. Many were the strictures delivered on the subject of handwriting, not only to the clerks but to British Ministers abroad. Not even the colour of ink escaped Palmerston's attention. He liked ink to be black and writing large. "Send this Despatch [from Madrid] back to Mr Bulwer, to be written over again in better Ink, and ask him where he got the Ink in which it is written", ordered the Foreign Secretary in 1847.[26] A minute to his whole staff read: "The greater portion of the Foreign Office Hands are excellent and admired by all but there are some few on the Establishment who might improve their Handwriting if they would take more pains to form their letters distinctly."[27] The efforts of particular individuals were denounced as "like running Penknives into one's eyes", or as sloping backwards hands "like the raking masts of an American schooner".[28] In what spirit did the chief clerk receive Palmerston's letter on leaving office in December, 1851? "I can assure you that I feel great regrets at finding myself separated from my fellow-labourers in the Foreign Office, to whose assistance I have been so much indebted for the success which has attended our united exertions."[29]

Pressure of work and his own arrogance made Palmerston notoriously unpunctual. Even at official banquets when members of the royal family were present, Palmerston would arrive after the meal had started. At the Foreign Office he took a perverse delight in making visitors, however important, wait their turn. Talleyrand complained of this treatment and Pozzo di Borgo, the Russian ambassador, once waited for two hours. Yet Palmerston was scarcely ever late in attending the House for a debate or to answer questions.

Palmerston's entry to the Foreign Office followed a few months after the accession of William IV. William, although not highly gifted, gave careful attention to business and was more respected than his brother. His influence on foreign policy was therefore important. "Viscount Palmerston", wrote William, "is doubtless responsible for the advice he gives but there is no positive obligation on the King to sanction that which he does not approve, and the very Process which is observed of submitting Instructions for his Approval, establishes the necessity of such approval."[30] In point of fact there were few disagreements, although there were occasions when Palmerston did not press a policy because he knew the King would oppose it. The King read all important despatches received and sent, most were marked "appr[ove]d" or sometimes "highly approved" and on occasion Palmerston could risk sending a despatch before it had received official consent. The relationship worked well but there is little doubt that Palmerston welcomed the inexperience of Victoria when she succeeded in 1837.

In the early part of Victoria's reign Palmerston spent long hours with the young Queen going through despatches and briefing her in advance of audiences with foreign ministers. Rather touchingly, after she had been on the throne for a few weeks, she wrote, "As the Queen has got a great many Foreign Despatches which, from want of time she has been unable to read as yet, she requests Lord Palmerston not to send her any more until she has done with those which she already has with her".[31]

As time went on the relationship altered: the Queen became more interested and better informed; Albert, whom she married in 1840, was influential, and Palmerston's policies diverged more and more from the royal couple's own views. The central issue, on which all others depended, was Palmerston's failure to seek royal approval before sending despatches or, more devious, his tendency to alter despatches after they had been approved. Apart from finding royal influence unwelcome, Palmerston could claim that the overwhelming pressure of affairs made short-cuts inevitable. The breach really developed after Palmerston's return to the Foreign Office in 1846. Victoria and Albert showed a marked preference for the autocratic monarchies, and suspected that Palmerston was working to undermine the Austrian position in Italy. For his part, the Foreign Secretary suspected that royal correspondence with European relatives and other rulers secretly worked against his policies. Matters of a more personal nature affronted the Queen. During an interview with Russell, the Prime Minister, Albert denounced Palmerston for his "worthless private character". In Windsor Castle itself Palmerston had apparently attempted to violate one of the Queen's ladies in waiting and "would have consummated his fiendish scheme by violence had not the miraculous efforts of his victim and such assistance attracted by her screams saved her".[32] On the constitutional issues Russell took the Queen's side, partly because there were times when he and the Cabinet had not been consulted either. As to the venery of the Foreign Secretary, Russell was reassuring, pointing out to Albert that at the age of sixty-five Palmerston would be unlikely to cause future offence.

With every appearance of surrender Palmerston agreed to the Queen's requirements that she should be fully informed. But in fact he conceded very little. Only a few months afterwards Palmerston clashed with the Crown again over the case of the Austrian General Haynau. While visiting Britain, Haynau, who was thoroughly detested in the country as a result of his cruel repressions in Hungary, was set upon by a group of workers belonging to Barclay's Brewery in Southwark. Palmerston took some delight in the incident and wrote to the Home Secretary: "The draymen were very wrong in the particular course they adopted. Instead of striking Haynau . . . they ought to have tossed him in a blanket, rolled him in the kennel and then sent him home in a cab".[33] Nevertheless, in the case of an assault on a seventy-year-old general, an apology to Vienna was necessary. Palmerston's despatch for presentation to the Austrian government gave such an inadequate apology that the Queen objected. To Victoria's fury, by the time she saw a copy of the despatch it had already gone off. She did succeed, however, in instructing Palmerston to write another, and although he talked to Russell of resignation he did not go through with it.

Palmerston again followed the popular line in 1851 on the visit to Britain of Kossuth, the Hungarian nationalist leader in exile. It would have been tactless, to say the least, for Palmerston to have received him, as he wished, but it was only with considerably difficulty that the Queen and Cabinet dissuaded him. Nevertheless, Palmerston did receive a delegation of Radicals whose address contained Kossuth's own words describing the Emperors of Austria and Russia as "odious and detestable assassins".

In December, 1851, Palmerston went too far. The occasion was Louis Napoleon's successful *coup d'état* of which Palmerston, in an interview with the French ambassador in London, showed his clear approval. The ambassador's report to Paris gave the Foreign Secretary's utterance the full weight of Britain's official endorsement. Neither Crown nor Cabinet had been informed; Victoria and Russell combined to secure Palmerston's dismissal. He never held the Foreign Secretaryship again.

In his first period at the Foreign Office, Palmerston encountered "more opposition in Cabinet than any other Foreign Minister of the nineteenth century except Canning in his first two years".[34] The Whig majority never fully accepted him, they were jealous of him and disliked his methods. In order to survive Palmerston depended upon his own unrivalled knowledge of foreign affairs, his popularity in the country, and the appeal he had to both Radicals and Tories in the House. But he was fortunate also in the support he received from his first two prime ministers. Grey and Palmerston were at one on almost all major issues; the Prime Minister rarely altered despatches, although he did tone down language, and he supported the Foreign Secretary's policies in Cabinet. "The initiative and conduct of policy remained in Palmerston's hands throughout."[35] Melbourne was, from the start, more critical of Palmerston's policies than Grey had been. However, Melbourne and Palmerston were close friends and the Prime Minister's loyalty was never in question.

Palmerston's dealings with his third Prime Minister, Lord John Russell, were complicated by his relationship with the Crown. Russell disapproved of Palmerston's methods but, although under great pressure from Victoria and Albert, was unable to act decisively because of the popularity of the foreign policy in the country. Therefore, on a number of occasions, Russell defended Palmerston to the Crown. However, Palmerston was furious at his dismissal in 1851 and blamed Russell.

Palmerston spent much time in the Commons. Although lacking Canning's great gifts of oratory, he was able to influence and cultivate the House in other ways. Palmerston placed more documents before Parliament than any of his predecessors. This was a recognition of his dependence on parliamentary and public opinion, and this importantly affected not only his diplomacy but that of his successors. His expression of liberal principles won support in the House and outside, as did his devotion to the cause of stamping out the slave trade. However, his greatest triumph in the House—"one of his few outstanding speeches"[36]—was over the Don Pacifico affair. For some time British subjects and interests had suffered interference and affronts in Greece. Don Pacifico, a Portuguese Jew whose claims to British citizenship rested on his having been born in Gibraltar, had failed to gain compensation from the Greek Government for damage done to his property in riots in 1847. In 1850 Palmerston used a British squadron to blockade Piraeus, the port of Athens, and seized public and private property as surety until pending British claims were met. This action caused a tremendous furore at home and abroad. The Cabinet was divided, the Queen complained explosively, and a vote of censure was carried in the Lords.

The debate in the Commons took the form of an attack on Palmerston's foreign policy across the board. His defence, in a speech lasting four and a half hours, was equally wide-ranging. It was a remarkable demonstration of his mastery of the issues (he used only half a sheet of paper for his notes) and of his stamina. He saved the government and his position, maintaining that "as the Roman, in the days of old, held himself free from indignity, when he could say *Civis Romanus sum*; so also a British subject, in whatever land he may be, shall feel confident that the watchful eye and strong arm of England will protect him against injustice and wrong".[37]

Palmerston surpassed his predecessors not only in laying information before Parliament but also in his use of the press. In doing so he demonstrated his reliance upon public opinion as well as recognizing its growing importance, especially as represented by the commercial and professional classes. In Palmerston's time parliamentary debates were more fully reported in the newspapers than before and, particularly relevant, there was a wider coverage of foreign news. Alone in Europe, British newspapers were generally independent of the government and, apart from the placing of government advertisements, could not be directly bought. Although *The Observer* was paid out of secret service funds politicians had to seek other means of influencing the press. Palmerston became an adept practitioner in this field. "The only influence", he wrote to Lady Cowper in 1831, "which my office possesses over the *Courier* or any other paper is positive not negative. I could get [the Editor] to insert any article I wished today but I have no means or power of preventing him from inserting any other of quite a different kind tomorrow. I can compel but I cannot control."[38] Palmerston took direct responsibility for supplying the newspapers with information and was most forthcoming with those journals which gave general support to his policies. Remarkably, for a man with such a huge workload, Palmerston wrote for the newspapers himself. He contributed mainly to the *Globe*, an evening newspaper, which enabled him to make an immediate reply to the morning journals. His articles, which were anonymous, show him to have been an excellent journalist with a shrewd awareness of the extent to which British foreign policy rested on public opinion.

"English interests continue the same, let who will be in office", wrote Palmerston to his brother in 1835.[39] Thirteen years later the same pragmatism was in evidence in a speech to the House. "We have no eternal allies, and we have no perpetual enemies. Our interests are eternal and perpetual, and these interests it is our duty to follow."[40] In spite of examples of bluster and gunboat diplomacy, Palmerston pursued British interests soberly and with restraint. Nor was he unaware of Britain's moral influence. "I hold that the real policy of England—apart from questions which involve her own particular interests, political or commercial—is to be the champion of justice and right; pursuing that course with moderation and prudence."[41]

He spoke in favour of liberal causes in Europe; recognized that constitutional states were Britain's natural allies; maintained a benevolent stance towards the nationalist movements in Italy and encouraged the parties of moderation in the Iberian peninsula. But intervention was quite another thing, except where absolutist states sought to intervene in the internal affairs of others. Like Canning he was generally opposed to the calling of congresses, although he did take part in conferences on specific issues such as Belgium, the slave trade or the Eastern Question. Although he condemned the reactionary character of Austria and enjoyed the humiliation of Haynau, he saw that Austria and Prussia were essential bulwarks against French or Russian expansion in Central Europe. Austria had to be maintained as a great Power, especially north of the Alps. For this reason among others he welcomed a reduction of Austrian influence in Italy, although he was anxious that it should not be replaced by French influence. Since Britain's interests lay in the maintenance of peace and stability in Europe he was far from being in favour of the destabilizing effects of revolution. He knew that detaching Hungary from Austria would be a crippling blow, although he welcomed Kossuth in Britain. The Balance of Power was to be pursued, not for any abstract reason of principle but because, once again, this best suited British interests, Palmerston saw it as a "System of Practical Mediation whereby British support was shifted from one side to the other according as the opposite Side may manifest a Spirit of Encroachment and Injustice".[42] In short, Palmerston had no "system".

It has been argued that Palmerston's greatest triumphs were won between 1830 and 1841. He was determined, for example, that Belgium should become independent and neutral. This objective was largely achieved by 1832 and confirmed in 1839. When the French army seemed likely to remain in Belgium after the expulsion of the Dutch he wrote to the British ambassador in Paris, "One thing is certain, the French must go out of Belgium or we have a general war, and war in a given number of days".[43] Having achieved French withdrawal he employed a technique that he was to use time and again in future: he allied with a potential rival, in this case France, reaching a settlement whilst restricting the rival's freedom of action. He combined with France again to achieve stability in the Iberian peninsula by the Quadruple Alliance of 1834. This he described as "a capital hit and all my own doing".

Webster argued that Palmerston's triumph in settling the crisis in the Near East in 1840 "was perhaps the greatest he ever won in his long connexion with foreign affairs".[44] The dissolution of the Ottoman Empire would not only have damaged the particular interests of Britain but would have had serious consequences for Europe as a whole. The more obvious danger at that time was that Mehemet Ali would undermine it, but of almost equal concern was that Russia's apparent support of the Turks would result in taking Constantinople rather by "sap than by storm". In the same way that he worked with France over Belgium, so he co-operated with Russia over the Eastern Question. Throughout the crisis, and with a deeply divided Cabinet, he showed patience in negotiation and coolness of mind. As appropriate, and with impeccable timing, he used threats and conciliation, flattery and straight-talking. Although Palmerston is criticized for his pursuit of narrow national aims, the settlement of 1840–41 was truly international in its scope and conception.

Palmerston was also capable of grave errors of judgement. His provocative despatch to Madrid in 1846 over the Spanish marriages surrendered the advantage to the French. The premature recognition of the Bonaparte coup of 1851 played into the hands of enemies at Court and in the government. His attempt to send Stratford Canning as ambassador to St Petersburg was highly imprudent and almost bound to fail. John Bright regarded Palmerston's tenure of the Foreign Office as "one long crime";[45] his treatment of non-European countries, especially China, would sorely try the conscience of the second half of the twentieth century. Yet his policies struck resonant chords with British public opinion and his qualities won the respect of rival diplomats abroad. For sheer professionalism and grasp of foreign policy he has few equals. "Lord Palmerston", wrote Talleyrand, "is certainly one of the most able, if not the most able man of business whom I have met in my career."

In style and aims the contrast between Aberdeen and Palmerston is striking. Twentieth-century labels might identify Aberdeen as an appeaser and Palmerston as an imperialist. "Tact and calmness were [Aberdeen's] greatest assets."[46] When he took up the Foreign Secretaryship for the second time in 1841, Aberdeen aimed to shift British foreign policy from the directions followed by Palmerston over the previous eleven years. Although he could do little but confirm the results Palmerston had obtained in China and Afghanistan, Aberdeen deliberately set out to improve relations with the United States and to revive the French entente.

In his dealings with France Aberdeen benefited from the desire for better relations on the part of Louis Philippe and his leading minister Guizot, with whom he was able to develop a friendship. The Queen also favoured an Anglo-French rapprochement and, more generally, regarded Aberdeen with high favour. He accompanied her to both meetings with Louis Philippe in 1843 and 1845. In this second period at the Foreign Office Aberdeen also enjoyed a much freer hand in his dealings with the Prime Minister. Aberdeen was on much more equal terms with Peel than with Wellington, and Peel showed less interest in foreign policy than the Duke. Moreover, a policy of tact and conciliation abroad fitted in with Peel's plans for reform at home.

Not surprisingly, the initiative to improve Anglo-American relations stemmed to a large extent from an appreciation of the commercial benefits which would accrue as well as from Aberdeen's broad, conciliatory approach to diplomacy. His selection as his envoy of Ashburton, a member of the banking family of Baring and married to an American wife, was significant. A number of disputes were settled, including the Maine boundary question, but the general amity for which Aberdeen had hoped was only partly achieved. The Oregon boundary question, for example, remained intractable, but the chief obstacle was simply hostile public opinion on both sides of the Atlantic.

With all his good intentions for international understanding Aberdeen's achievements were limited. He was too inclined to listen to the views of strong personalities, such as Guizot and Wellington, while failing to heed and respond to the voice of public opinion, and especially to its nationalistic tones. By 1845 he was accustomed almost daily to see himself "characterized as pusillanimous, cowardly, mean, dastardly, truckling and base".[47] Once again the contrast with Palmerston is clear. A sensitive and peace-loving man, his greatest test was yet to come. Under his premiership Britain became embroiled in the blood-letting of the Crimea.

The Foreign Secretaryship is one of the few Cabinet posts which an ex-Prime Minister can accept with dignity. Lord John Russell was Prime Minister from 1846 to 1852 and from 1865 to 1866. In between he was Foreign Secretary twice: briefly from 1852 to 1853, and throughout Palmerston's premiership from 1859 to 1865. A leading Whig, with experience as Home Secretary, Colonial Secretary and Leader of the House, he was given the Foreign Office for political reasons rather than for his obvious talent or fitness for this particular post. "In person diminutive and rickety", he reminded one contemporary[48] of a "pettifogging attorney" who "wriggled round, played with his hat, and seemed unable to dispose of his hands or his feet; his voice was small and thin". He had had the distinction, however, of moving the first reading of the Great Reform Bill and his great popularity in the country dates from this time.

In Aberdeen's Coalition Russell's chief responsibility was to lead the government in the Commons and after two months he handed over the Foreign Office to Clarendon. He therefore had little chance to make an impact, although during this short period certain lines of policy were laid down which, inherited by Clarendon, led to the outbreak of the Crimean War. Above all, it fell to Russell to reject the Tsar's proposals for a partition of Turkey.

In 1859 Palmerston wanted Clarendon at the Foreign Office, but Russell insisted upon it for himself. Russell's own considerable influence, together with Palmerston's difficulties in forming the ministry, secured the appointment. As it happened, Palmerston and Russell worked well together. Rather surprisingly, although he was tempted, Palmerston interfered little with Russell's department. The Foreign Secretary was left to handle negotiations and draft despatches. From time to time the Prime Minister altered despatches, or amplified them in his own letters to foreign ministers or ambassadors, but he never interfered in appointments to the diplomatic service or in the Foreign Office. On the Italian question their views closely coincided. Although they were suspicious of Napoleon III's intentions in Italy, and were anxious to see Austria retain her Great Power status, they wanted to achieve a settlement with the use of Britain's "moral influence". Here they ran into trouble with Victoria and Albert, who were committed to the Austrian position. Palmerston and Russell found themselves being undermined in Parliament and Cabinet by the Queen. They stuck together, circumvented Cabinet control and lectured the monarch on constitutional principles. Eventually "those two dreadful old men", as Victoria called them, were able to get their own way. "I soon became aware", wrote Clarendon, "how easy it was for a Foreign Secretary to act dishonestly towards his colleagues without being detected."[49]

Russell's most lasting achievement in the Foreign Office was his setting up, in 1861, of the Select Committee on the Diplomatic Service. Its work led to important changes: notably, the raising of salaries and the payment of allowances for proficiency in languages, which greatly improved the professional standards of diplomats. In future wealth and influence counted for less.

In most respects, however, Russell's tenure of the Foreign Office was undistinguished. He bungled the *Alabama* affair and later conceded that he should have prevented the ship sailing from Liverpool. Nevertheless, he held out to the end in refusing to offer compensation or accept arbitration, and Anglo-American relations suffered for some years as a result. In Europe, by his mishandling of Napoleon III, Russell forfeited the chance of Anglo-French co-operation in checking Prussia in Schleswig-Holstein. The Queen of Holland told Clarendon that Russell's answer to Napoleon's suggestion of a European Congress on the Polish question was "deplorable" and "the death blow of an alliance which ought to have dominated the world, managed the affairs of the Continent, and secured an era of peace".[50]

Clarendon held the Foreign Secretaryship on three occasions, 1853–58, 1865–66 and 1868–70. He had the unenviable distinction of presiding over foreign policy through the crisis which led to the Crimean War as well as during the conflict itself. It was he himself who coined the phrase "drifting towards war".[51] By experience and character he was well fitted for the Foreign Office and his reputation stands high. His administrative reforms were of considerable importance. The work of the Office had continued to grow. By 1853 as many as 49,000 despatches were being handled and Clarendon gave close attention to the professional quality of his staff. A qualifying entrance examination was introduced in 1856; in 1858 an

Assistant Under-Secretaryship was created; there was closer co-ordination of the functions of the two Under-Secretaries. In 1856, also, the decision was made to commission new buildings for the Foreign Office. Clarendon maintained a very different régime in the Office to Palmerston's. At first the clerks brought Clarendon the day's despatches at eleven o'clock at night, as in Palmerston's day. But Clarendon had gone to bed by this time and therefore despatches came to be delivered at seven in the morning. A cigarette-smoker like his friend Napoleon III, Clarendon allowed the clerks to smoke in the office.

As a young man he had been on the British embassy staff in St Petersburg, and from 1833 to 1839 was British minister in Madrid. The complications and difficulties of his post had led him to write to his sister: "I am convinced that I have improved more in my profession during the two years here than I should in twenty as ambassador in Paris".[52]

His succession to the family title in 1838 brought him home and into the Cabinet as Lord Privy Seal. In the 1840s he was Palmerston's principal critic in the government, taking an opposite line on Mehemet Ali. He served as Lord Lieutenant of Ireland from 1847 to 1852 but refused the Foreign Office in 1852 and, on two occasions in his life, the Governor-Generalship of India.

When Aberdeen's Coalition was formed in 1853, Clarendon's experience and personal qualities made him a strong candidate for the Foreign Secretaryship. He had an excellent grasp of European languages and affairs, was hard-working and a good judge of character, with courtly and dignified manners. In approach he was cosmopolitan rather than narrowly patriotic and lacked Palmerston's consuming devotion to British interests. Instead, he saw himself as the guardian of civilization and peace.

Clarendon not only inherited a first-class crisis in the Middle East but sat in a Cabinet divided between compromise (Aberdeen and Gladstone) and resolution (Palmerston and Russell). Far from pursuing his own line, the Foreign Secretary found himself trying to devise a policy which would hold the ministry together. Moreover, the Cabinet contained no fewer than four former Foreign Secretaries—Palmerston, Aberdeen, Russell and Granville. A further difficulty for Clarendon was the position of Stratford Canning, who had once more been despatched as ambassador to Constantinople, in April, 1853, by Clarendon's predecessor Russell. Clarendon believed Canning to be too powerful and did not trust him, but any attempt to have recalled him would probably have provoked some ministerial resignations. Rarely has an ambassador played such an important role in Britain's affairs. Stratford Canning "came to Constantinople, the historic figure, armed with the dignity of his office, the prestige of his personality, the long reach of his experience; armed with the authority he rightly had, and the contempt of authority that he boldly dared; hating the Russians, despising the French, dominating the Turks; a man, the like of whom is not found in the annals of our diplomacy—he came to Constantinople, he saw, and swiftly he conquered".[53] Clarendon mistakenly believed not only that Canning encouraged the Turks to resist the Vienna Note but that he wanted war. The depths of his suspicion of the ambassador are clearly shown in his correspondence. "He is bent on war and on playing the first part in settling the great Eastern Question",[54] wrote Clarendon to the diplomatist Earl Cowley. To the same correspondent he later complained: "What a pest the man is! If I recalled him, however, he would make peace impossible".[55]

The making of peace was, for Clarendon, a much more congenial task. In Paris the Foreign Secretary played a major part in the negotiations and the treaty owed a very great deal to his influence. Although the Peace of Paris did not provide a permanent solution to the Eastern Question it gave a degree of stability and quiet for twenty years. Against a background of the French cultivating the former enemy, Russia, the inherent rottenness of the Ottoman Empire and the abiding ambitions of the Tsar, Clarendon secured the best obtainable settlement.

Clarendon's second period at the Foreign Office was short; although on the fall of Russell's government in 1866 the Queen attempted to persuade him to stay on by changing parties, he refused. Yet she objected to his being Foreign Secretary when Gladstone formed his Liberal government in 1868. As well as policy differences, she took exception to his sarcasm and lack of tact. However, Gladstone stuck out for his choice. Clarendon's most important task in this third term was to attempt to reconcile Prussia and France. He did this by using his reputation as an honest broker and by his influence with Napoleon III. His efforts were doomed to failure, perhaps inevitably, but in 1871 Bismarck observed to Clarendon's daughter: "Never in my life was I more glad to hear of anything than I was to hear of your father's death . . . What I mean is that, if your father had lived, he would have prevented the war".[56]

Two men held the Foreign Office for brief spells in this period, Wellington and Malmesbury.

When Melbourne resigned in 1834, Peel was out of the country. For a short while Wellington held the offices of Prime Minister, Home Secretary, Secretary for War and Colonies and Foreign Secretary all at the same time. On Peel's return he retained only the Foreign Secretaryship. As a result of the uncertain stability and, in the event, shortness of Peel's first ministry, Wellington behaved cautiously and made little impact on the Foreign Office. Nevertheless, his military reputation and status as an ex-Prime Minister, his involvement in the foreign policy of the Congress period and personal acquaintance with foreign rulers and statesmen, the esteem in which he came to be held by Queen Victoria, all gave him a very special influence on foreign affairs for much of the first half of the nineteenth century. His was a conservative influence; he was heartily opposed to democratic movements and to the press, and he frequently clashed with Palmerston.

James Harris, third Earl of Malmesbury, was Foreign Secretary in Derby's short Conservative ministries of 1852 and 1858–59. It has been said that he owed his appointment more to the diplomatic distinction of his family than to his own. His grandfather, the first Earl, had been minister at Berlin, ambassador in St Petersburg and Pitt's special envoy on a number of important continental missions. His father had been Under-Secretary to Canning in 1807. The third Earl was widely travelled in Europe. Of particular significance was his friendship with Louis Napoleon, whom he met for the first time in 1827 and visited again in 1845, when the Prince was imprisoned at Ham. It is also of interest that Malmesbury had studied his grandfather's copious papers and prepared them for publication under the title, *The Diplomatic Journal and Correspondence of the first Lord Malmesbury*. "Without this accidental education I should have been as great a novice in political business as were most of my colleagues", he later recorded.[57] In office Malmesbury was able to draw on the advice of Palmerston, his grandfather's ward.

Whatever his abilities, or lack of them, Malmesbury's periods in office were too short a test. In his first term a principal aim was to keep on good terms with France, and he was the first to recognize the Second Empire. On his return in 1858 his long-standing friendship with Louis Napoleon superficially made Anglo-French relations more congenial. Nevertheless, like most British statesmen he was concerned about the growth of French influence on Italy and a French-dominated Europe. In 1859 he despatched a special mission to Vienna to prevent the outbreak of war between the Austrians and the French-backed Piedmontese. His efforts in this direction were considerable and praiseworthy but stronger forces than British diplomacy were at work. War broke out in Lombardy in the late spring of 1859, by which time Derby's ministry was on its last legs. Malmesbury left the Foreign Office in June.

**NOTES TO CHAPTER THREE**

1  See Paul Kennedy, *The Realities Behind Diplomacy: Background Influences on British External Policy 1865–1980* (Fontana, 1981), p. 20.

2  M. E. Chamberlain. *British Foreign Policy in the Age of Palmerston* (Longman, 1980), p. 54.

3  See above.

4  At this time, on the first occasion in an international crisis, the British government were able to use the electric telegraph as far east as Belgrade. In October, 1853, Clarendon wrote to Russell that "these telegraphic dispatches are the very devil. Formerly Cabinets used to deliberate on a fact and a proposition from foreign governments; now, we have only a fact". See E. L. Woodward, *The Age of Reform, 1815–1870* (Oxford, 1938), pp. 246–247.

5  Woodward, p. 253.

6  Quoted by Woodward, pp. 308—09.

7  Quoted by Bourne, p. 374.

8  Quoted by Middleton, p. 117.

9  Sir Henry Bulwer (1801–72). Widely experienced diplomatist. Attaché at Berlin 1827; Vienna 1829; the Hague 1830; chargé d'affaires at Brussels 1835; ambassador at Madrid 1843–48; ambassador at Washington in 1849—52; minister at Florence 1852; ambassador at Constantinople 1858—65.

10  Quoted by Woodward, p. 213.

11  Quoted by Jasper Ridley, *Lord Palmerston* (Panther Books, 1972), p. 170.

12  Sir C. Webster. *The Foreign Policy of Lord Palmerston* (London, 1951), pp. 13–16.

13  Quoted by Webster, p. 156.

14  Emily Lamb, wife of Earl Cowper and sister of Lord Melbourne, the Whig Prime Minister. Married Palmerston in 1839 when she was 52 and he was 55.

15  Quoted by Ridley, p. 167.

16  Quoted by Webster, p. 58.

17  Middleton, p. 118.

18  Quoted by Jones, p. 14.

George William Frederick Villiers, fourth Earl of Clarendon, drawn by George Richmond. *The Mansell Collection*

Robert Arthur Talbot Gascoyne Cecil, third Marquess of Salisbury.

*The Mansell Collection*

19  In 1841 after Palmerston had carried through reforms in the Foreign Office the establishment and salaries were as follows:

| | |
|---|---|
| Secretary of State | £5000 |
| 2 Under-Secretaries (one called Permanent) | £2000 |
| (one called Parliamentary) | £1500 |
| Chief Clerk | £1000 rising to £1250 |
| 6 Senior Clerks | £600 „ „ £1000 |
| 10 Clerks | £350 „ „ £545 |
| 7 Junior Clerks | £100 „ „ £150 |
| Librarian | £600 „ „ £800 |
| Sub-Librarian | £350 „ „ £545 |
| 2 Clerks attached to Chief Clerk's Department | £350 |
| 4 Clerks attached to Slave Trade Department | £80 „ „ £300 |
| 2 Clerks attached to Librarian's Department | £80 „ „ £300 |
| Translator | £300 |
| Private Secretary | £200 |
| Printer | £150 |

see Tilley and Gaselee.

20  Quoted by Ridley, p. 164.

21  Granville George Leveson-Gower, Second Earl Granville. Palmerston's Under-Secretary of State 1840–41. Three times Foreign Secretary.

22  Quoted by Tilley and Gaselee, p. 50.

23  Sir George Shee, until 1835 Palmerston's "Governmental" Under-Secretary (an office later defined as "Parliamentary" Under-Secretary). Of all the officers, he was closest to Palmerston and carried out confidential duties such as the management of the Press.

24  John Backhouse, Permanent Under-Secretary 1827–40 until his health broke down. The mainstay of the Office.

25  Quoted by Tilley and Gaselee, p. 3.

26  Quoted by Sir Edward Hertslet, *Recollections of the Old Foreign Office* (London, 1901), p. 81.

27  Quoted by Tilley and Gaselee, p. 59.

28  Quoted by Hertslet, p. 79.

29  Quoted by Hertslet, p. 64.

30  Quoted by Middleton, p. 85.

31  Quoted by Middleton, p. 93.

32  Quoted by Ridley, p. 532.

33  Quoted by Cecil, p. 186.

34  Webster, p. 31.

35  Webster, p. 34.

36  Bourne, p.70.

37  Speech to the Commons, 25 June, 1850. Quoted by Bourne, p. 302.

38  Quoted by Webster, pp. 47–48.

39  Quoted by Middleton, p. 31.

40  Speech to the Commons 1 March 1848. Quoted by Bourne, p. 293.
41  Speech to the Commons 1 March 1848. Quoted by Bourne, p.292.
42  Quoted by Middleton, p. 40.
43  Quoted by Cecil, p. 142.
44  Webster, p. 621.
45  Quoted by Ridley, p. 793. John Bright (1811–89) Radical statesman; leading member of
    Anti-Corn Law League; member of Peace Society which opposed the Crimean War.
46  Middleton, p. 114.
47  Speech to the House of Lords, 4 April 1845. Quoted by Hayes, p. 94.
48  Charles Sumner see *D.N.B.*
49  Quoted by Hayes, p. 116.
50  Quoted by Woodward, p. 309.
51  In a letter to his wife. Quoted by Cecil, p. 238.
52  Quoted by Cecil, p. 232.
53  Cecil, p. 244.
54  10 November, 1853. Quoted by Cecil, p. 238.
55  9 March, 1855. Quoted by Cecil, p. 238.
56  Quoted by Cecil, p. 253.
57  Quoted by Hayes, p. 113.

**CHAPTER FOUR**

SECRETARIES OF STATE

| | |
|---|---|
| Edward Henry Stanley, Lord Stanley, afterwards fifteenth Earl of Derby | June 1866–December 1868 |
| Clarendon | December 1868–July 1870 |
| Granville | July 1870–February 1874 |
| Derby | February 1874–April 1878 |
| Robert Arthur Talbot Gascoyne Cecil, third Marquess of Salisbury | April 1878–April 1880 |
| Granville | April 1880–June 1885 |
| Salisbury | June 1885–February 1886 |
| Archibald Philip Primrose, fifth Earl of Rosebery | February 1886–August 1886 |
| Stafford Henry Northcote, first Earl of Iddesleigh | August 1886–January 1887 |
| Salisbury | January 1887–August 1892 |
| Rosebery | August 1892–March 1894 |
| John Wodehouse, first Earl of Kimberley | March 1894–June 1895 |
| Salisbury | June 1895–October 1900 |

# Imperialism and Isolation

## Foreign Policy 1865–1900

ALTHOUGH Britain remained in the first rank of the great powers in the final decades of the nineteenth century, she suffered a relative decline. Her early industrial lead was whittled away as the advantages of industrialization, large populations and political unity came to benefit other powers. The new German Empire and the post-Civil War United States provide outstanding examples, but Japan and Russia also made powerful advances. In 1870 Britain possessed 32% of the world's manufacturing capacity and 25% of the world's trade. By the eve of the First World War these shares had fallen to 25% and 14% respectively. In 1870 Britain produced twice as much steel as Germany. Forty years later the position was exactly reversed.

"European policies were becoming more and more world policies, through Russian expansion into Asia and the competitive intrusion of other European Powers into Africa."[1] Almost everywhere Britain found increasing competition. Trading in Europe became more difficult and she faced stiffer colonial rivalry, notably in Africa. Whereas in the eighteenth and earlier nineteenth centuries France had been Britain's only serious imperial rival, now others emerged, principally Germany. In the Far East the modernization of Japan and the eastward drive of Russia resulted in a scramble for China where, hitherto, Britain had maintained the principal influence. Westwards, the United States flexed its muscles in the Caribbean and, in due course, the Pacific. Older anxieties about French maritime power, or the possibility of a Franco-Russian naval combination, were by 1900 being replaced by the challenge of a German fleet.

The possession of a colonial empire had long influenced British foreign policy. What was new in the last quarter of the nineteenth century was the strength of imperial sentiment and the extension of the Empire into Africa. This was partly a defensive reaction, as other powers entered the colonial race, but there was also a growing sense of pride in Empire. Disraeli's proclamation of Victoria as Empress of India in 1877 appealed to such sentiments (at the same time it infuriated the Liberals). Politicians who had previously denounced the colonies as millstones round the country's neck became ardent Empire-builders and public opinion, fed by an active press, took up the cause.

India remained the jewel in Britain's imperial crown and strategic considerations demanded the safeguarding of the Cape route as well as of the Near East. With the opening of the Suez Canal, and the purchase of a substantial number of shares in the Canal Company, Britain forged a new strategic chain whose links were Cyprus, Egypt, the Sudan and East Africa. Similarly, Britain's position in Cape Colony demanded control over the interior, including the Boer republics. Elsewhere, Russia's expansion into Central Asia concentrated British attention upon Afghanistan. The British Empire expanded at an astonishing rate in the closing decades of the nineteenth century but, even so, the trend was towards relative decline as the other powers successfully pressed their own claims.

As the Empire expanded there was a growing feeling that Britain was over-committed. Even Joseph Chamberlain, the greatest of the nineteenth-century Colonial Secretaries, spoke of "the weary Titan, staggering under the too-vast orb of its fate".[2] Britain, in the face of new rivals, could no longer afford the fleets and men to provide full protection to her ever-expanding territories. The solution was to relinquish naval preponderance in some areas while entering into regional agreements, although not alliances, with other powers. Eventually it was Britain's sense of over-commitment which led to the abandonment of what has been termed her "splendid isolation".

In part isolation was forced upon Britain, in part it was the choice of her own statesmen. At the time of Palmerston's death, and in the aftermath of the Schleswig-Holstein affair, Britain deliberately turned her back on Europe and had little influence on the recasting of the balance of power by Bismarck's Germany. Politicians of both parties were absorbed in the issue of parliamentary reform, and then Ireland, in these critical years. Later, particularly in the 1880s, the same questions again took attention away from foreign policy. Furthermore, Britain's lack of military forces meant that she could have little influence over such continental matters as the Austro-Prussian war. "We are fish", said Lord Salisbury, and until the continental balance was seriously upset, the British could remain comparatively isolated islanders. This sense of isolation was intensified by the lack of any international conferences in which Britain played a major part: the Congress of Berlin in 1878 and the later Berlin Conference on Africa were exceptions. As to international agreements, Britain was not prepared to enter into full-scale alliances. She limited herself to partial or regional understandings. Meanwhile the other great powers were prepared to develop full alliance systems. In 1879 Germany signed a secret alliance with Austria–Hungary which was expanded into the Triple Alliance in 1882 when Italy was included. Austrian and German relations with Russia were regulated by the Three Emperors' League. This was formalized by an alliance in 1881, although it was not maintained beyond 1887. The tightening of the bonds between Austria and Germany, and French investment in Russia, drew France and Russia into an alliance in 1894. Britain was left out.

In 1864 Disraeli announced that the Conservative party was "interested in the tranquillity and prosperity of the world, the normal condition of which is peace".[3] Forty years later Balfour was able to repeat the assurance that "the interest of this country is now and always—Peace".[4] For a great commercial power peace was the ideal, but there were certain conditions in which Britain would fight. These included an attack on Britain itself; a threat to the Cape or the Suez Canal; a determined assault by Russia on India; a serious challenge to Britain's naval supremacy; the collapse of the European balance of power, especially if this should threaten the Low Countries.

The fundamental questions to be resolved in Britain's foreign policy in this period may be reduced to two. How far, if at all, should Britain play the role of a European power? What limits, if any, should be placed upon imperial expansion? To some extent these questions were party matters but they also cut across party lines. The Liberal party continued to advocate free trade, to express disapproval of the European autocracies, to show support for national self-determination, to be unenthusiastic about acquiring more colonies. But, especially in office, the Liberals were forced to adjust these principles, and within their ranks the Liberal Imperialists grew in strength. Before Disraeli's period of leadership the Conservative party followed a cautious, non-interventionist line but Disraeli saw considerable opportunities in changing tack. "Disraeli's purchase of the

Suez Canal shares, his belligerent attitude towards Russia in 1878, and his 'forward' policies in Afghanistan and South Africa in 1879, were not just the result of his own interests and prejudices and misapprehensions. They were also, in a sense, an attempt to escape from the internal contradictions of Conservative domestic policy in the seventies by a brilliant display abroad."[5] Bolder policies raised further issues of an increase in expenditure on armaments and the desirability of firm alliances.

After Prussia's swift victories over Denmark in 1864, Austria in 1866 and France in 1870, Bismarck proclaimed the German Empire. As a result of this "German Revolution", which Disraeli regarded as more significant for the politics of Europe than the great French Revolution, the balance of power was entirely altered. But in these events successive Foreign Secretaries kept Britain neutral. Although British policy was ineffective, and was criticized as such, the outcome of these new events seemed by no means disadvantageous to Britain. After all, the old enemy, France, had been defeated and a strong Protestant Germany, which still favoured free trade, might be depended upon to check French and Russian aggression. Moreover, after her success, Bismarck's Germany was a conservative power out to maintain peace and the European *status quo*. She seemed to pose no obvious threat to Britain's concept of the balance of power or to British interests.

Right up to 1900, of all the European powers, it was Germany and her allies in the Triple Alliance with whom Britain was most likely to form an understanding. Some difficulties were bound to arise, of course, especially when Germany entered the colonial race. In 1884 Britain, already on bad terms with France and thoroughly isolated, was forced to give way to German pressure. German claims were recognized in South West Africa, Togo, Cameroon and Zanzibar as well as in Samoa and New Guinea. These humiliations in external relations typified the disasters of Gladstone's second ministry, and when Salisbury came into office in 1885 his principal task was to lead Britain out of isolation by improving relations with Germany. "The Liberal Government", stated the new Prime Minister, "have at last achieved their long desired 'Concert of Europe' . . . They have succeeded in uniting the continent—against England."[6] In 1885 Sir Philip Currie, an Assistant Under-Secretary at the Foreign Office, was sent to Berlin on a special mission to restore good understanding and, in particular, to enlist Germany's assistance in checking Russia in Persia and

Central Asia. These initial moves were unsuccessful but for the next ten years it was a foundation stone of British foreign policy to work with Germany and her Triple Alliance partners. Principal aims were to secure stability in the Mediterranean and Black Seas; to provide safeguards against France; to maintain the Turks in Constantinople. To this end the Mediterranean Agreements of 1887 were signed with Austria and Italy. Anglo-German co-operation reached its height between 1888 and 1892. In 1889 Bismarck secretly approached Salisbury for an alliance. Such a firm undertaking was avoided but important agreements were made. In 1890, for example, Heligoland was handed over to Germany in exchange for Zanzibar, thereby strengthening Britain's ability to control events on the Upper Nile.

The dismissal of Bismarck in 1890 opened new channels for German foreign policy. Pressure on Britain to join the Triple Alliance was stepped up but mutual suspicions in Africa, the Far East, and over the great fleet which Germany began to develop at the end of the century, all worked in an opposite direction. When relations between Britain and the Boers of the Transvaal deteriorated, Germany emerged as the self-appointed protector of the Boers. The Kaiser's telegram to the Boer leader, Kruger, expressing support was highly provocative. In the Far East Germany gained concessions for herself from China and it also became clear that she was not prepared to check Russian ambitions there. The German Navy Law of 1898 laid down a programme for the building of a powerful high seas fleet. But in spite of all this, in the summer of 1898 the British ambassador to Berlin was able to discuss with the Kaiser the question of an alliance. These negotiations fell through, but in the same year an agreement was reached on the possible partition of the Portuguese colonies in Africa in the event of Portugal's future collapse. The wider importance of this agreement was that it made sure that there would be no interference when Britain came to settle her accounts with the Boers.

Although there were some strains in the relationship in Disraeli's time, the Anglo-French understanding really broke down in the 1880s. Whereas Britain feared the consequences of the collapse of the Ottoman Empire, the French saw an opportunity of furthering their historic interests in the Near East and of inheriting sway in North Africa.

Attention came to centre chiefly upon Egypt. The opening of the Suez Canal in 1869 (Britain had originally opposed its construction) immediately placed Egypt across Britain's lines of communication with India. Disraeli's purchase in 1875 of 40% of the shares in the canal clearly demonstrated Britain's interest. Within three years the chaotic state of the Khedive's government and finances led Britain and France to protect their interests by imposing what amounted to a joint control of the country. A nationalist revolt in 1882 and anti-European rioting in Alexandria compelled further intervention. Indecisiveness on the part of the French resulted in a unilateral, though reluctant, military occupation by Gladstone's Liberal Government. What was meant to be a temporary occupation became permanent and the Egyptian question and connected issues bedevilled Anglo-French relations for the rest of the century. Although there were negotiations with France for withdrawal, principally in 1884, the chief consideration was that political stability had to be maintained. This was not easy. Furthermore, Cairo came to replace Constantinople as the key to Britain's Near Eastern route to India, and was one which could be defended more easily. In 1889 Salisbury made it clear that Britain meant to stay in Egypt.

Once established in Egypt, further responsibilities crowded in upon British governments. They had to concern themselves with the stability of the Sudan, which had been conquered by Egyptian forces in the 1820s. Especially important was the Mahdist revolt which broke out in the Sudan in 1881. Gladstone's policy of withdrawing garrisons from the Sudan led to the death of General Gordon at Khartoum in 1885. No event in the Liberal leader's career made him so unpopular. The Sudan was more or less abandoned by the British for more than a decade, but it was recognized that it was vital to prevent control of the upper Nile from falling into the hands of other powers. In 1892 Alfred Milner[7] wrote: "Who can say what might happen, if some day a civilized Power, or a Power commanding civilized skill, were to undertake great engineering works on the Upper Nile, and to divert for the artificial irrigation of that region the water which is essential for the artifical irrigation of Egypt?"[8] Such strategic considerations explain Britain's close interest in Zanzibar, East Africa and, in particular, the territory around Lake Victoria. These matters were Salisbury's concern in the Anglo-German Agreement of 1890.

It was not until 1896 that the reconquest of the Sudan was ordered. By then it was a pressing matter. The Italian defeat at the hands of the Abyssinians at Adowa jeopardised the south-eastern flank of the Sudan.

At the same time, from West Africa, the French were making a fresh attempt to establish themselves on the Upper Nile. Kitchener's victory in 1898 at Omdurman and his occupation of Khartoum secured the Sudan. However, within three days of his triumph, Kitchener learned that a small French force, under the command of Captain Marchand, had established itself at Fashoda five hundred miles upriver of his own position. Kitchener's march on Fashoda led to a crisis of the first order, bringing Britain and France to the brink of war. In the end British naval supremacy and Russian and German unwillingness to assist France led to an agreement in Britain's favour.

Thus Britain succeeded in safeguarding her position in Egypt from the south. To the north, in the Mediterranean, she had the French fleet to contend with and the Mediterranean Agreements of 1887 were partly intended to cope with this danger. The growth of the French fleet in the Mediterranean, fourteen ironclads in 1888 and twenty in 1891, led to the passing of the Naval Defence Act in 1889. This aimed to secure a Two-Power Standard for Britain. At this stage there was little doubt which two powers Britain most feared, and the Franco-Russian alliance of 1893 combined her two most serious colonial and naval rivals.

There were occasions when British statesmen indeed believed that Russia and France were planning a concerted assault on the British Empire. In 1893 the French, already firmly established in Indo-China, declared war on Siam. Britain's position in Burma and, indirectly, India itself was felt to be in danger but an ultimatum to France resulted in an acceptable agreement. These events coincided with new Russian pressure upon Afghanistan and in the Pamirs. There were also fears about Russia's intentions towards Constantinople and French interests in Cairo. In October, 1893, the Russian fleet visited Toulon.

Attempts in the 1880s and 1890s to rebuild an understanding with France were largely unsuccessful. But once the Fashoda crisis was over, and the French had accepted that the British were in Egypt to stay, the way was cleared for an improvement in relations. The Entente Cordiale was, perhaps, simply a matter of time.

Russia's ambitions in Asia Minor, in the Balkans, and towards Constantinople continued to trouble British statesmen. By 1900, however, Britain's firm position in Egypt and possession of Cyprus meant that her interest in Constantinople had significantly declined. So too had her influence with the Porte. Nevertheless anxieties about Tsarist expansion in Central Asia and the potential threat to India remained unabated. By the 1890s Russia was also causing Britain concern in the Far East.

Britain continued her traditional policy towards the Turks although the days of useful support were numbered. A revolt against the Sultan in Crete in 1866 placed severe strains on relations between Greece and the Turks. By now, too, the construction of the Suez Canal had increased Crete's strategic importance. Meanwhile the ambitious Prince Michael of Serbia was seeking an anti-Turkish coalition as a way of gaining final independence of the Sultan. In Britain the familiar arguments were rehearsed: whether to act to check possible intervention by Russia or to co-operate with her; whether the Ottoman Empire could be persuaded to reform and thus strengthen itself. As matters turned out, in this particular period of crisis British influence proved largely ineffective.

A much more important crisis began in 1875 with the revolt of Bosnia and Herzegovina against the Turks. Uprisings followed in Macedonia and Bulgaria. They were suppressed with extreme brutality. Serbia and Montenegro next declared war on the Sultan but were speedily routed. The prolongation of this widespread Balkan crisis forced the Powers to act. Disraeli, who had become Prime Minister in 1874, was broadly in favour of confronting the Tsar, should he decide to intervene, and of persuading the Turks to reform their empire. A major difficulty however, was the strength of anti-Turkish feeling aroused by the Bulgarian Massacres.[9] Those who believed the Ottoman Empire to be beyond redemption suggested partition, a solution also taken up by Bismarck. After a fruitless conference at Constantinople, Russia declared war on the Sultan in April, 1877. Although British public opinion was cool towards the Turks this latest move reawakened its Russophobia. When the Russians finally broke Turkish resistance, the British fleet, with Jingoism sweeping the country, was sent to Constantinople. The intervention of other Powers led Russia to conclude a hurried armistice and to impose the Treaty of San Stefano on the Turks. The terms were unacceptable to Austria as well as Britain. Their chief objection was to the creation of a so-called Big Bulgaria which would, it was thought, as a client of Russia, enable the Tsar to dominate the Balkans. It was at this point that Salisbury succeeded Derby at the Foreign Office. With the Prime Minister he attended the celebrated Congress of Berlin to resolve this latest development in the Eastern

Question. Big Bulgaria was split into three: an independent Bulgaria; Macedonia, which was returned to the Turks; Eastern Rumelia, which occupied a half-way house between independence and direct Turkish rule. In order to protect her own strategic interests Britain gained Cyprus. Disraeli and Salisbury returned home bringing, in the Prime Minister's words, "peace with honour". But they had not settled the Eastern Question, merely plastered up the cracks. Furthermore, although Salisbury had followed the traditional Palmerstonian line of defending Constantinople, he was doubtful of its value as the key to India. In the years ahead he developed different policies to safeguard Britain's connexions with the East. At the same time, Russia's own interests seemed to be moving from the Balkans to Central Asia. In these circumstances, although there was no sudden or complete desertion of the Sultan, Britain's commitment to Constantinople steadily declined.

Britain's changing policies were illustrated in the Bulgarian crisis of 1885 when Eastern Rumelia revolted and demanded union with Bulgaria. The independent attitude towards Russia which Prince Alexander of Bulgaria had increasingly shown led Britain to encourage such a union. In contrast to the view Britain had formed in 1878, Bulgaria now seemed a useful check on Russia. The crisis was complicated by an invasion of Bulgaria by a jealous Serbia. Serbia's defeat served to strengthen Alexander but he was then kidnapped and forced to abdicate by the Tsar. This crisis was serious on two main counts. Russia might establish her own puppet in Bulgaria; and this most recent turbulence in the Balkans could lead to the collapse of the Ottoman Empire. Once again the Powers intervened to restore stability. The union of Bulgaria and Eastern Rumelia was agreed and Prince Ferdinand of Coburg was chosen to succeed Alexander. From Britain's point of view the principal result of the Bulgarian crisis had been to focus attention upon her strategic weaknesses in the Mediterranean. The Mediterranean Agreements of 1887 should therefore be seen not only as a response to a French threat, but also to a Russian challenge. Negotiations were carried out while the Bulgarian crisis was still in progress. By the first Agreement Britain, Austria-Hungary and Italy underwrote the *status quo* in the Aegean and Black Seas as well as the Mediterranean and resolved to resist any threat towards Constantinople. The second Agreement was intended to uphold the *status quo* in the Balkans as well as Turkish independence and integrity. "The corner-stone of British policy had been laid, and was not disturbed until 1895."[10]

A new series of crises affecting the Ottoman Empire in the mid-1890s revealed a further shift in British policy. In 1895, in order to check the growth of Armenian nationalism, a series of massacres was ordered in various parts of the Empire. In addition, in 1896, Crete once again rebelled. These events persuaded Salisbury that the Ottoman Empire was incapable of reform and that its collapse could not long be delayed. Meanwhile he was advised by experts that Britain no longer had the military and naval capability to intervene in the Straits to check a Russian advance. In 1896 Britain failed to renew the Mediterranean Agreements because she was unable to agree to Austria's demand for a more binding agreement to defend Constantinople. Goluchowski, the Austrian Foreign Minister, was convinced that "whatever might occur in the Turkish capital [Great Britain would] certainly neither move nor interfere . . . Great Britain had practically renounced her traditional policy in the East of the Mediterranean".[11] Defence of the route to India now came to be based upon Egypt.

After the Crimean War the check to Russia's ambitions in Europe and the Black Sea led her to take up the policy of further expansion in Central Asia. This gave rise to fears for the future independence of Afghanistan, an essential buffer-state for British India. On the whole British policy was defensive, although it took a war against the Afghans (1878–79) before they would accept a British military mission in Kabul. Disraeli was criticized by the Liberals for this forward policy. In Gladstone's second ministry (1880-85) a refusal to advance British interests in Persia led to increased Russian influence there. But the Liberals were forced to make a stand when in 1885 the Russians, having occupied Merv, violated Afghan territory and defeated an Afghan force at Penjdeh. The Penjdeh crisis is of particular interest since it highlighted Britain's over-commitment, as she was already heavily engaged in Egypt, and her isolation. Reaction in Britain was intense; posters announcing the outbreak of hostilities with Russia were printed ready and there was a panic on the Stock Exchange. Finally caution won the day.

In the Far East Britain was presented with few problems until the 1890s. Since 80% of the China trade was in her hands, Britain was concerned to maintain peace and stability and to prevent any attempt at partition by other powers. In its implications for international relations, therefore, China bore important similarities to the Ottoman Empire; its weaknesses made it vulnerable to interference and its rulers were highly resistant to suggestions for reform. The relatively untroubled state of affairs in the Far East was transformed by the rise of Japanese power, by Russia's construction of the Trans-Siberian railway, and by a growing German interest. In such circumstances there were considerable doubts whether Britain possessed sufficient naval power to protect the Chinese Empire or to shut other powers out.

In 1894, partly in order to forestall Russia, Japan established a puppet government in Korea. Soon afterwards, as a result of years of rivalry, war broke out between Japan and China. The Japanese carried all before them. The Chinese were forced to cede the Pescadores, Formosa and the Liaotung peninsula, including Port Arthur, and to agree to the independence of Korea. This was too much for Russia who, with the assistance of Germany and France, forced Japan to restore the Liaotung peninsula. Fortunately for Britain, her non-involvement in this move laid the basis for future co-operation between her and Japan.

In 1897 a potentially very dangerous scramble for China began. Germany demanded, and gained, the concession of Kiaochow. Russia, encouraged by Germany,[12] sent warships to Port Arthur. Britain, anxious to prevent an uncontrollable scramble for territory, negotiated for a settlement with Russia but protected her own interests by gaining Weihaiwei. The resentment of the Chinese, provoked by European opportunism, was expressed in the anti-foreigner Boxer Rising of 1900 and the siege of the legations in Peking.

In the 1890s, too, especial care was required in Britain's relations with America. Immediately after the Civil War the United States concentrated upon internal reconstruction. But in the 1890s an expansionist foreign policy was adopted, associated with the building of a powerful fleet. In 1895 the American Secretary of State, in a reassertion of the Monroe Doctrine, demanded that Britain should submit to arbitration in her dispute with Venezuela over that country's frontier with British Guiana. The British Cabinet agreed to this, against Salisbury's advice. Although the arbitration found in Britain's favour, the Venezuela crisis was highly significant. Britain had signified her acceptance of a wide-ranging interpretation of the Monroe Doctrine. The affair also further underlined her isolation since it coincided with the Kaiser's expressed support for the Boers in the Kruger Telegram. Fortunately, after 1896, relations with the

USA rapidly improved, largely because of Britain's scrupulous neutrality in the United States' war with Spain over Cuba.

Between 1865 and 1900 Britain's foreign policy assumed a more global character. This was in contrast to the largely European-centred policies of the age of Palmerston. In these last decades of the nineteenth century Britain pursued imperialist goals with great success; it was significant that that formidable politician Joseph Chamberlain should, of all the Cabinet offices open to him, have chosen the Colonial Secretaryship. To a greater extent than before, colonial questions affected Britain's relations with other powers. Foreign policy became almost indistinguishable from colonial policy, whether it concerned the Transvaal, Egypt, Afghanistan or Weihaiwei. As a global power, Britain found her interests challenged at all points of the compass. In the 1890s she clashed somewhere with all the major powers. Although there were still hopes of an understanding with Germany, and the worst was over between Britain and France, relations were demonstrably improving with only two powers. Both of these, the United States and Japan, lay outside Europe. Britain's understanding with them, at the very beginning of the twentieth century, marked her first steps out of isolation.

## The Foreign Secretaries 1866–1900

After 1886 the conduct of British foreign policy was characterised by stability and continuity. This was chiefly a result of the dominance of Lord Salisbury but there was also a growing tendency to take party politics out of foreign policy. In 1890 Lord Rosebery affirmed that he would "never be party to dragging the foreign policy of this country into the arena of party warfare".[13]

Between the death of Palmerston and the beginning of Salisbury's second ministry, however, British foreign policy was less consistent in direction and of uncertain success. Rosebery's own party, the Liberals, was sharply divided over foreign affairs for the whole of the period from 1865 to 1900. In Gladstone's fourth ministry (1892–94) the Prime Minister and his Foreign Secretary, Rosebery, who sought to continue the Conservative Salisbury's policies, disagreed on virtually every issue of foreign policy. Indeed, a substantial wing of the Liberals had more in common with sections of the Conservative party than with their own colleagues. Until 1886 at least there were serious divisions even within the Conservative ranks. Disraeli's Cabinet was split over the Eastern Question and the Foreign Secretary saw fit to reveal its secrets to the Russians. The two broad issues of whether Britain should play a major role in Europe and the extent to which she should expand her Empire cut across party lines.

The general impression of instability in the twenty years after Palmerston's death is strengthened by the fumbling nature of much of Britain's foreign policy. The conduct of affairs in Gladstone's second ministry (1880–85) provides an outstanding example. Between 1865 and 1886 Foreign Secretaries of both parties, notably Derby and Granville, rather than attempting to influence events positively were content to be carried along by them. Salisbury's appointment in 1878 offered the chance of a fresh start.

With serious party divisions at home and challenges of a novel and even threatening nature from abroad, the personalities and abilities of the Foreign Secretaries were more than usually important. So too were the relations between Prime Ministers and Foreign Secretaries. It is of especial significance that Lord Salisbury combined these two offices for the whole of his first ministry and for the substantial bulk of his second and third.

With the fall of Russell's government in 1866 and the formation of a Conservative ministry under the fourteenth Earl of Derby, the Prime Minister's eldest son, Edward Henry Stanley, became Foreign Secretary. Although he had sat in the Commons since 1848, Stanley's experience in office was limited; he had served as Under-Secretary for Foreign Affairs in 1852 and as Colonial Secretary and Secretary of State for India in his father's second Cabinet (1858–59).[14]

In his first period at the Foreign Office, between 1866 and 1868, Stanley showed excessive caution and, worse still, proclaimed it. Clarendon recorded that on handing over the office he had begged Stanley "not to proclaim our determined inaction on every opportunity that arises—the policy of not meddling is of course the right one but it is not necessary that all mankind should be let into our secret twice a day".[15] It would probably have been impossible for a British statesman to have headed off the developing conflict between France and Prussia, but Stanley's muddled thinking and inaction simply brought Britain into disrepute. "By the end of 1867 [the European powers] were inclined to write off England, very largely because of Stanley's attitude."[16]

Despite his unhappy record Derby (Stanley had succeeded his father in

Archibald Philip Primrose, fifth Earl of Rosebery, speaking in the House of Lords, by Sidney P. Hall. *The Mansell Collection*

Henry Charles Keith Petty-Fitzmaurice, fifth Marquess of Lansdowne.

*The Mansell Collection*

the peerage in 1869) returned to the Foreign Office when Disraeli formed his second Cabinet in 1874. It was because of his electoral and party influence that Derby was included. The contrasts between the Foreign Secretary and his chief were marked. Disraeli, supported by the Queen, was an activist while Derby, favouring a minimum of intervention, was perhaps "the most isolationist foreign secretary that Great Britain has ever known".[17] At one time they were close personal friends but this relationship crumbled. The Prime Minister intervened more and more in the Foreign Secretary's sphere of responsibilities. In 1876 Disraeli told Derby, "I must again complain of the want of order and discipline in your Office".[18] From 1874 until his resignation in 1878 Derby was one of the weakest members of the Cabinet and, added to his extreme cautiousness, he seemed incapable of making decisions.

In his hesitant acceptance of the purchase of the Suez Canal shares Derby demonstrated his anxieties about Disraeli's boldness, but it was over the Eastern Question crisis of 1876–78 that the most serious differences arose. Despite the outbreak of war between Russia and the Turks, Derby opposed any action which might run the risk of armed intervention to check the Tsar. In a misguided attempt to convince the Russians that there was a peace party in the government, Derby and his wife revealed the Cabinet disagreements to Shuvalov, the Russian ambassador. Meanwhile, unknown to the Foreign Secretary, Disraeli established a private correspondence with Layard, the British ambassador in Constantinople, and in August, 1877, again without telling Derby, despatched a secret emissary to the Tsar with the message that the British Cabinet was united in its resolve to declare war if necessary.

In December, 1877, when the Turkish stronghold of Plevna surrendered to the Russians, Disraeli demanded a vote of credits to raise forces. Derby opposed the Prime Minister and in January, 1878, when the Cabinet decided to order British warships to the Dardanelles, he resigned. The reversal of this order enabled Derby to make a brief return, but in March he finally departed on the issues of mobilizing the reserve in Britain and transferring troops from India to the Mediterranean. By this time the strain had brought him to the verge of a nervous breakdown, and he was drinking heavily.

At heart a Liberal, Derby left the Conservative party in 1880; from 1882 to 1885 he served under Gladstone as Colonial Secretary.

When Granville succeeded Clarendon in 1870 as Gladstone's Foreign Secretary the international horizon seemed to him to be relatively clear. Within a month of his accepting the seals of office, however, the Franco-Prussian War was under way. "I felt that our position was very much that of a man trying to prevent a fire with inflammable materials all around him, and with matches all ready to ignite."[19] Thus Granville revealed his principal weaknesses, his unwillingness to seize initiatives and an over-readiness to accept events as they were. Although he managed to get both combatants to agree to the neutrality of Belgium, he failed to exert any influence in the greater issue of the European balance of power.

Granville George Leveson-Gower, second Earl Granville, was the son of a diplomatist. Born in the year of Waterloo, and educated at Eton and Christ Church, he was briefly an attaché at the British Embassy in Paris before being elected to the Commons in 1836. He succeeded to his father's title ten years later.

Granville built up wide experience in office. He was Palmerston's Under-Secretary for Foreign Affairs in 1840–41 but had to wait for ten years for Cabinet rank—Paymaster General in Russell's Cabinet and then Foreign Secretary for two months in the winter of 1851–52. In Aberdeen's Cabinet he served as Lord President of the Council and held the same office in both of Palmerston's governments. When Gladstone became Prime Minister in 1868 Granville went to the Colonial Office, transferring to foreign affairs on Clarendon's death.

Calm, patient and tactful, Granville was known to his colleagues as 'Puss'—he purred his way through business. He spoke French, we are told, with a slight Court accent which recalled the *ancien régime*.[20] When dealing with ambassadors he was masterly, but in treating with great foreign statesman such as Bismarck he lacked the necessary forcefulness. Although the charge of indolence might be too strong, he was, nevertheless, unenthusiastic about the burdens of office. After his party's overthrow at the polls in February, 1874, he wrote: "When the first bitterness of defeat was over, you cannot conceive how pleasant it is to be without the 'lumbering of the wheels'. I look at a few empty boxes and say 'D---n the parade'."[21] Yet he made a determined and successful stand in reminding Gladstone of the constitutional relationship between Prime Minister and Foreign Secretary. This had permanent significance in the conduct of foreign policy. Gladstone showed great interest in foreign affairs and was accustomed to making statements without consulting the Foreign Secretary or Cabinet. Granville therefore wrote to Gladstone: "I imagine that the Prime Minister has an undoubted right to communicate directly either with our representives abroad or with Foreign Ministers in London. But I think it is in his interests as much as in that of the Foreign Secretary that he should only appear as the *deus ex machina*".[22] Thereafter Gladstone observed the constitutional proprieties.

Granville's second period as Gladstone's Foreign Secretary (1880–85) "presented no greater appearance of strength than the first".[23] He faced considerable problems: the influence of the Queen; differences of opinion with the Prime Minister; deep divisions within the Cabinet. Nevertheless, he himself must take a major share of the blame for the foreign disasters and humiliations of the Liberal Government. Victoria had plain views on the matter. "The Queen blames Lord Granville very much", she wrote, "for he is as many say 'quite past'—weak and indolent and not able to work hard."[24] Her influence was sufficiently powerful to prevent his being Foreign Secretary again.

Lord Salisbury is not unique in combining the offices of Foreign Secretary and Prime Minister but the length of his joint tenure of the posts is unparalleled. His first spell at the Foreign Office covered the last two years of Disraeli's premiership; he was then Foreign Secretary in his own first, short ministry; throughout his second, apart from the first five months; and for all but the last two years of his third. Altogether he was Foreign Secretary for some twelve years and eight months. He actually preferred the Foreign Office and at times neglected the Premiership for the sake of his principal interest. On forming his first Cabinet he informed the Queen that "he was anxious to be Foreign Secretary as well as Prime Minister, because none of his colleagues were well acquainted with foreign affairs".[25]

Salisbury did not take the Foreign Office at the outset of his second ministry. He appointed Stafford Northcote, first Earl of Iddesleigh, a former Chancellor of the Exchequer. After a matter of months Iddesleigh resigned, dying suddenly within hours of his resignation. Salisbury returned to the Foreign Office. At the end of this ministry, in 1892, he wrote to Cranbrook: "The Foreign Office leaves you no holiday—not for a weekend. After six years one gets to hate the sight of a red box and to feel doubtful whether one is giving the necessary attention and thought".[26] Yet on his return to office in 1895 he once again assumed the dual responsibility.

Robert Arthur Talbot Gascoyne Cecil was born at Hatfield in February, 1830. The death of his older brother in 1865 and of his father three years later brought him the title of third Marquess of Salisbury. A lonely child, he was mercilessly bullied at Eton and was taken away aged fifteen to be privately tutored. In later life, even as Prime Minister, he shunned company and was aloof to all but a small circle. When asked about his intimate knowledge of the alleys and obscure streets around his London home, he explained that he had got to know them as a means of avoiding meeting his fellow-Etonians in the holidays. His daughter, Lady Gwendolen Cecil, recorded that to take a walk with her father "through a frequented place—excepting London where everyone is safe from undesired observation—was to realize with some accuracy what must be the feelings of a criminal escaping justice. One went in constant terror of recognition and of its possible consequences, knowing that any overt expression of admiration from some passing group would cast him into the profoundest gloom".[27] Throughout his life he suffered from depression. He left Christ Church, Oxford, after only two years, suffering from physical and mental illness, and in later years spoke of the "nerve-storms" which still afflicted him. Fortunately, a highly successful marriage and happy family life, as well as a strong Christian faith, supplied the stabilizing elements in his life. In office he possessed an entirely unneurotic view of the responsibilities which lay upon him. At the moment of stepping outdoors on a storm-threatened autumn day he remarked, "I don't understand what people mean when they talk about the burden of responsibility. I should understand if they spoke of the burden of decision—I feel it now, trying to make up my mind whether or no to take a great-coat with me. I feel it in exactly the same way, but no more, when I am writing a despatch upon which peace or war may depend".[28]

Salisbury was an intellectual of wide interests. He was well read in the Classics and in French. His favourite authors were Euripides, Virgil, Horace, Tacitus and Shakespeare. When travelling he took with him a case of their works in small leather-bound volumes. He had a particular interest in the French Revolution and possessed a large collection of books and pamphlets on the subject. At Hatfield he had a laboratory built for his work in botany, photography, physics and electricity and explained that politics distracted him from his studies.

Although he had an "almost fanatical belief in personal liberty"[29] he opposed any measures which would substantially increase the electorate. He was suspicious of untrammelled democracy and of those elements which sought to stir up class hatred. His ideal was rule by an enlightened and benevolent élite tempered by constitutional safeguards and influential public opinion. He was forward-looking on social issues, being particularly concerned about working-class housing and education. Drunkenness and squalor were the results, he believed, of poor housing and ignorance. At the beginning of his third ministry he was able to say to the Lords: "It is the improvement of the daily life of the struggling millions and the diminution of the sorrows that so many are condemned to bear which is the blessed task that parliaments are called into existence to perform".[30] On colonial questions he deplored the ill-treatment of native peoples and believed that their welfare was "the one justification" for British rule in India.

Salisbury first entered active politics in 1853 as Member of Parliament for Stamford. He remained on the back benches until 1866 when he became Secretary of State for India with a seat in the Cabinet. Within less than a year he resigned over the Conservatives' introduction of the Second Parliamentary Reform Bill, which he regarded as a betrayal of the party's principles. This established a rift between Salisbury and his party, especially its new leader, Disraeli. It took years to repair it. Nevertheless, when Disraeli formed his second ministry in 1874 Salisbury returned to the India Office. This was an important experience for him and gave him insight into a whole set of issues spanning imperial, foreign and strategic policies. At this time, too, the India Secretary's influence over the Viceregal government was increased by the laying of the Red Sea cable.

It was as India Secretary that he was sent to the Constantinople Conference in November, 1876. As he travelled out he visited Berlin, Vienna, Paris and Rome and met Bismarck, Kaiser Wilhelm I, Andrássy and Decazes. In Constantinople he was able to form first-hand impressions about the Eastern Question, a problem which was to occupy so much of his time as Foreign Secretary. His sympathies tended to be with the Russians and he wished to co-operate with them. He believed that the Ottoman Empire was on the verge of collapse, that Constantinople was undefendable, and that Russia no longer constituted a serious threat to India. "It is clear enough", he wrote to Disraeli, "that the traditional Palmerstonian policy is at an end."[31]

"English policy", wrote Salisbury in March, 1877, "is to float lazily downstream, occasionally putting out a boat-hook to avoid collisions".[32] Yet his own appointment as Foreign Secretary in April, 1878, gave new direction to British foreign policy and rescued it from the fumbling efforts of his immediate predecessors. Salisbury modestly claimed that in 1878 he "was only picking up the china that Derby had broken".[33] But his circular despatch written on the eve of his formal acceptance of the seals "showed clearly to the world that Britain had at last made up her mind".[34] His handling of negotiations at the Congress of Berlin bore the hallmarks of a new effectiveness for Britain in international affairs.

The decisions reached at Berlin shored up Constantinople, but Salisbury believed that the Turkish breakwater was "now shattered, I fear, beyond repair, and the flood is pouring over it. Another dyke may have to be established behind".[35] Constantinople survived longer than Salisbury believed possible, but it was not until 1897 that he made it clear that it was no longer a cardinal aim of British policy to sustain it at all costs. In 1878 Bulgaria was divided to prevent undue Russian influence in the Balkans. By 1885 Salisbury supported an enlarged Bulgaria, this time as a check on Russia. It was not so much that Salisbury's views changed, more that his methods adjusted to fresh circumstances. In the case of Constantinople it was manifestly clear by 1895 that Britain lacked the military and naval resources to protect it. Furthermore, the chances of internal reform by the Sultan were so remote as not to be worthy of consideration.

Salisbury believed war to be "the final and supreme evil". The principal object of his diplomacy was to avoid it. He saw that the application to warfare of modern technology could inflict immense suffering. In general, therefore, he acted cautiously and defensively. Where it was necessary to stand firm he did so. Constantly occupied with the problem of defending India, he set out to impose strict limits upon Russian expansion in central Asia. In 1888, for example, Russian pressure on Afghanistan led him to instruct his ambassador in St Petersburg that an advance on Herat "means war". An equally determined line was maintained over the Pamirs dispute in 1891–92.

Diplomatic triumphs could be dangerous, however, since they inspired desire for revenge. Thus Salisbury's work was characterized by patient negotiation rather than by dramatic coups, and by an avoidance of permanent commitments to foreign powers. Even short-term engagements were to be avoided, unless the contracting powers shared mutual and specific interests. He entered into the Mediterranean Agreements but shrank from wider and more general undertakings. His avoidance of alliances, at a time when other European powers were entering into them, made his policies seem isolationist. In fact the international problems with which Salisbury had to deal made it impossible for Britain to be truly isolationist even had Salisbury wished it, and he did not. He sought international co-operation as the most effective way of upholding the country's interests. In 1878 he publicly denounced the view that Britain should "confine herself to her own insular forces" and went on to maintain that "the commerce of a great commercial country like this will only flourish—history attests it again and again—under the shadow of empire, and those who give up empire in order to make commerce prosper will end by losing both".[36] Salisbury was an imperialist. Although he was cautious about taking on new commitments, the British Empire expanded enormously during his administrations. He "regarded the defence of the Empire as the most important task facing British statesmen in the last quarter of the nineteenth century".[37] Yet the acquisition of territories, the forestalling of other powers, even the defence of empire were not ends in themselves. The real problems of an imperial power lay not in the gaining of territories but in presiding over them with justice and good government.

With Salisbury's abhorrence of war and of "racial arrogance" his policies were rooted firmly in moral principles. Similarly, in his dealings with other powers, good faith was paramount. Despite his Olympian reputation he was equally scrupulous in his regard for public opinion, an influence strengthened during the course of his own career by a widened franchise and the growth of the popular press. Thus in 1895 and 1896, although it might have suited Britain's interests to guarantee Constantinople against a Russian onslaught, he drew back from doing so because he feared that British repugnance for Turkish atrocities would leave him without support for war. It was a surprising and major failing, therefore, that throughout his time in office he made so little effort to frame and lead public opinion at home.

Egypt, a problem which he inherited from Gladstone's second ministry, lay at the centre of Salisbury's policies. In some ways the British position in Egypt was a liability and an embarrassment. By disturbing relations with France it made Britain dependent upon Bismarck's support. Even so

Salisbury became convinced that Britain could not pull out. From this decision a long train of consequences followed: the Mediterranean Agreements; the abandonment of the traditional policy towards Constantinople; Salisbury's encouragement of Cromer, the British Consul-General, in reforming Egyptian administration; the defence of Britain's position on the Nile by the division of African territories; the eventual decision to send Kitchener into the Sudan; the crisis and triumph of Fashoda.

The Foreign Office which Salisbury took over in 1878 had already been affected by a series of changes which better fitted it for its growing burden of work and responsibility. Reforms in the Civil Service as a whole, including competitive examinations, higher professional standards in the diplomatic service, and a more structured departmental organization of the Office itself all played their part. After 1871 the Foreign Office examination consisted of eight papers, including spelling, arithmetic, English composition, French translation, dictation and conversation, Latin, German translation, and an intelligence test.[38] By Salisbury's last period at the Foreign Office, geography and history were included in the compulsory papers with Italian, Spanish, Russian and Portuguese as options. Even so, candidates required the Foreign Secretary's personal nomination before being allowed to take the examinations, and as late as the 1890s "men from families totally unknown to Lord Salisbury or his private secretary did not apply".[39] In the Foreign Office patronage and aristocratic connections continued to matter.

As to departmental organization, by 1895 the Office was divided into four political departments and five administrative.[40] Meanwhile, although important and heading departments, the senior clerks were still occupied with mainly clerical tasks. The junior clerks handled the routine work of copying despatches, ciphering and deciphering and keeping the register. The Foreign Secretary still concerned himself with much of the drafting of telegrams and despatches.

"Foreign policy did not emerge through a process of consultation within the Foreign Office. Lord Salisbury was the master of his house; he made his own decisions and expected them to be carried out."[41] Salisbury's view of the role of civil servants in the making of policy was clear—it was not for them to trespass upon the preserve of elected governments. Civil servants were to give advice only when asked and it was not their function to make decisions. This was understood by Salisbury's Permanent Under-Secretaries, but these officials were far from being nonentities. Sir Philip Currie, Permanent Under-Secretary from 1889 to 1894, was a close friend of Salisbury; they worked closely together and the Foreign Secretary relied upon him for advice on matters of the highest importance. Currie's successor, Thomas Sanderson (known as "Lamps"), has been described as the last of the great super-clerks.[42] He saw himself as the head of a department concerned with implementing the instructions of the Secretary of State. Nevertheless, Sanderson shared in the shaping of policy.

Most of Salisbury's work was done at Hatfield, not because he was concerned to by-pass the Office but because he required privacy and solitude. His boxes were sent from the Office daily and he worked on them until the small hours. By his reluctance to delegate he imposed additional strains upon himself, and his doctors came to insist that he take several weeks' holiday and rest in the course of each year. As a result of the burden of business, Salisbury's habits of work and Sanderson's special qualities (he was a brilliant draftsman and had an astonishing memory), the Permanent Under-Secretary inevitably became a policy-maker. He acted as the link between the Foreign Office and the Secretary of State, interviewed ambassadors in Salisbury's absence, dealt with important correspondence and played a key role in the wording of agreements with foreign countries. But even Sanderson was no *éminence grise*; ultimate responsibility for foreign policy remained firmly in Salisbury's hands. To the Foreign Office staff as a whole Salisbury remained an aloof figure. His wife is supposed to have said that he knew no more about his clerks than about the housemaids at Hatfield.[43]

In 1895, when he took on the Foreign Office for the fourth time, Salisbury was at the height of his influence and reputation at home and abroad. Having been made all the more powerful by an election victory which had given him a majority of 152 in the Commons, he seemed set fair to deal successfully with the international problems facing Britain. In some ways, however, in spite of the successes of Omdurman and Fashoda, his last five years as Foreign Secretary were disappointing. Faced once again by the Eastern Question, he wished to avoid a radical breach with Britain's traditional policies. However, the Armenian massacres dissolved any remaining hopes of reform of the Ottoman Empire. Meanwhile military and naval experts were making it clear that Britain could no longer strike through the Straits to save Constantinople. Unable to gain Russia's co-operation or to engage the Powers collectively, Britain virtually abandoned her traditional policy in the Near East. The Mediterranean Agreements were not renewed.

After 1898 Salisbury's ascendancy in his Cabinet was far less certain. As a result of ill-health, failing eyesight and increasing obesity he was not able to cope with the heavy work-load. There were signs that he was losing his enthusiasm for the Foreign Office. In addition, he found Joseph Chamberlain exceptionally difficult to control. With Salisbury still at the helm Britain drifted into the Boer War. The opening campaigns proved disastrous. To most people's relief, including his own, Salisbury resigned the Foreign Office at last in October, 1900. He remained Prime Minister for a further year and a half but it was a sad exit for a very great Foreign Secretary.

As Foreign Secretary and then Prime Minister Rosebery forged the links of continuity in foreign policy between the three Salisbury ministries. A Liberal Imperialist, Rosebery was at odds with Gladstone and other Cabinet colleagues but his presence in the Government was essential to Liberal party unity, already riven by the Irish question. Moreover, he was the Queen's nominee for the Foreign Office.

Archibald Philip Primrose, fifth Earl of Rosebery, was a somewhat reluctant politician who had had little experience of office when appointed Foreign Secretary for the first time in 1886. Rich and talented, he was a keen sportsman and racehorse-owner with three Derby winners to his credit. He was a noted authority on eighteenth-century literature and, as a historian, wrote on Peel, Pitt, Napoleon and Chatham. His tenure of high office was short: his two spells at the Foreign Office totalled a little over two years, his Prime Ministership lasted from March, 1894, to June, 1895. He resigned the leadership of the Liberal party in 1896.

Rosebery was a vigorous Foreign Secretary, particularly in the imperial field, and earned a considerable reputation without reaching the heights. He was very well travelled and well informed. He worked long hours and maintained a taut, personal control over the Foreign Office. In his determination to continue Salisbury's policies he faced great problems in dealing with his Prime Minister, Gladstone, and senior colleagues such as Harcourt and Morley. Their fundamental doubts about the wisdom of the Mediterranean Agreements meant that Rosebery avoided discussing the matter in Cabinet. Gladstone was therefore led to complain of the Foreign Secretary's "outrageous assumption of power apart from both the First Minister and from the Cabinet".[44] As to Egypt, Rosebery determinedly opposed any suggestion of British withdrawal, and strongly supported Cromer against the Khedive. The Prime Minister's preparedness to sacrifice Cromer caused Rosebery to threaten resignation and, as a result, the Foreign Secretary got his way. In Europe Rosebery followed a policy of general rapprochement, but eventually failed to achieve a better understanding with Russia and France and actually worsened relations with Germany.

In his difficulties with his colleagues Rosebery had an important ally in the Queen, who once wrote to him: "The Queen thanks Lord Rosebery for his letters and telegrams wh. are all she wishes but the decision of the Cabinet is *dreadful*. How *can* they be so shortsighted & weak!"[45] At the Foreign Office he finally broke with the remaining traditions of Gallic diplomatic language by insisting that in notes to foreign ambassadors and ministers the style of address should no longer be "Monsieur l'Ambassadeur" or "Monsieur le Ministre" but "Your Excellency" or "Sir".

When forming his own Cabinet Rosebery chose John Wodehouse, first Earl of Kimberley, as his Foreign Secretary. A popular elder statesman, Kimberley's previous experience in office had been wide and relevant: lengthy periods as Under-Secretary under Aberdeen and Palmerston; British minister to St Petersburg; Colonial Secretary 1870–74[46] and 1880–82; Secretary of State for India 1882–85, 1886 and 1892–94. In his short period at the Foreign Office Kimberley followed the Salisbury line. A careful and cautious man, he used black blotting paper to avoid the risk of the contents of his letters being discovered by spies.[47]


**NOTES TO CHAPTER IV**

1  L. Penson. *Foreign Affairs under the Third Marquess of Salisbury* (London, 1962), p. 4.

2  Quoted by Kennedy, p. 35.

3  Quoted by Kennedy, p. 27.

4  Quoted by Kennedy, p. 27.

5  P. Adelmann, *Gladstone, Disraeli and Later Victorian Politics* (London, 1970), p. 19.

6  Paul Hayes, *Modern British Foreign Policy: The Twentieth Century 1880–1939* (London, 1978), pp. 31–32.

 7  Sir Alfred Milner (Viscount Milner, 1902), Under-Secretary for Finance in Egypt, 1889–92; High Commissioner for South Africa, 1897–1905; member of the War Cabinet, 1916–19; Colonial Secretary, 1919–21.

 8  Quoted by M. C. Morgan, *Foreign Affairs 1886–1914* (London, 1973), p. 25.

 9  Gladstone wrote a pamphlet entitled *The Bulgarian Horrors and the Question of the East.* It sold 40,000 copies within a few days and demanded that the Turks should clear out "bag and baggage" from "the province (Bulgaria) which they have desolated and profaned".

10  Hayes, p. 39.

11  Quoted by Bourne, p. 159.

12  Germany's part in this and her unwillingness to check Russia was not realized by the Foreign Office. Had it been realized then, relations between Britain and Germany might well have taken a completely different course and the Foreign Office would have saved itself a good deal of trouble.

13  Quoted by Hayes, p.30.

14  In 1863 he had been offered the throne of Greece but had refused it. (*D.N.B.*).

15  Quoted by Bourne, p. 119.

16  Bourne, p. 119.

17  A. J. P. Taylor, *The Struggle for Mastery in Europe*, (Oxford, 1954), p. 233.

18  Quoted by Hayes, *Nineteenth Century*, p. 126.

19  Speech in the Lords 28 July, 1870, quoted by Hayes, p. 111.

20  *D.N.B.*

21  Quoted by Hayes, p. 112.

22  Quoted by Cecil, p. 257.

23  *D.N.B.*

24  Quoted by Hayes, *Twentieth Century*, p. 27.

25  Quoted by Hayes, p. 31.

26  Robert Taylor, *Lord Salisbury* (London, 1975), p. 148.

27  Quoted by Taylor, p. 2.

28  Quoted by Morgan, p.10.

29  Lord Robert Cecil quoted by Taylor, p. 192.

30  Quoted by Taylor, p. 156.

31  Quoted by Bourne, p. 132.

32  Quoted by Bourne, p. 132.

33  Quoted by Bourne, p. 133.

34  Penson, p. 1.

35  Quoted by Bourne, p. 134.

36  Quoted by Morgan, p. 31.

37  J. A. S. Grenville. *Lord Salisbury and British Foreign Policy* (London, 1970), p. 19.

38  See Steiner, pp. 116–17.

39  Steiner, p. 17.

40  In 1895 the Foreign Office consisted of four political departments (Western, Eastern, American and Asiatic, African and Protectorates) and five administrative (Chief Clerk's Office, Commercial and Sanitary, Consular, Library, Treaty). In 1899 American and

Asiatic affairs were separated. All the political work was in the hands of the "first-division" clerks who were collectively known as the diplomatic establishment. There were some fifty first-division clerks. See Steiner, p. 11.

41  Steiner, p. 44.
42  Steiner, p. 33.
43  Tilley and Gaselee, p. 5.
44  Hayes, p 39.
45  Robert Rhodes James. *Rosebery* (London, 1963), p. 279.
46  During this period Griqualand West was annexed and the town of Kimberley was named after the Colonial Secretary.
47  Tilley and Gaselee, p. 138.

116

**CHAPTER FIVE**

SECRETARIES OF STATE

| | |
|---|---|
| Henry Charles Keith Petty-Fitzmaurice, fifth Marquess of Lansdowne | November 1900–December 1905 |
| Sir Edward Grey | December 1905–December 1916 |
| Arthur James Balfour | December 1916–December 1919 |

# Entente and Armageddon

## Foreign Policy 1900–1918

THE YEAR 1900 marked a period in British foreign policy. The Franco-Russian alliance and the Fashoda crisis had already demonstrated the dangers of isolation and the Cabinet was half-prepared for change, but two considerations made a new diplomatic initiative essential. These were the disasters of the opening months of the Boer War and increased fears for British interests in the Far East. In South Africa the tide had turned by the summer of 1900 and the relief of Mafeking was wildly celebrated, but grave doubts were being expressed about Britain's imperial role. Her discomfiture at the hands of the Boers had been watched with some satisfaction by the continental Powers while Russia had been able to bring fresh pressure to bear on Afghanistan and to increase her influence in Persia. Britain was over-stretched militarily and financially; the Secretary of State for War was soon to warn of the shortage of soldiers and the First Lord of the Admiralty of the difficulty in maintaining the two-power naval standard.

Lord Salisbury capitalised on the better turn of events in South Africa by calling a General Election. His party was returned to office with an acceptable majority. In the ensuing Cabinet reshuffle Salisbury handed over the Foreign Office to Lansdowne. Although the Prime Minister remained very influential, the new Foreign Secretary followed new paths, many of his own making. Lansdowne was not alone in perceiving the dangers of isolation. Balfour, Hamilton, the Secretary of State for India, and Chamberlain at the Colonial Office all shared his views. Britain herself could shelter behind her fleet but her commitments around the world, particularly in the Far East, were more difficult to maintain. Germany had already demonstrated her willingness to give comfort to the Boers and the Fashoda affair had led Britain and France to the brink.

Even so, there were strong reservations about coming out of isolation.

Lord Salisbury himself was an obstacle. It was believed that undertakings with other Powers would lead to firm alliances and costly entanglements on the Continent. There were preoccupations nearer home, in Ireland, and, when the Liberals came to office in 1905, an ambitious programme of social reform. The Liberals themselves were divided between Liberal Imperialists and those of the opposite persuasion, at one time labelled pro-Boers. Increasingly too, especially after the Entente Cordiale with France in 1904, foreign policy was a matter of party politics. Conservatives tended to be imperialist and pro-French, which meant more expenditure on armaments. An influential section of the Liberals sought an understanding with Germany who was, after all, Britain's best customer. Public opinion was of crucial importance, Britain was a democracy with a free press and politicians needed to win elections. In due course, public opinion swung strongly behind the Anglo-French entente, especially once the German challenge was appreciated, but it had to be cultivated and won over. Lord Salisbury wrote in May, 1901: "I do not see how, in common honesty, we could invite other nations to rely upon our aid in a struggle, which must be formidable and probably supreme, when we have no means whatever of knowing what may be the humour of our people in circumstances which cannot be foreseen".[1]

Developments in the Far East set Britain on the road away from isolation; the weaknesses of the Manchu Empire had precipitated a scramble for China. Britain, long established in the China trade and handling the vast majority of it, watched Russia and Germany uneasily. Russia caused particular alarm by gaining a concession to extend a branch of the Trans-Siberian railway across Manchuria to Vladivostok. This was followed by a Russian occupation of Port Arthur and a general mêlée in which the European powers gained leases on Chinese ports and territories on very favourable terms. An anti-European movement, known as the Boxer Rising, led to a dramatic intervention in China by the Powers in 1900 and a march on Peking. Although Britain took part in the expedition her fears deepened when the Powers demanded compensation, Russia despatched troops to occupy Manchuria and then gained economic concessions in Korea.

Britain's anxieties about the Far East lay behind negotiations with Germany in the later 1890s and with Russia herself. These talks failed and, largely as a result of her fear of Russia's Far Eastern fleet, Britain

Sir Edward Grey.                                     *The Mansell Collection*

George Nathaniel Curzon, first Earl Curzon and afterwards first Marquess Curzon.
*The Mansell Collection*

negotiated with Japan, who was equally concerned about Russian expansion. A treaty was signed in January, 1902, which pledged them to maintain peace in the Far East and to safeguard the territorial integrity of China and Korea. In naval terms the British and Japanese had a clear superiority in Far Eastern waters over the combined fleets of any two other powers. The treaty was renewed in 1905 to run for a further ten years.

The second step out of isolation was the entente signed with France in 1904. At the Quai d'Orsay, the French Foreign Minister, Delcassé, had for some time been concerned to create an atmosphere of greater understanding. This was the burden of Delcassé's instructions to Paul Cambon on Cambon's appointment as ambassador in London in 1898. Although the Boer War was brought to a victorious conclusion it represented a grave psychological blow to Britain, and the peace treaty turned out to be remarkably generous to the Boers. In such circumstances Lansdowne strongly desired better relations with the European powers. Balfour's succession to the premiership in July, 1902, helped to clear the way. The negotiations were largely concerned with an accommodation over colonial disputes. French interests in Morocco had led to a policy of penetration there, and in return for an agreement by Britain in France's favour similar assurances could be given on the British position in Egypt. "In a word", remarked Cambon, "we give you Egypt in exchange for Morocco."[2] Conflicting claims in Newfoundland and the Gambia were also dealt with. International and strategic considerations provided additional interests in common. French fear of Germany was of long standing, and it was already clear to the Admiralty that the German fleet was being developed to take on the British. Events in the Far East again proved decisively important. As relations between Russia and Japan deteriorated, France feared that her ally Russia would call upon her aid and Britain that Japan would invoke the alliance of 1902. Only by a close understanding between themselves could Britain and France avoid the possibility of being on opposite sides in a war. Japan and Russia declared war in February, 1904, and the Anglo-French Entente was signed in April. Britain and France did not become allies; they had a colonial understanding. Nevertheless, in the years ahead, and as German power menaced them both, they drew closer together until British troops fought on French soil in 1914.

The Entente was first tested in Morocco. In March, 1905, the Kaiser made an appearance in Tangier and, in a deliberately provocative speech, championed Moroccan independence. Germany's intention was to break the Entente and in the words of her Chancellor, von Bülow, "to confront France with the possibility of war, cause Delcassé's fall, break the continuity of aggressive French policy, knock the continental dagger out of the hands of Edward VII and the war group in England and, simultaneously, ensure peace, preserve German honour and improve German prestige".[3] Before the crisis had been resolved the Conservative Government had made way for the Liberals in December, 1905, and Sir Edward Grey had replaced Lansdowne at the Foreign Office. Grey and the Liberals stuck by the Entente, the Germans were warned of its popularity in Britain and the French were assured of diplomatic support. At an international conference at Algeçiras, early in 1906, the British delegate, Sir Arthur Nicolson,[4] stood firmly by the French. The upshot of the crisis was a rebuff for Germany, a strengthening of the Entente and the beginning of informal naval and military conversations between Paris and London.

The Russians were impressed by Britain's display of loyalty. They too looked for an understanding, shaken as they were by defeat at the hands of Japan in 1905 and by subsequent internal revolution. For her part, Britain saw Germany's developing interests in Turkey and the Near East as a possible threat to her communications with India. The new Russian Foreign Minister, Izvolsky, who strongly favoured closer ties with Britain, therefore met with an encouraging response. Nicolson was despatched as ambassador to St Petersburg with instructions to pursue an entente. As in the Entente with France, Britain began by seeking to ease some existing irritants, principally in Persia, Afghanistan and Tibet. An agreement covering these areas was signed in August, 1907. In the years ahead the agreement sailed through choppy waters: Britain did not back Russia in every single international dispute, particularly in the Balkans; disagreements arose over Persia, where different sides were taken in the struggle between the Shah and constitutional forces; important sections of British political and public opinion objected to closer links with Tsarist Russia. But the Anglo-Russian Entente survived and was converted into an alliance after the outbreak of war in 1914.

It might be argued that Germany's policy in Morocco, and her creation of a powerful fleet, drove Britain towards firmer international agreements than she had ever intended. Certainly by the time of the Moroccan crisis of

1905–06, British public opinion was running strongly in an anti-German direction. The Kaiser was seen as an aggressive meddler. Such views had already been anticipated by some politicians and a growing band of professionals in the Foreign Office who saw issues very much in terms of the balance of European power. In the forefront of Anglo-German rivalry stood the question of naval might. Under Tirpitz[5] the German fleet was powerfully expanded by the Navy Laws of 1898 and 1900. It was quickly realized by the Admiralty that the design and range of the new ships fitted them not so much as defenders of far-flung colonial possessions as for deployment in the Baltic and North Sea. Britain jealously guarded her naval supremacy and still aimed to maintain the two-power standard.

It was partly in response to the German challenge that Sir John Fisher, First Sea Lord, and Earl Cawdor, First Lord of the Admiralty, carried out their naval reforms. The most dramatic step was the laying down of H.M.S. *Dreadnought*. Launched in 1906, this super-battleship rendered all other battleships obsolete. In a curious way this was to Britain's disadvantage, since her lead over any other power was now reduced to one-nil. Britain and Germany started on almost equal terms; Britain, at vast expense, had to keep ahead. The naval race was on; Germany also began to lay down ships of the dreadnought type. From 1908 to 1911 Britain tried to negotiate with Germany on a limitation of naval programmes. This was met with suspicion and failed. In 1909 there was a naval scare when, to public alarm, it seemed that Germany was narrowing the gap. The building programme was stepped up but at the price of deeper divisions in the Liberal Cabinet and Party.

Meanwhile, Britain's withdrawal from diplomatic isolation was accompanied by military developments to fit her for a new role. In 1902 the Committee of Imperial Defence was established. Under the chairmanship of the Prime Minister the Committee was to co-ordinate military and naval policies; to develop a general strategy for the defence of the Empire and Britain; and to bring the armed services into the sphere of political decisions. It is significant that before the end of 1905 the committee was discussing a possible strategy in the event of an Anglo-French war against Germany. Among the reforms and reorganisation of the army carried out by Haldane, Secretary for War 1905–12, was an expeditionary force for rapid mobilization overseas, possibly to the continent of Europe.

In spite of the uneasy relations between Britain and Germany a clash of arms was not seen as inevitable. Indeed, in the years before 1914 there was a surprising degree of fluidity in European relations; there were attempts at Austro-Russian, Anglo-German, Russo-German, and Franco-German collaboration. Right up to 1914 Britain was able to conclude two agreements with Germany, one over the German-backed Berlin–Baghdad railway, the other on a joint policy towards the Portuguese colonies in Africa. But on two fundamental issues negotiations always broke down. Britain's attempts to lessen the tension over the growth of fleets by arranging an agreed limitation, or "naval holiday", met with German resistance. Germany was unable to gain a pledge from Britain that she would remain neutral should a continental war break out.

For her part, Germany made a further dramatic attempt to drive a wedge into the Anglo-French Entente, and the continued French expansion in Morocco provided an opportunity. When French troops occupied Fez in 1911, the Germans responded by sending a warship, the *Panther*, to Agadir, a small port on the Atlantic coast of Morocco. Such naval activity, even on a small scale, alarmed the British government and public. When the Germans demanded compensation elsewhere in Africa, in return for giving the French a free hand in Morocco, Britain feared a carve-up of territory behind her back. A stiff warning was delivered to Germany by Lloyd George, the Liberal Chancellor of the Exchequer, in a speech at the Mansion House, and there seemed a real prospect of Anglo-German conflict. War was averted, although the crisis dragged on for some months. At last, in November, 1911, an agreement was signed which recognised the French position in Morocco and gave compensation to Germany in the French Congo. The affair gave added strength to the Entente but Germany stepped up her naval programme.

When war broke out in 1914 its immediate cause was the last of a series of crises in the Balkans. Important interests were at stake there. The further decline of the Ottoman Empire had encouraged the Slav peoples in the hope that they might drive the Turk from Europe. Austria–Hungary watched with some apprehension lest successful Slav nationalism should spark off similar upheavals among her own subject-peoples. It was remarked that once Turkey vacated the bed allocated to the sick man of Europe, Austria–Hungary would fall into it. Another scenario, however, was that the Habsburgs might profit in the Balkans from Turkey's demise, especially if backed by their ally Germany. For her part, Germany had been steadily expanding her influence in Turkey, particularly with the shrinking of British interest there, and in the years before 1914 held the chief sway in Constantinople. Her economic ambitions in the Middle East were considerable, including the Berlin–Baghdad railway. Russia, for her part, held firm to her historic policies of protecting and encouraging the Orthodox Christian Slavs and setting herself across the Straits.

Rather oddly, perhaps, the Balkan crisis of 1908 was closely bound up with an attempted Austro-Russian deal. The activities of the Young Turks[6] roused Austrian fears of a Turkish resurgence and, in particular, a revival of claims on Bosnia and Herzegovina which the Habsburgs had administered since 1878. Arising from this, Izvolsky came to an agreement with Aehrenthal, the Austrian Foreign Minister, whereby Austria would annex Bosnia and Herzegovina in return for supporting Russia in an attempt to open the Straits. Austria went ahead and annexed the provinces but did not fulfil her part of the bargain with Russia. Serbia was incensed; the majority of the annexed population was Serb, and Russia backed her up. Izvolsky made a personal visit to London to call for support but there was little chance of British intervention. In the event Russia, still weak from recent military defeat and revolution, drew back, while Germany strongly supported Austrian claims. The Bosnian affair caused much anxiety, and bitterness remained. Russia and Serbia did not forget.

Four years later fresh sparks in the Balkans threatened a European conflagration. In the autumn of 1912 the independent Balkan states of Serbia, Montenegro and Bulgaria, in alliance with Greece, succeeded in overrunning most of the territory still left to Turkey in Europe. Quick action by the Powers stopped the fighting and, on British initiative, a settlement was worked out at a conference in London. Sir Edward Grey played a key role and the danger seemed to have passed. But hardly had the terms been announced than Bulgaria attacked Serbia and Greece in a quarrel over the spoils of their joint victories. Bulgaria was swiftly defeated and, to a large extent because of the harmony established in London, the Great Powers were not drawn in. A dangerous situation had been created: although Serbia was bitterly disappointed not to have gained Albania she was, nevertheless, greatly expanded and Austria watched her with justifiable suspicion; Bulgaria was consumed by resentment; Germany saw the success of Russia's protégé as a challenge to her own advances towards the Middle East; Turkey was left with but a fingerhold in Europe.

The final spark was struck in Sarajevo, the capital of Bosnia. There, on 28th June, 1914, the heir to the Habsburg throne, the Archduke Franz Ferdinand, was assassinated by a Serbian nationalist student. The nearest parallel would be the murder of a Prince of Wales in Ulster but, although there was considerable shock, the reaction of the Powers was surprisingly low-key. Until almost the end of the following month the British Cabinet talked of war but they had Ireland in mind, not the Balkans; Lloyd George was able to remark that relations with Germany had not been better in years. But on 23rd July, having been assured of Germany's full support, Austria decided to seize her chance of settling scores with Serbia. A savage ultimatum was presented. It virtually accused Serbia of having been behind the Archduke's murder. In spite of Serbia's conciliatory reply, Austria pressed ahead and declared war on 28th July. There was a chain reaction: Russia mobilised, was warned by Germany to stand down, and when she did not, Germany declared war on 1st August; when Germany demanded neutrality from France, she refused and a declaration of hostilities followed on 3rd August. Britain's attitude was crucial; there was no guarantee that she would stand by France. The decision was made easier when Germany, in order the more quickly to strike down France, invaded Belgium. Britain was able to invoke the pledge she had given in 1839 to uphold Belgian neutrality and declared war on Germany on 4th August.

With the outbreak of the Great War the purposes and nature of diplomacy altered. In peace it had been the chief aim of British policy to prevent war and, if this failed, to ensure that Britain did not lack friends. During the war foreign policy occupied a subordinate position. Sir Edward Grey wrote that "in war words count only so far as they are backed by force and victories".[7] After December, 1916, when David Lloyd George became Prime Minister, the traditional diplomacy and the means of conducting it suffered a further blow. Already in eclipse, the Foreign Office suffered further loss of influence under his administration. Lloyd George brought in his own expert advisers and his personal dynamism was matched by a determination to put the whole sweep of policy under his own hand.

Nevertheless, the importance of diplomacy in these years should not be underestimated. There was, for example, the possibility of a negotiated peace. This was seriously considered in government circles, notably at the end of 1916. Lord Lansdowne publicly advocated such a policy in a letter to the *Daily Telegraph* in November, 1917. Furthermore, as the stalemate of trench warfare on the Western Front became more obvious, it was felt necessary to recruit fresh allies so that new theatres of operations could be opened up. Italy joined the Allies in 1915.

The Dardanelles and Gallipoli campaign of 1915 attempted to find an alternative to the trench deadlock by seizing Constantinople, knocking Turkey out of the war and giving direct aid through the Black Sea to the hard-pressed Russians. More widely, it was hoped that by such an action Bulgaria and Greece could be won over and the Balkans gained for the Allies. In addition, by a secret treaty in March, 1915, Russia was promised Constantinople. Diplomacy and military operations combined in one strategy.

Care was taken to ensure that neutrals such as Sweden and the United States were not irreconcilably offended by the policy of blockade, and British diplomacy played some part in bringing the Americans into the war on the Allied side in April, 1917. Meanwhile, faltering or exhausted allies had to be kept in the struggle, perhaps with promises of future gains. A change of régime, as in Russia in 1917, complicated diplomacy still further. Finally, schemes were negotiated among the Allies for the eventual peace treaties and future division of conquered territory.

**The Foreign Secretaries 1900–1919**
Henry Charles Keith Petty-Fitzmaurice, fifth Marquess of Lansdowne, is not generally placed among the greatest of British Foreign Secretaries, yet he presided over what amounted to a revolution in British foreign policy. His "appointment paved the way for a departure in British policy and for a major upheaval within the Foreign Office".[8] Born in 1845, he was educated at Eton, where he was Arthur Balfour's fag-master, and Balliol. He inherited his father's title at the age of twenty-one, sitting in the House of Lords as a Liberal and holding office in Gladstone's first ministry. His appointment as Governor-General of Canada came in 1883 during a Liberal government but, chiefly over the Irish question, he joined the drift of Whigs and Liberal Unionists towards the Conservatives. It was Salisbury who in 1888 appointed him Viceroy of India, an office he held until 1894, after which he was offered, but refused, the ambassadorship to St Petersburg. In 1895 he entered Salisbury's Cabinet as Secretary of State for War. His five years in this office convinced him of Britain's military weaknesses and the necessity of changing the traditional policies of

isolation. He made a real stand for the army, but Lansdowne's opponents blamed him for the early military failures of the Boer War.

Although his acquaintance with Parliament was somewhat limited, Lansdowne was otherwise well fitted for the Foreign Secretaryship. He was an able administrator of varied experience with a command of fluent French. At first Salisbury continued to wield considerable influence over policy, but Lansdowne was a cipher neither of his Prime Minister nor his officials in the Foreign Office. Lansdowne had a mind of his own and the initiatives in the making of the new policies were to a large extent his. Although Queen Victoria had agreed to Lansdowne's appointment only on the "strict understanding" that Salisbury would continue to supervise policy very closely, the new Foreign Secretary progressively shook himself free to set his own stamp on affairs. He benefited from a swing of Cabinet opinion in his favour and from Balfour's succession to the Premiership in July, 1902. "I shouldn't call him clever," the new Prime Minister remarked; "he was better than competent".[9] Lansdowne certainly lacked Balfour's intellectual brilliance but his modesty and tact were considerable advantages and he was a very skilled negotiator. Above all, perhaps, he remained cool in a crisis.

On taking office, Lansdowne had few preconceived ideas about the precise direction British policy should follow. Nevertheless, he was anxious about Britain's isolation and alarmed by the experiences of the Boer War. During his first four months, policy took shape as a result of the crisis in the Far East caused by Russian aggression towards China. He recognized the need to redeploy British naval and military resources and saw the importance of friends should the Russian danger prove overwhelming. He began by attempting a closer understanding with Germany. At the end of 1900 he informed Sir Frank Lascelles, the British ambassador in Berlin, that "we should use every effort to maintain and, if we can, to strengthen the good relations which at present exist between the Queen's Government and that of the Emperor".[10] Lansdowne did not discount even an Anglo-Russian agreement, but repeated attempts to secure it, which went on until the autumn of 1902, broke down. Approaches to Germany also failed, on the grounds of Germany's reluctance to endanger her own relations with Russia. There were also objections within the Cabinet. Negotiating mistakes were made on both sides and the result was, if anything, a deterioration in relations. Lord George Hamilton, the

Secretary of State for India, wrote to Curzon that he was "coming round to the opinion that they, the Germans, are a detestable race, and that the more we kick them the better friends we shall be".[11]

In these circumstances a radical shift of policy was necessary and Lansdowne proposed the adventurous step of an Anglo-Japanese alliance. He conducted most of the negotiations himself and by November, 1901, had won a majority in Cabinet. Strong support was given by Selborne, the First Lord of the Admiralty, for whom the alliance promised relief for his overstretched fleets.

Closely related to the strategic consideratons explicit in the Anglo-Japanese alliance was the Hay–Pauncefote[12] Treaty with the United States. It was signed in November, 1901, and "was perhaps [Lansdowne's] greatest achievement as Foreign Secretary".[13] Relations between the United States and Britain were uneasy over a number of issues: the Canadian–Alaskan frontier; the question of a Pacific–Atlantic canal; conflicting interests in Venezuela. The essence of the treaty was a recognition of American naval supremacy in the Caribbean. This rapprochement remained unbroken by later disagreements and was of profound significance for the future.

More generally, Lansdowne's negotiations with the United States and Japan marked a new awareness of the interdependence of strategy and diplomacy. His experience at the War Office had been of considerable importance and, as Foreign Secretary, he continued to rely upon the advice of the service chiefs.

As with the Anglo-Japanese alliance, Lansdowne himself took part in the detailed negotiations leading to the Anglo-French Entente. He met his opposite number, Delcassé, to agree on some preliminaries but the real work was done with Paul Cambon. "Just as Lord Lansdowne and Count Hayashi[14] were the real authors of the Anglo-Japanese Agreement, Lord Lansdowne and M. Cambon deserve the chief credit for the successful negotiation of the Anglo-French Entente."[15] Having made the Entente, Lansdowne was prepared to stick to it in the face of German sabotage. During the first Moroccan crisis of 1905 he wrote to Lascelles, "I am afraid that we can hardly regard the Tangier ebullition as an isolated incident. There can be no doubt that the Kaiser was much annoyed by the Anglo-French Agreement . . . We shall, I have little doubt, find that the Kaiser avails himself of every opportunity to put spokes in our wheels".[16]

Unlike Salisbury, Lansdowne did most of his work at the Foreign Office and sought the advice of his senior staff. Salisbury had always tended to deride the experts. Moreover, Lansdowne's Secretaryship coincided with the beginnings of a period of change in the Office itself. The chief features of this were greater efficiency and a determined attempt to secure effective influence over policy for senior officials. Sanderson remained as Permanent Under-Secretary. Lansdowne relied heavily upon him, particularly in the early stages, and allowed him considerable initiative. It has been suggested that Lansdowne's *éminence grise* at the Foreign Office was Francis Bertie,[17] an Assistant Under-Secretary since 1894. He was certainly intimately concerned with the Anglo-Japanese alliance and for some time before its conclusion had pressed his view of the Far Eastern situation on Lansdowne. Bertie was also increasingly anti-German. Others in the department who shared his views and were influenced by him included Louis Mallet,[18] who became Lansdowne's assistant private secretary, William Tyrrell[19] and Eyre Crowe.[20] Nevertheless, although Bertie was very influential, Lansdowne did not consistently follow his line and never gave up hope that Anglo-German détente might be achieved.

Lansdowne also differed from Salisbury in his attitude to public opinion. Lansdowne "had no respect for public opinion, but he lived in constant apprehension of it; and yet, in spite of the constricting influence it had on his policy, and especially on his German policy, he never attempted to influence it."[21] Again, while Salisbury believed the days of secret diplomacy to be over, Lansdowne saw that it was necessary because of the new challenges to British power, and returned to it.

Lord Lansdowne had no master plan for a system of alliances; he proceeded piecemeal in response to challenges and opportunities as they arose. He did not go so far as to reverse Salisbury's policies, for like his predecessor he drew back from a general alliance system. The chief plans of his policy were to confine possible conflicts and to reduce British commitments to attainable levels. "He was not a great Foreign Secretary; but, all things considered, Britain was fortunate in having him in charge of her foreign policy during five years of rapid changes and extreme danger."[22]

Sir Edward Grey accepted office with some reluctance. His hesitation in December, 1905, almost cost him the Foreign Secretaryship itself. Earlier, after Grey had been appointed as Rosebery's Under-Secretary, Sir William

Harcourt[23] advised him to break up his fishing rod for the ball was at his feet. Grey replied that he wasn't sure that he wanted the ball.[24] A highly developed sense of duty to his country, his party and family traditions kept him in the public service, and his eleven-year tenure of the Foreign Office eventually endangered his health and ruined his eyesight. He grew into the office. "Every year he loomed larger in the eyes of Europe and America, at least until the guns spoke and diplomacy became the handmaid of war."[25]

Grey's interests of the heart were in the countryside: he was a naturalist, ornithologist and fisherman and published expert books on all these subjects. Whenever he was able to do so, and especially before he attained high office, he spent his time at his beloved Falloden in Northumberland, or fishing from his cottage at Itchen Abbas in Hampshire, or walking and fishing in Scotland. He felt a keen sense of deprivation when not able to follow country pursuits. In 1906, at the height of a foreign crisis, he missed visiting his favourite beech-wood to see the trees at the height of their perfection. "There are a few days in the first part of May when the beech-trees in young leaf give an aspect of light and tender beauty to English country which is well-known but indescribable. The days are very few; the colour of the leaves soon darkens, their texture becomes stiffer; beautiful they are still but 'the glory and the dream' are gone . . . I had now to wait another twelve months to see the great beech-wood as I knew it in its greatest beauty."[26]

These interests were shared by Grey's first wife, Dorothy, whom he had married in 1885. Her death, in a carriage accident in February, 1906, was a shattering blow. On the very day, he wrote to his friend Haldane, "I shall feel the need of friends, a thing I have never felt while I had her love every day and could give all mine to her".[27] Dorothy's death happened within weeks of Grey becoming Foreign Secretary, within a few days of the conclusion of an arduous election campaign and during the Algeçiras Conference in the aftermath of the first Moroccan crisis. Fortunately he had conducted the most crucial of his talks with Cambon. With characteristic sense of duty, as well as for solace, he was back at his desk in a few days and immersed in his work. But the loss left its mark. "His nature grew under the pressure of private sorrow and public care. His face, in youth beaked and bright-eyed like a hawk's, became like that of the king of the birds. Men spoke of his 'sad eagle eyes'."[28]

Grey became Foreign Secretary in December, 1905, after the fall of the Conservatives had made way for Campbell-Bannerman's Liberal government. He was not the new Prime Minister's first choice—the post was first offered to Lord Cromer[29]—and, for some time, Grey and his political friends, Asquith and Haldane, had worked against Campbell-Bannerman's leadership of the Liberal Party. The ministry could not have done without Asquith, who persuaded Campbell-Bannerman to take Grey in. Having accepted, Grey wrote to Rosebery: "The decision is taken at last and I have today agreed to go into the Cabinet and take all the consequences which that entails. I go to the F.O."[30]

The Foreign Secretaryship was Grey's first and, indeed, only Cabinet office. He was the first Foreign Secretary to sit in the Commons since 1868 and parliamentary pressures placed heavy burdens upon him. "One of the [Foreign Secretary's] most depressing moments", he wrote, "is after a long Foreign Office debate in the House of Commons. The debate may have begun at four o'clock and ended at dawn. It will have been necessary for him to sit through it and speak, possibly to make a difficult and important speech. When the debate is over he enters his room at the House of Commons and sees the pile of red boxes that have accumulated."[31]

In some respects Grey seemed ill fitted for his new post. He had a reputation for cleverness but his academic achievement at Winchester and Balliol had been undistinguished. Certainly his parliamentary career was substantial. He had sat for Berwick since 1885, but the only office he had held hitherto was Parliamentary Under-Secretary to the Foreign Office. He spoke no language with any confidence, although he read and wrote French well. In his dealings with Cambon, Grey spoke English and the ambassador French, an arrangement which generally worked satisfactorily. Grey was also relatively untravelled, he had no first-hand experience of European countries and knew no foreign statesmen. Yet his very Englishness was an advantage and his lack of personal ties freed him from the clouded view which could affect ambassadors long resident in a particular country. Among the Liberals he commanded considerable respect, and was widely regarded as the party's expert on foreign affairs. He was an effective speaker in the House and had a reputation for straightforwardness, honour and integrity. Aged forty-three in 1905, he was an athletic man and, as befitted a six-times national real tennis champion, lithe and elegant in his movements. He made an impressive figure, and was to become one of the greatest of Foreign Secretaries, but within a few weeks of taking office he was writing: "The mud of foreign politics is deeper than any I have been in yet".[32]

The Foreign Office which Grey inherited had begun a process of change under his predecessor. This came to fruition during Grey's own tenure and may be summarized under three heads: the attempt to make the Foreign Office into a policy-making bureaucracy instead of a "department of scribes" who only gave advice when specifically asked; the reorganization of the internal structure of the Office to make it more efficient and modern; and the development of what has been identified as an influential anti-German stance on the part of some of the most senior officials. It was this anti-German view which "became the prevailing orthodoxy under Sir Edward Grey".[33] The key figures in these interrelated changes were Francis Bertie, Charles Hardinge,[34] Eyre Crowe and, in the second rank in this period, Louis Mallet and William Tyrrell. Since the new Secretary of State was relatively young and inexperienced the officials took the opportunity of asserting their influence. Grey's appointment coincided with that of "Capability" Hardinge, who as Permanent Under-Secretary had a very different approach from that of his predecessor, Sanderson. The new Foreign Secretary found that his officials were now taking initiatives. For example, the despatches in his boxes were augmented by the opinions of the Permanent Under-Secretary and appropriate heads of department. "A group of extremely able men had come into the key positions of influence, men who had decided views and were all too anxious to make these views known."[35] But Grey was no cipher. Whilst he sought advice and had considerable respect for the "professionals" he made his own decisions.

Hardinge remained the permanent head of the Foreign Office until 1910. Older than Grey and with wide experience abroad, he was intensely loyal to the Foreign Secretary. For his part, Grey was wise enough to appreciate the qualities of his principal official and their partnership was very much that of equals. Both men were agreed on the necessity of containing Germany and continuing the French Entente, but Hardinge was also concerned to achieve a closer relationship with St Petersburg, where he had been ambassador. "I fully believe", he wrote in 1911, "in the theory of Germany's intention, if possible, to dominate Europe to which we are the only stumbling block."[36] Hardinge's views were held, perhaps to a more extreme degree, by Eyre Crowe who in 1906 was appointed to head the Western Department of the Office. In 1907 he produced a remarkable memorandum on Anglo-German relations and came to be recognized as the foremost German expert. There is little doubt that Grey was served by an exceptionally able, hard-working and ambitious group of men.

Edward Grey's relations with his second Permanent Under-Secretary, Arthur Nicolson, were less happy. Nicolson lacked Hardinge's administrative ability, he was rather anxious to return to an ambassadorship, and he and Grey differed on some fundamental issues. From an extreme pro-Russian stance, he was anxious to go much further than Grey in turning the understanding with France and Russia into arrangements more like alliances. Otherwise, he feared, Russia at least would come to terms with Germany, leaving Britain isolated. The Foreign Secretary was more concerned to maintain a policy of balance. Until a late stage he continued to hope and work for an improvement in Anglo-German relations.

Loyally supported by his officials, Grey was given considerable freedom by Cabinet colleagues and by the two Prime Ministers under whom he served. Campbell-Bannerman had no specific interests in the field of foreign policy, while Asquith (who replaced Campbell-Bannerman in 1908) was a long-standing political friend and in close agreement with Grey's views on Europe. The majority of the Cabinet was immersed in domestic policy-making and, in addition, had to concern itself with Ireland and issues like the constitutional crisis over the House of Lords. Despite Grey's reputation for honesty and openness, he played his departmental cards remarkably close to his chest. Only a handful of Cabinet ministers were privy to his plans and he made strenuous efforts to prevent the participation of his more radical colleagues. Lloyd George, a leading radical, later claimed that "the Cabinet as a whole were never called into genuine consultation upon the fundamental aspects of the foreign situation. There was a reticence and a secrecy which practically ruled out three-fourths of the Cabinet from the chance of making any genuine contribution to the momentous questions then fermenting on the continent of Europe".[37]

Grey inherited the Japanese alliance and the Entente with France. There was little difficulty in his continuing with them; in opposition he had welcomed both arrangements. His principal objective was to preserve the peace of Europe, but he had already come to the conclusion that Germany represented the main obstacle to his plans. More than ever he believed that "what really determines foreign policy in this country is the question of sea-power".[38] His attendance at meetings of the Committee of Imperial Defence was meticulously regular. But although he extended Britain's commitments to France and entered into an entente with Russia, he stopped short of an alliance with either country. After exactly a year in office he wrote to President Theodore Roosevelt, "Now, a word as to our policy. It is not anti-German. But it must be independent of Germany. We wish to keep and strengthen the Entente with France . . . The economic rivalry (and all that) with Germany do not give much offence to our people, and they admire her steady industry and genius for organisation. But they do resent mischief making . . . The long and short of the matter is that, to secure peace, we must maintain the Entente with France, and attempts from outside to shake it will only make it stronger".[39] Once Germany had embarked on the policy of building a great naval fleet her relations with Britain were possibly irreconcilable, but Grey persisted in his attempts to restore understanding. One important avenue of approach was the naval question itself and he gave considerable energy and time to unsuccessful negotiations over armaments limitation and "naval holidays". On other matters patient and protracted talks bore fruit. He signed agreements with Germany concerning the Portuguese colonies in Africa in 1913 and over the Berlin–Baghdad Railway in 1914. But this was small beer compared to the naval rivalry. Meanwhile, the other great stumbling-block to the preservation of peace, the instability of the Balkans, was soon to prove insurmountable.

In handling his first major test, the Moroccan crisis which had begun in March, 1905, Grey had to decide how far Britain could go in support of the French. The German ambassador, Metternich, was warned that in the event of conflict between France and Germany public opinion might demand that Britain should not remain neutral. At the same time, Cambon pressed Grey on the crucial question of military conversations between their countries. These had already been taking place in Lansdowne's time but after consulting the Secretary for War, Haldane, Grey agreed to place them on an official footing. This decision was crucial on two counts. First, did it commit Britain to something altogether different from an entente—an alliance? Certainly the British plans involved sending an army of 80–100,000 to fight alongside France, and the military conversations drew the two countries together as time went by. But even in 1914 it was not at all assured that Britain would in fact fight alongside France. It was only the German invasion of Belgium which clinched matters. Second, the conversations went ahead without the authorization of the Cabinet and, up to 1911, Grey informed only a small group of his colleagues, which included the Prime Minister. In a sense, Grey discharged his responsibility by informing Campbell-Bannerman. Such limited confidences may well have been the result of fears of Cabinet leaks, of which the *Manchester Guardian* was a favoured recipient. On a number of occasions in 1907 Grey took the opportunity of reaffirming the Anglo-French Entente, thus upholding it as the chief principle of his system.

"It was not so easy to create friendship with Russia as with France. Russian despotism was repugnant to British ideals, and something was constantly happening in Russia that alienated British sympathy or stirred indignation."[40] Nevertheless, an agreement with Russia was concluded; it was very much Grey's own achievement and he maintained a close personal oversight during the negotiations. He paid generous tribute to his principal assistants. "Nicolson [then ambassador in St Petersburg] has, as usual, been invaluable, never missing a point, and with excellent judgement. So has Hardinge, with his knowledge both of the Russian Government and of Persia, and his clear view as to the good policy of an agreement."[41]

Better relations with Russia offered Grey the chance of improving the situation in the Balkans. At the time of the Bosnian crisis Grey lent diplomatic support to Russia; it was important, for example, that Izvolsky, who was pro-British, should not be discredited. But although Izvolsky had personal talks with Grey in London the radical section of the Cabinet prevented outright British support.

Before 1914, Grey's most difficult period in office was in 1911 when he came under increasing pressure inside and outside Parliament. Early in the year, the radicals in the Cabinet pressed successfully for a small committee to oversee negotiations with Germany. Grey's officials believed this to be a watchdog on their chief. Later in the year when the Agadir crisis threatened war, Grey's handling of affairs brought a stream of criticism, from press and backbenchers, that the Foreign Secretary was a Germanophobe and that the Foreign Office was too independent of parliamentary influence. In a delicately balanced Cabinet Grey strove successfully to gain the necessary support for France; the Entente emerged stronger from the Agadir crisis and so did Grey. Two of the leading radicals, Lloyd George and Churchill, were convinced of the German threat and shifted their weight towards the Entente. Grey's defence of his policy in the House provides an excellent summary of his views: "Our friendship with France and Russia is in itself a guarantee that neither of them will pursue a provocative or aggressive policy to Germany. Any support we would give to France or Russia in times of trouble would depend entirely on the feeling of Parliament and public feeling here when the trouble came, and both France and Russia know perfectly well that British opinion would not give support to provocative or aggressive action against Germany."[42]

The Balkan Wars showed Europe to be on a knife-edge, but Grey's handling of the problem took him to the zenith of his prestige. His handling of the London Conference, which he had called and presided over, was masterly. Although the Conference did not end the fighting for long, Grey kept Britain out, restrained Russia without alienating her, and successfully prevailed upon Germany to moderate Austrian action.

Grey's greatest task was in 1914; he passionately wanted to preserve the peace, yet he saw that Britain's interests and honour were at stake if he did not uphold the Entente against Germany. As the crisis following the Archduke's murder deepened, Grey was active in urging calm on the other Powers. But his suggestion of mediation by international conference, the Concert of Europe, was turned down by Germany. His problem was to decide whether Germany was determined on war and whether demonstrations of support for France and Russia, such as fleet movements, would deter Germany. On the one hand he warned Lichnowsky, the German ambassador, that Britain could not be depended upon to stand aside in the event of a Franco-German war; on the other he was not sufficiently able to reassure an anxious and emotional Cambon. After the German occupation of Luxembourg, he vigorously addressed a Cabinet meeting on 2nd August and was able to persuade his colleagues that any breach of Belgian neutrality would necessitate British action. It was on this matter, and the wider implications of the Entente, that he addressed the House on Bank Holiday Monday, 3rd August. "His face was passionless", wrote an observer, "and sharply cut like a bird's, his voice was clear, with no warm tones in it, his language was wholly unadorned, precise, simple, accurate, austerely dignified."[43] On the evening of the same day as Grey stood in his room at the Foreign Office, watching the lamps being lit in St James's Park, he remarked to his companion: "The lamps are going out all over Europe; we shall not see them lit again in our lifetime".[44]

Although Grey had united the nation on the issues of August, 1914, he felt no cause to congratulate himself; indeed he experienced a sense of failure. "I hate war", he lamented to Nicolson, and in the days ahead he would "go out of his way to avoid a company of Kitchener's recruits marching down the cheering street; the sight merely cut him to the heart".[45] The thought of resignation occurred to him and perhaps he should have gone through with it. He was conscious, perhaps over-conscious, that in war diplomacy is swallowed up by the conflict. Moreover, the July days had overstrained him fearfully, his eyesight was failing, he was bone-weary and sick at heart.

In the early stages of the war Grey's chief preoccupation was with the Near East and the Balkans. Turkey's decision to fight alongside Germany was an early diplomatic reverse and Grey then took up the task of wooing Bulgaria. However, the failure of the Dardanelles campaign gave him nothing to bargain with and Bulgaria also joined Germany. As for relations with the neutral U.S.A., Grey aimed to keep negotiations in his own hands. There were three main difficulties: Britain's blockade of Germany and its effect on American commerce; the suppression of the Irish Easter Rebellion in 1916, which turned important sectors of American opinion against Britain; and President Wilson's attempts to secure a negotiated peace, which Grey believed would solve nothing without a complete change of heart by Germany. Grey enjoyed considerable success. He was basically pro-American, and the United States, whose friendship he had always sought, joined the Allies in April, 1917.

The complicated questions of blockade and contraband meant a big increase in Foreign Office work. This added to Grey's load and he found such work tedious. A special section of the Office was established to deal with these matters and was directed by Grey's Parliamentary Under-Secretary, Lord Robert Cecil, who was given a seat in the Cabinet. Thus foreign policy was under dual control.

Grey's last eighteen months in office were the most miserable period of his whole career. He was increasingly tired and ill and his diplomacy came under mounting fire. He was not sorry to give up his seals of office when Asquith resigned at the end of 1916. In looking back over his years as Foreign Secretary, he believed them to have been a time of almost continuous storm, of vast forces beyond the control of individuals. "We could take an honourable part", he wrote to Rosebery, "but we could not control the whirlwind."[46] Above all, he experienced a tremendous sense of relief. "I feel like a man who has walked 1000 miles without rest and has at last been told he may lie down."[47]

On the formation of Lloyd George's Coalition government in December, 1916, the choice for the Foreign Secretaryship was Arthur James Balfour. "He was an ideal man for the Foreign Office and to assist the Cabinet on big issues."[48] Prime Minister and Foreign Secretary were in direct contrast: Lloyd George the dynamic and highly professional politician, a radical Liberal and avowedly a man of the people; Balfour nonchalant, even lazy, the Conservative politician who probably regarded his new chief as an upstart and a careerist. A product of Eton and Trinity College, Cambridge, a nephew of the great Lord Salisbury, Balfour came from a charmed circle. Beatrice Webb described him as "strong-willed, swift in execution, utterly cynical, and honestly contemptuous of that pitiful myth 'Democracy'."[49] Yet the relationship between Balfour and Lloyd George was one of considerable mutual admiration. Lloyd George respected Balfour's intelligence, while Balfour once wrote to Bonar Law that Lloyd George was "the most remarkable single figure produced by the war". The partnership worked also because Balfour was content to allow a dyarchy in the handling of foreign affairs and for Lloyd George to be the major figure at the Paris Peace Conference.

Tall, gangling and languid, Balfour had great personal charm and verbal brilliance. He was a philosopher of some distinction, although his intellectual gifts sometimes made for difficulties. In 1918, at an Allied conference, he had given a brilliantly reasoned analysis of the matter under discussion. Having asked Balfour whether he had finished, and Balfour saying that he had, Clemenceau, the French Premier, then demanded, "But are you for or against?"[50]

His entry into politics was in 1874, at the instigation of Salisbury. He rose steadily and in 1902 succeeded his uncle as Prime Minister. But his ministry fell apart in 1905 in a welter of party disputes. After further disagreements, he resigned his leadership of the Conservatives in 1911. When Asquith's Coalition was formed in May, 1915, Balfour became First Lord of the Admiralty. His knowledge was therefore wide, but he was almost seventy when he entered the Foreign Office.

Almost immediately, he was faced with further American initiatives for a negotiated peace. These he strongly resisted. Before long, however, Germany's use of unrestricted submarine warfare, and the consequent loss of American lives and shipping, led the United States to break off relations. Thus it fell to Balfour to woo America, to guide her at last into the British camp and to build an effective alliance. The United States were finally pushed into the war by the Zimmermann Telegram[51] and it was Balfour's dramatic task to hand over the text of it to Walter Page, the Anglophile American ambassador in London.

The United States declared war on Germany on 6th April, 1917, and within days Balfour, at his own request, was despatched across the Atlantic at the head of a goodwill mission. He addressed Congress, struck up an understanding with Wilson and discussed means of collaboration. Sir Ian Malcolm, Balfour's private secretary, observed that he "had gained for us (in all but name) an ally whose sympathy sprang not only from the head but now from the heart".[52]

During his American visit Balfour met Louis Brandeis, the noted jurist and Zionist. At the end of a long discussion Balfour had remarked "I am a Zionist".[53] The Sykes–Picot Agreement (between Britain and France), providing for the future partition of the Ottoman Empire, including Palestine, had already been made. By 1917, however, the British saw the Agreement as less than satisfactory. To alter it to include provision for a British-sponsored homeland for the Jews would, it was hoped, gain useful support in America and protect the Suez Canal. At the same time Chaim Weizmann[54] and his colleagues, who had caught wind of the Sykes–Picot Agreement with some dismay, were preparing their case. They presented a memorandum to the British Cabinet in July, 1917. It proposed "the establishment *of* Palestine *as* a national home for the Jewish people".[55] The formula eventually agreed by the Cabinet was by no means as clear as Weizmann's, but on 2nd November, 1917, Balfour wrote his celebrated Declaration in the form of a letter to Lord Rothschild, the President of the British Zionist Federation. "His Majesty's Government view with favour the establishment in Palestine of a national home for Jewish people, and will use their best endeavours to facilitate the achievement of this object",[56] ran the initial phrases. Balfour has been described as a man with no sense of mission. Opportunism, propaganda and strategic considerations all played their part in the Balfour Declaration, but idealism was far from absent. Blanche Dugdale records that "near the end of his days [Balfour] said to me that on the whole he felt that what he had been able to do for the Jews had been the thing he looked back upon as the most worth his doing".[57] On later occasions he strongly defended the Zionist cause and when it came up at the peace conference he was able to influence the settlement to its advantage.

Curzon, his successor, maintained that Balfour betrayed the independence of the Foreign Secretary and Foreign Office by allowing Lloyd George the dominant role. The crucial period was during the peace negotiations. "From an early stage", maintained Curzon, "he—a former Prime Minister and the Foreign Minister of the British Empire—allowed himself to be displaced in Paris and pushed aside."[58] Curzon went on: "I regard him as the worst and most dangerous of the British Foreign Ministers with whom I have been brought into contact in my political life".[59] Balfour was certainly complacent at the conference while Lloyd George was a whirlwind of activity. Lord Robert Cecil, Balfour's cousin and Under-Secretary, believed that he looked "in the last stages of exhaustion". Nevertheless, Harold Nicolson recorded that when he chose to rouse himself to intervene in proceedings "he is a whale among minnows". Nor was his stay in Paris inactive socially, far from it. At one musical evening a singer asked whether anyone objected to German songs. Balfour's witty, if cynical, reply was: "I don't; I will take them as part of the reparations that they owe us".[60]

In the later stages of negotiations concerning Germany Balfour played little part. His responsibility for the resulting treaty, Versailles, is therefore limited. However, once this was signed, Lloyd George departed and Balfour's part in deciding the fate of Germany's partner, Austria, was much more important. His signing of the Treaty of St Germain was his last significant act as Foreign Secretary. By now, like many of his predecessors in the post, he was exhausted and asked Lloyd George to be relieved. He exchanged posts with Curzon in October, 1919.

**NOTES TO CHAPTER FIVE**

1  M. D. R. Foot. *British Foreign Policy Since 1898* (London, 1956), p. 28.

2  Quoted by C. M. Andrew, *The Entente Cordiale from its Origins to 1914* in Neville Waites, ed., *Troubled Neighbours: Franco British Relations in the Twentieth Century*, p. 11.

3   Quoted by Morgan, p. 80.

4   Sir Arthur Nicolson entered the Foreign Office in 1870. Ambassador to St Petersburg 1906–10; Permanent Under-Secretary 1910–16.

5   Grand-Admiral Alfred von Tirpitz. German Minister of Marine 1897–1916. Built up the German High Seas Fleet. Responsible for the decision to develop battleships to rival the British Dreadnoughts.

6   A movement dedicated to the reform of the Ottoman Empire. Especially important among young army officers. Their attempt, in 1908, to establish constitutional government eventually failed.

7   Quoted by Keith Robbins, *Sir Edward Grey* (London, 1971), p. 305.

8   Steiner, p. 46.

9   Quoted by Steiner, p. 46.

10  Lord Newton. *Lord Lansdowne* (London, 1929), pp. 196–197.

11  Quoted by Grenville, p. 421.

12  John Hay, United States Secretary of State. Sir Julian Pauncefote, British ambassador in Washington.

13  Grenville, p. 389.

14  The Japanese ambassador in London. Later foreign minister, 1906–08.

15  Newton, p. 294.

16  Quoted by Newton, p. 334.

17  Francis Bertie: Head of African and Asian Departments; Assistant Under-Secretary 1894–1903; ambassador in Rome 1903–05; ambassador in Paris 1905–18.

18  Louis Mallet: précis writer to Lansdowne 1902–05; private secretary to Grey 1906–07; Assistant Under-Secretary 1907–13; ambassador to Constantinople 1913–14.

19  William Tyrrell: private secretary to Sanderson 1896–1903; secretary to Committee of Imperial Defence 1903–04; précis writer to Grey 1905–07; private secretary to Grey 1907–15; Head of Political Intelligence Department 1916; Permanent Under-Secretary 1925–30.

20  Eyre Crowe: educated in Germany; joined Foreign Office, 1885; as Head of the Western Department, in 1907 he submitted to Grey his *Memorandum on the present state of British relations with France and Germany*; Assistant Under-Secretary 1912–20; Permanent Under-Secretary 1920–25.

21  G. W. Monger. *The End of Isolation: British Foreign Policy, 1900–1907* (London, 1963), p. 234.

22  Monger, p. 235.

23  Sir William Harcourt: Home Secretary 1880–85; Chancellor of the Exchequer 1886 and 1892–95; Liberal Leader 1896–98.

24  Robbins, p. 71.

25  G. M. Trevelyan. *Grey of Falloden* (London, 1937), p. 107.

26  Viscount Grey of Falloden. *Twenty-Five Years, 1892–1916* (London, 1925), Vol. I, pp 127–129.

27  Quoted by Trevelyan, p. 146.

28  Trevelyan, p. vi.

29 Evelyn Baring, Earl of Cromer (1841–1917). Appointed British Agent and Consul-General in Egypt, 1883. For the next twenty-four years he was ruler of Egypt in all but name. Restored finances, established efficient government, carried through military reforms which enabled Kitchener to reconquer the Sudan.

30 Quoted by Robbins, p. 124.

31 *Twenty-Five Years,* Vol. II, p. 262.

32 Quoted by Foot, p. 33.

33 Steiner, p. 70.

34 Charles Hardinge: entered Foreign Office, 1880; first secretary at St Petersburg 1898–1903; Assistant Under-Secretary 1903–04; accompanied Edward VII on a tour of western capitals, 1904; ambassador at St Petersburg 1904–06; Permanent Under-Secretary 1906–10; Viceroy of India 1910–16; Permanent Under-Secretary 1916–20. Known as 'Capability' Hardinge.

35 Steiner, p. 91.

36 Quoted by Steiner, p. 101.

37 David Lloyd George. *The War Memoirs of David Lloyd George* (London, 1938), Vol. I, p. 28.

38 Quoted by Trevelyan, p. 110.

39 Quoted by Trevelyan, pp. 114–15.

40 *Twenty-Five Years*. Vol. I., p. 154.

41 Grey to Campbell-Bannerman, *Twenty-Five Years*, Vol. I, p. 165.

42 27 November 1911. Quoted by Trevelyan, p. 113.

43 Quoted by Robbins, p. 296.

44 Quoted by Trevelyan, p. 266.

45 Quoted by Trevelyan, p. 266–67.

46 Quoted by Robbins, p. 345.

47 Quoted by Robbins, p. 345.

48 Lloyd George. *War Memoirs*, Vol. I, p. 607.

49 Quoted in John P. Mackintosh (ed), *The British Prime Ministers* (London, 1977), Vol. I, p. 24.

50 Lloyd George. *War Memoirs*, Vol. I, p. 606.

51 Arthur Zimmermann, German foreign minister, sent a coded telegram to the German representative in Mexico suggesting a German–Mexican alliance. In the event of war between the United States and Germany, Mexico would receive territory in Texas, Arizona and New Mexico. The message was intercepted by British naval intelligence and the United States informed.

52 Quoted by Max Egremont, *Balfour* (London, 1980), p. 290.

53 Quoted by Egremont, p. 293.

54 Chaim Weizmann, Leader of British Zionism; head of the World Zionist movement 1920 and of the Jewish Agency 1929; first President of Israel 1948.

55 Quoted by Howard Morley Sachar, *The Course of Modern Jewish History* (New York, 1958), pp. 374–375.

56 Quoted by Sachar, p. 375.

57  B. E. C. Dugdale. *A. J. Balfour* (London, 1936), Vol. II, p. 235.
58  Quoted by Leonard Mosley, *Curzon: The End of an Epoch* (London, 1960) p. 205.
59  Quoted by Mosley, p. 207.
60  Quoted by Egremont, p. 304–305.

**CHAPTER SIX**

SECRETARIES OF STATE

| | |
|---|---|
| George Nathaniel Curzon, first Earl Curzon afterwards first Marquess Curzon | October 1919–January 1924 |
| James Ramsey MacDonald | January 1924–November 1924 |
| Sir Austen Chamberlain | November 1924–June 1929 |
| Arthur Henderson | June 1929–August 1931 |
| Rufus Daniel Isaacs, first Marquess of Reading | August 1931–November 1931 |
| Sir John Simon | November 1931–June 1935 |
| Sir Samuel Hoare | June 1935–December 1935 |

# In Pursuit of Peace

## Foreign Policy 1919–1935

WHEN the victorious Powers assembled in January, 1919, for the Paris Peace Conference, Britain was in a uniquely powerful position in that she had already achieved virtually all of her war objectives. The military preponderance of Germany in continental Europe had been broken; the German fleet had surrendered; Britain, with her Dominions, was in possession of the lion's share of Germany's colonies and well placed to share in the dismemberment of the Ottoman Empire.

British public opinion cried out for the Kaiser to be hanged and for Germany to be made to pay. But these demands moderated, and by the early 1920s the current opinion in favour of reconciliation was running strongly. Lloyd George, who kept the British negotiations largely in his own hands, anticipated these sentiments at the Conference itself and consistently argued in favour of relatively lenient terms for Germany. He upheld British interests such as the retention of mandated territories in the Middle East, with consequent control of oil supplies, and claims to Germany's African colonies. In other matters, however, he was concerned not to make the terms so burdensome as to leave Germany open to a Bolshevik revolution or to create a series of Alsace-Lorraines in reverse. In all this there was a sense of realism, though not unaffected by national interest. Within two weeks of the Armistice he had remarked: "Of course the Germans must pay to the uttermost farthing. But the question is how they can be made to pay beyond a certain point. It could only be done with gold or goods—and goods would prejudice our trade".[1]

The policy of moderation did not altogether succeed and, to make matters worse, the Treaty of Versailles left France feeling insecure. By the end of 1919 France and Britain were drifting apart, and it became the prime dilemma of British foreign policy in the 1920s and early 1930s to balance the French desire for security with the aim of reconciliation with

Germany. Amidst controversy, German reparations were eventually fixed at £6,600,000,000 in cash and kind, spread over some thirty years. During the course of 1922 Germany rapidly subsided into a deep economic crisis, and by the end of the year declared herself unable to meet her obligations. Thereupon, France and Belgium, without the approval of the British, occupied the Ruhr. Although they were able to overcome the passive resistance of the Germans, the French found themselves enmeshed in an adventure they could not win and one which inflicted economic damage on themselves. The solution was an expert committee, under the chairmanship of the American General Dawes, which took steps for the stabilization of the German currency, the provision of loans for Germany and the resumption of reparations in a modified form. The Dawes Plan was agreed in August, 1924; the French were able to extricate themselves from the Ruhr, and the British and French Premiers, MacDonald and Herriot, met in Geneva to settle the wider issues of French security. The Covenant of the League of Nations was to be strengthened by a process of compulsory arbitration in international disputes. This scheme, known as the Geneva Protocol, did not come to fruition, but the Rhineland Pact, signed at Locarno in 1925, guaranteed the frontiers of Belgium, France and Germany and promised a solution to the general problems of European security. Locarno seemed to open a new period of co-operation between Germany and her former enemies. Germany entered the League of Nations in 1926.

In the Middle East the treaty-makers ran into serious difficulties. By the Treaty of Sèvres, imposed on the Sultan in August, 1920, Turkey was truncated. But any chance of implementing the Treaty was virtually destroyed by the resistance of a Nationalist Government established at Ankara in opposition to Istanbul. Under their newly elected President, Mustapha Kemal, the Nationalist Turks fought a bloody war against the Greeks who, by the Treaty of Sèvres, had been allowed control of Smyrna. In September, 1922, Smyrna fell to the Kemalists, who then marched upon Istanbul. A potential clash with British forces occupying the neutralized Straits at Chanak almost led to war, but the crisis was averted. There was no alternative but to renegotiate terms with the new Kemalist government. The Treaty of Lausanne was signed in 1923.

The assumption of office by Labour in 1924 not only offered a fresh approach to the problem of international relations in Western Europe but also raised the question of Britain's own relations with Soviet Russia. So far, the response of British governments to the Bolsheviks had been open hostility, followed by a marked coolness. Labour's Prime Minister, Ramsay MacDonald, gave diplomatic recognition to the Soviet Union and proposed a collection of trading agreements. These arrangements were repudiated by Baldwin's Conservative government and Anglo-Soviet relations continued to languish in mutual suspicion.

If the First World War was "the war to end wars", then the League of Nations, with its Covenant embedded in the Treaty of Versailles, seemed to provide the means by which this aspiration might be realized. However, the authority of the League was tested to breaking-point by Japan and the European dictators. Alone among the Great Powers, France and Britain were members throughout; the United States never joined, Germany, Japan and Italy all left in the 1930s. Britain could not be "the policeman of the world". It took years to prepare for a disarmament conference. When it finally met in February, 1932, Franco-German differences proved insoluble, and Hitler's arrival in power in January, 1933, finally ended any chances of agreement. In October Germany announced its withdrawal from the League.

Closely connected with the rise of Hitler was the world economic depression and the associated Wall Street Crash of October, 1929. As manufacturing industry and trade shrank and unemployment rose, the nations took refuge in economic nationalism and, not only in Germany, populations demanded extreme measures from their governments. These developments were far from propitious for international co-operation, and the League had no machinery for curbing the self-destructive forces present in world capitalism.

The first great challenge to the League, which virtually smashed its authority, came in the Far East. In September, 1931, a section of the South Manchurian railway was blown up. Japanese troops, guarding the railway under treaty rights, responded by occupying the city of Mukden. Manchuria, the most highly industrialized province of China, had been developed first by the Russians and later by the Japanese. The combination of the effects of the economic depression and the rising influence of military interests in Japan led to a forward policy which found expression in Manchuria. In November, 1931, the League agreed to send a commission of enquiry to the Far East under the chairmanship of Lord

Lytton. Its report was completed at the end of 1932; while recognizing that Japan had genuine grievances against China it condemned her aggression. The Lytton Report was adopted by the League; Japan resigned in protest, and had in any case already overrun the whole of Manchuria and reduced it to a puppet state.

Well before Hitler came to power as Chancellor of Germany, the Foreign Office had recorded its deep suspicions of the Nazis. In April, 1933, Austen Chamberlain, who had previously argued for conciliation with Germany, denounced the new regime in the House of Commons. Whatever Hitler's long-term aims, and these seemed cloudy, his immediate plans seemed to centre more and more on Austria and the possible achievement of *Anschluss*.[2] British official opinion was thoroughly alarmed, especially when in July, 1934, the Austrian Chancellor, Dollfuss, was murdered in an attempted *putsch* by Austrian Nazis. The *putsch* failed and, as a warning to Hitler, Mussolini ordered 100,000 troops to the Austrian frontier. Nevertheless in March, 1935, in clear breach of the Treaty of Versailles, Hitler announced the existence of a German air force and the reintroduction of conscription. The response was the Stresa Conference when France, Britain and Italy condemned Germany's action and sought a common front to resist Hitler. This was the last expression of unity by the three former allies. In June Britain earned the censure of France for condoning further breaches of the Treaty by making a naval agreement with Germany. More immediately serious, however, was Mussolini's preparations against Abyssinia, a fellow-member of the League, and Italian troops invaded in October, 1935. Once again the authority of the League was set at nought. The aggressor was condemned but, although Britain took the lead in recommending economic sanctions, oil sanctions were never imposed. Britain had hoped to keep Mussolini as a counterpoise against Germany but the Italian dictator felt ostracized and fell into Hitler's embrace.


**The Foreign Secretaries 1919–1935**
With Lloyd George and Balfour so deeply involved in the Paris Peace Conference it was thought necessary to appoint an Acting Foreign Secretary. In January, 1919, the post was offered to George Nathaniel, Earl Curzon of Kedleston, who was already Lord President of the Council

and a member of the War Cabinet. Curzon accepted with alacrity, especially since he was given to understand that he would succeed to the Foreign Secretaryship proper on Balfour's return at the end of negotiations. This he duly did in October, 1919. Curzon was no stranger to the Foreign Office. He had been Lord Salisbury's Under-Secretary, and straightway he noted a change in the furniture of the Foreign Secretary's desk. "In Lord Salisbury's time", he remarked "there stood here an ink-stand of alabaster. What is this contraption of glass and brass?"

Curzon was well qualified for the office. Although he had not taken his expected First at Oxford, he had a brilliant mind allied to a remarkable capacity for hard work. He had travelled widely, particularly in the East, and had written authoritative volumes on Persia, the Far East, and the frontiers of India and Asiatic Russia. After a parliamentary career, he was appointed Viceroy of India in 1898 at the age of thirty-nine—the youngest man in history to hold the office. Having resigned amidst controversy in 1905, he retired into private life but was called into the war-time Coalition in 1915.

In spite of his wide experience and great ability, Curzon made enemies rather too easily and he was obsessed with holding office. Although he expressed serious opposition to the Coalition in February, 1918, he still clung to office. He wrote letters of resignation to Lloyd George but never sent them; in the early part of 1922 he had incontrovertible evidence that Lloyd George had by-passed him and was in effect running a second Foreign Office but, although he went to the brink, he simply filed the missive which was, by implication, his resignation.

Curzon's love of the panoply of power was notorious; the American Ambassador referred to him as 'His Royal Pomp', while officials at the Foreign Office found him imperious and contemptuous. Vansittart, a future Permanent Under-Secretary, recalled: "He always made one aware that one was subordinate, and never that one was necessary!"[3] His work and effectiveness could not but be affected by a suspiciousness that bordered on a persecution complex. This was compounded by ill-health and chronic insomnia. He was undoubtedly in great pain for long periods from a deformed back and hip, and his sleeplessness and taste for work regularly kept him at his boxes until the small hours.

It was inevitable that Lloyd George, "the man who won the war", should have dominated the peace negotiations, but he continued to stride the world stage after the Conference dispersed. Curzon recognized the inevitability and necessity of the Prime Minister playing the predominant role in the immediate aftermath of war, but attacked the "fatal ascendancy and interference" of Lloyd George in foreign policy. At other times Curzon complained of the difficulty of maintaining regular communications with his Prime Minister. Letters and memoranda went unanswered and Lloyd George "had the habit of going to bed and to sleep and refusing to be disturbed!" For his part, Lloyd George rightly calculated that Curzon would hold on to office in almost any circumstances, that opposition would never be pressed and that the Foreign Secretary would be a pliant subordinate; in Curzon's own words, a "valet and a drudge".

Lloyd George's determination to keep a wide sweep of Foreign Office business directly in his own hands proved, on occasion, perilous in the extreme. In the war between Greece and Turkey the Prime Minister took a consistently pro-Greek line; he was contemptuous of Mustapha Kemal— "a carpet-seller in a bazaar!" With the failure of the Greek forces to reach Ankara in September, 1921, their Prime Minister, Gounaris, plied anxiously between Athens and London to beg for money and arms. Curzon's policy was to persuade the Greeks to accept Allied mediation and for Britain to shun direct involvement. He therefore refused to give aid to the Greeks and, in Churchill's words, Gounaris "was confronted by Lord Curzon, who soused him in sonorous correctitudes".[5] Meanwhile, Lloyd George pursued an exactly opposite policy. Using his private secretary Philip Kerr as an intermediary, he encouraged the Greeks and promised them aid. The Greek Ambassador was able to inform his government that Britain stood behind them. Correctly suspecting a deception, Curzon instructed Foreign Office experts, who had broken the Greek diplomatic code, to provide him with copies of the Ambassador's telegrams. All was revealed, but although Curzon railed against the "Second Foreign Office" he declined to confront Lloyd George: the Foreign Secretary's pusillanimity was as blameworthy as the Prime Minister's deceitfulness.

It was, nevertheless, in the Near East that Curzon won his greatest triumph. His expertise in the area was recognized, not least by Lloyd George, and his long connection with India made him aware of the necessity of safeguarding and stabilizing every approach to the subcontinent. He worked hard for a new Anglo-Persian Treaty, for example. This was signed in August, 1919, but was unfortunately short-lived.

By the late summer of 1922 the war between Greece and Turkey had produced a state of extreme crisis and the Allied policies embodied in the Treaty of Sèvres were in ruins. In mid-August the Greek armies on the Sakaria River collapsed in the face of advancing Turkish Nationalist forces and, having fallen back on Smyrna, were swept from Turkish soil. The Turks then proceeded to advance towards the neutral zone of the Straits held by British, French and Italian forces. In a Cabinet held on 16th September, 1922, from which Curzon was absent, Lloyd George, supported by Churchill, Birkenhead and Austen Chamberlain, decided to call a halt to Kemal's progress. To this end Churchill drew up a Manifesto, later printed in the newspapers, which rallied the country and called upon the Dominions to give military backing. Curzon, having returned from his country retreat, protested that he had not been consulted and that the Manifesto was provocative. The crisis deepened a few days later when France and Italy announced their intention of withdrawing their troops from the neutral zone, thus leaving Britain alone. The British Government's first task was to persuade the French to stand by their obligations. Curzon insisted on going to Paris himself to meet Poincaré, who was at that time Premier and Foreign Minister. Although the Cabinet wanted Birkenhead to accompany Curzon, on the grounds of his recent ill-health, the Foreign Secretary opposed this, suspecting that Birkenhead would be instructed to provoke a crisis. In the event, Birkenhead's support might have been beneficial; the discussions with Poincaré turned out to be emotional shouting-matches which left Curzon totally exhausted. Nevertheless, Curzon and Poincaré were eventually able to agree on a joint approach to the Turks, and the British Foreign Secretary returned home to the congratulations of his Cabinet colleagues.

Such congratulations proved premature when Kemal decided to advance into the neutral zone once more and confront the British occupying forces under General Harington at Chanak. An explosive situation developed and the Cabinet ordered their forces to stand firm. Harington showed good sense by not actually delivering an ultimatum; the Turks did not press forward but agreed to negotiate.

Curzon claimed the credit for delivering Britain from the Chanak crisis and avoiding war. He argued that he had consistently favoured negotiation and moderated the antics of a war-mongering Cabinet. Certainly the newspapers took this line, although it could be argued that Churchill's

Manifesto had warned Kemal off or that the man on the spot, Harington, had shown more prudence than his political masters in London.

There is far less disagreement that a longer-term solution to the problems of the Near East owed much to Curzon; the Treaty of Lausanne was a personal triumph for him. The conference opened in November, 1922, and presented exceptional difficulties; the Turks no longer saw themselves in the role of a defeated power and dug in their heels, while the British felt that they could not trust their Italian and French allies. Curzon was present only for the first session of the conference. He departed in February, 1923, but although the eventual treaty was not signed until July, the second session simply confirmed his successful work. He was at his very best at Lausanne, freed at last from Lloyd George, who had fallen from power in the wake of the Chanak crisis. The new Prime Minister, Bonar Law, did not interfere and Curzon negotiated with patience and determination. The Turks received back a good deal of what they had lost at Sèvres but agreed to British demands for the continued neutrality of the Straits. In addition, the arrangements made for the Mosul oil-wells ensured that effective control by British companies was maintained.

In the political upheavals after the fall of Lloyd George, Curzon, as usual, showed the propensity to hold on to office. Although Bonar Law was preferred to Curzon as leader of the Conservative Party and Lloyd George's successor as Prime Minister, Curzon accepted the Foreign Secretaryship back from the hands of his successful opponent. When Bonar Law resigned in May, 1923, and Baldwin was offered the Premiership, Curzon was deeply wounded. Even so, after a brief hesitation in replying to Baldwin's invitation to serve, he wrote that he would "for the present continue at the Foreign Office".

Although Lloyd George had drawn much of the direction of foreign policy into his own hands, Ramsay MacDonald was the first British Prime Minister since Lord Salisbury actually to combine the office with the Foreign Secretaryship. Not only was he deeply interested in foreign affairs but he believed that there was no one else among his colleagues who was capable of filling the post. But although his diplomacy was very successful, even admirers admit that the choice of a dual role was a mistake. The strain was enormous, particularly in the summer of 1924; he neglected domestic affairs, and things were made worse by his reluctance to delegate.

During the war, and for some time after it, it was almost universally believed that MacDonald was a pacifist and perhaps even pro-German. For years he was the best-hated man in Britain. His stand in 1914 was not in fact that of an outright pacifist; he was never that. He believed that Britain had entered the war for the wrong reasons but he wanted Britain, once involved, to win an early victory lest after a long-drawn-out conflict the eventual peace would be revengeful. Even though he encouraged his fellow-citizens to join the armed forces and to work in munitions factories, he was widely misunderstood. Further suspicions were aroused by his attitude to revolutionary Russia. His welcome for the Fourteen Points[6] was matched by his denunciation of the Versailles Settlement. Although losing his seat in the election of 1918 and out of Parliament for four years, he was able to return in October, 1922, to the leadership of a reunited Labour Party.

Thus when MacDonald formed the first Labour Government in January, 1924, he was well fitted by conviction and record to catch the breezes of conciliation then blowing in European affairs. "The 'weather' must be improved", he noted in his diary. Unlike some of his colleagues, including Arthur Henderson who had badly wanted the Foreign Office, MacDonald had no previous ministerial experience. But he was a skilled parliamentarian with a striking appearance. As Foreign Secretary he was an excellent negotiator, gracious in manner and conciliatory in style and intentions.

The new Government sought to present a specifically Socialist and international approach to foreign policy, and Labour's arrival in office marked an important period. MacDonald lasted only eight months but he helped to mould British policy for a decade ahead. His method and approach were very different from Curzon's, especially in such matters as relations with the French, but circumstances also favoured a change. Both France and Germany wished to extricate themselves from the Ruhr crisis. Measures were already in hand to deal with the reparations issue, and there was wide support for improving relations between the former enemies. For MacDonald the great problem of the day could be solved by "the strenuous action of good-will".

Relations with France were quickly improved by a personal letter to Poincaré, and after Poincaré's electoral defeat the good work was continued. The new French premier, Herriot, was invited to Chequers in June, a cordial relationship was established and it was agreed to implement the Dawes Plan. The details were settled by an allied conference in London in August to which a German delegation, including the new foreign minister Stresemann, was invited. MacDonald's skilful chairmanship made the occasion a personal triumph for him; he steered a tactful course between Germans and French, and the outstanding questions of a new scheme of reparations and the evacuation of the Ruhr were resolved. "It was the high point of his Government—perhaps of his career."[7]

Labour had strongly argued the case for a lessening of international tension to allow a reduction of armaments. This, in turn, would provide the foundation for a more secure economic future. The realization of these objectives, it was believed, depended upon the effectiveness of the League of Nations. As the first British Foreign Secretary and the only British Prime Minister to attend the Assembly of the League, MacDonald aimed to strengthen the machinery of internationalism. He withheld agreement to the Treaty of Mutual Assistance, which would have involved automatic military intervention on behalf of victims of aggression, but promoted the Geneva Protocol. This ingenious plan provided for compulsory arbitration in international disputes, with sanctions as a last resort, and disarmament by agreement. The Assembly accepted it unanimously.

Labour's relations with the Soviet Union, becoming entangled with domestic politics, were less successful than other aspects of foreign policy and brought about the fall of the Government. Soon after coming to office MacDonald recognized the Soviets. This was not only a gesture of friendship but a practical appreciation that they formed the *de facto* and effective government of Russia. When MacDonald moved on to negotiate commercial and general treaties, he ran into trouble. The main stumbling-block was that the Russians would agree to the repayment of pre-Revolutionary debts only if the British would guarantee fresh loans. Negotiations broke down. As a minority government, Labour was dependent upon the support of the Liberals who, after some hesitation, decided to oppose the treaties. The Conservatives and Lloyd George, now back with the Liberals, were already in full cry. Meanwhile, MacDonald's decision not to prosecute a *prima facie* case of incitement to mutiny against the Communist journalist J. R. Campbell kindled fresh anxieties about Labour's democratic credentials. The Government was defeated on a motion of censure and lost forty seats in a General Election complicated by the notorious Zinoviev letter.[8]

The return of Baldwin and the Conservatives in November, 1924, brought Austen Chamberlain to the Foreign Office. The son of "Radical Joe" Chamberlain, Austen was a political heavyweight. In 1924 he was a Member of Parliament of nearly thirty years' standing; he had been Chancellor of the Exchequer twice, Secretary of State for India in the war-time Coalition and subsequently a member of the War Cabinet. During Bonar Law's illness he had led the Conservative party and on two occasions, in February, 1922, and April, 1923, he passed up the chance of the Premiership itself. To all outward appearances he seemed stiff and aloof, even forbidding, while his top hat, frock coat and monocle seemed to place him in a previous age. But the young Eden, his Parliamentary Private Secretary, found him "warm-hearted, considerate and generous" and had "the greatest affection for him".[9] His reputation as an honourable man was deserved but was one he himself cultivated. This made him vulnerable, and led Birkenhead to say that "Austen always played the game and always lost it". Nevertheless as a negotiator he was patient and persuasive and his influence in Europe was unrivalled by any British Foreign Secretary of the inter-war years. His view of his predecessors proved interesting when, in 1927, portraits of the six greatest Foreign Secretaries were to be hung in the Foreign Office. Chamberlain's selection was Castlereagh, Canning, Palmerston, Salisbury, Lansdowne and Grey.

The chief plank in Chamberlain's foreign policy was France. He "loved France like a woman, for her defects as well as her qualities"; an attitude which was not infrequently misunderstood and even vilified. As a young man he had paid lengthy visits to both France and Germany, comparing Berlin unfavourably with Paris, and spoke French fluently and well. In 1924 he informed the House that he would "make the maintenance of the entente with France the cardinal object of our policy". Nevertheless, it is clear that he thought it vital for Britain to move with France towards an understanding with Germany. The rapport he later enjoyed with his opposite numbers Stresemann and Briand ("the true heart of chivalrous France") added substance to his aspirations.

The new Conservative Foreign Secretary could not swallow his Labour predecessor's policies whole, particularly since a dominant theme of the General Election had been Labour's relations with Soviet Russia. For many Tories the Campbell case and the Zinoviev Letter were clear evidence of reds under beds. The newly negotiated treaties with Russia were repudiated and by the summer of 1925 relations with the Soviets had reached a state of almost complete breakdown. Chamberlain also had grave doubts about the Geneva Protocol and, shortly after taking office, informed the League that the British Government could not accept it. Nevertheless, the Dawes Plan was taken on board and the consequent flow of loans to Germany (mainly from the United States) was a crucial step in rapprochement.

Chamberlain was conscious that he represented a great power. On his visits abroad all the trappings of Foreign Office prestige were paraded for him, with the harbourmaster of Dover, the mayor of Calais and the full Foreign Office staff turning out at appropriate stages of the journey. As for the substance, his policies were founded on a traditional Foreign Office pattern and under him the department worked smoothly. At the conclusion of the Locarno negotiations Chamberlain wrote of the spirit of teamwork from typists upwards. He was well served by his Permanent Under-Secretaries, at first Sir Eyre Crowe and later Sir William Tyrrell. The major ambassadorships were filled by men of exceptional talent and Chamberlain was quickly on cordial terms with them. However, Lord Robert Cecil's appointment as Lord Privy Seal, with special responsibility for the League of Nations, threatened to trespass on the Foreign Secretary's territory. When Cecil asked to see all Foreign Office papers, Chamberlain refused permission and received Baldwin's support. Tension was never far from the surface and intensified after 1925.

Baldwin left his Cabinet colleagues to run their own departments and the Foreign Office was no exception. The relationship might have been uneasy: Baldwin was the junior and had earlier served under Chamberlain as Financial Secretary to the Treasury. They had taken different paths after the Carlton Club vote, and when Baldwin was forming his first ministry in May, 1923, Chamberlain avoided an invitation to serve, deliberately remaining out of the country. The two were reconciled at a dinner-party given by Neville Chamberlain, Austen returned to the front bench and his appointment to Baldwin's second Cabinet was a foregone conclusion. Relations between Prime Minister and Foreign Secretary were friendly but never intimate. Chamberlain appreciated the free hand given by Baldwin, although in part he attributed his independence to the Prime Minister's lack of knowledge. This arrangement worked well and the sentiments expressed in a letter written by Baldwin in 1926 should probably be taken at their face value: "It has been a great comfort throughout this year that I never need worry about foreign affairs and to feel perfect confidence in the judgement and wisdom of the Foreign Secretary, and for all this I am grateful".[10]

Chamberlain's greatest achievement in these years was the Locarno Treaties which were carried through in the teeth of fierce opposition in Cabinet and Parliament. The British rejection of the Geneva Protocol caused consternation in France and Belgium but Chamberlain quickly made it clear that Britain did not intend to withdraw into isolation; his aim was "to supplement the Covenant by making special arrangements in order to meet special needs". With the end of the Ruhr crisis and the acceptance of the Dawes Plan, Franco-German relations had eased. For this hopeful situation to continue, and for the health of Anglo-French relations, an alternative to the Geneva Protocol would have to be found. Chamberlain sought an international agreement which would offer direct guarantees to France but stop short of unlimited commitments by Britain. In so doing he met an initiative by Stresemann in favour of a mutual security pact. Chamberlain's plans were limited in scope partly because of his sense of realism but also in anticipation of fierce opposition in Cabinet. "A practical idealist" is the verdict of Sir Charles Petrie, Chamberlain's biographer. In the midst of the battle with his colleagues and public opinion at home, he was engaged in anxious conversations with the French. At last Cabinet opposition was overcome, an achievement for which Baldwin deserves great credit, and thereafter Chamberlain's negotiations went virtually unhindered. Agreement was reached at Locarno in October, 1925, and signed in London the following December. The most important of the treaties, signed by Britain, France, Belgium, Germany and Italy, provided for a mutual guarantee of the Franco-German and Belgo-German frontiers.

The effects of the treaties were perhaps largely psychological but they did usher in a period of international co-operation in which the the League could work fruitfully. In 1926 Germany joined the League and the trio of Chamberlain, Briand and Stresemann gave public expression to the new amity. Chamberlain himself was realistic about Europe's chances of a more permanent peace. In a debate in the House of Commons he said: "We regard Locarno not as the end of the work of appeasement and reconciliation, but as its beginning"[12] The treaties have been criticized for their failure to deal with the frontiers of eastern Europe in the same way as they had in the west. Chamberlain was aware of this limitation but it was one imposed by his own countrymen's unwillingness to commit themselves too far. They would not, for example, have agreed to defend the Polish Corridor, "for which no British government ever will or ever can risk the bones of a British Grenadier".[12]

On his brother's triumph, Neville Chamberlain remarked, "a great moment for him, the greatest of his life up till now, perhaps in the future". In fact Austen never touched such heights again. He seemed to age rapidly after this; he was ill in 1927 and again, more seriously, in 1928. Perhaps he should have been replaced. Relations with America were uneasy in 1927 and 1928, initially because of the breakdown of the talks for the further limitation of navies but compounded by the lack of contacts and understanding between the Foreign Office and the State Department. Chamberlain must take some of the blame and it was left to Hoover and Baldwin to restore harmony. In China, in 1927, as part of an anti-foreigner campaign, Communist forces seized the British concession of Hankow. At home Chamberlain was criticized for failing to recover it, although it is doubtful whether there would have been sufficient support for the kind of expedition required for the task. Nevertheless, he persuaded the Cabinet to send a strong force to Shanghai to prevent repetition. Meanwhile, relations with Russia deteriorated still further. From the contents of intercepted Russian telegrams, Chamberlain was aware that unrest in India was being exacerbated by Soviet propaganda. In an attempt to find evidence, a raid was ordered upon the offices of Arcos, the Russian trade delegation in London. This was an ill-judged action ordered, it seems, by Chamberlain, Baldwin and Joynson-Hicks.[13] Although nothing seriously incriminating was discovered, the Government decided to bluster it out and broke off diplomatic relations.

However, the central theme of Chamberlain's foreign policy held firm; the peace of Europe could best be safeguarded by the maintenance of the Anglo-French Entente and the cultivation of Germany. Chamberlain maintained excellent relations with Briand and Stresemann, and Locarno seemed to provide the necessary guarantees. It was to become clear, however, that the stability of Europe also depended on American money and, ominously, United States loans were beginning to be called in before the end of 1928. Stresemann died in October, 1929, by which time Chamberlain had lost office with the Conservative defeat at the polls. The "spirit of Locarno" did not long survive their departure.

Arthur Henderson's appointment as Foreign Secretary in June, 1929, was agreed only after a serious row among the Labour leaders. Henderson was ambitious for the post and had been disappointed not to receive it in 1924. MacDonald would have preferred J. H. Thomas,[14] whom he liked and trusted, and also considered keeping the Foreign Office for himself. After considerable manoeuvring Henderson got his way, having refused to serve at all otherwise. Such a major figure could not be left out without considerable damage to the incoming Government, but relations between Henderson and MacDonald grew worse as a result of his surrender. The Prime Minister did not forget that he had been put under pressure; he interfered in the Foreign Office and took charge of Anglo-American relations himself, including the vital negotiations on naval disarmament.

Henderson's credentials for major office in a Labour Cabinet were excellent. The son of a Scottish cotton-spinner, he was by trade an iron-moulder and by religious faith a Nonconformist. Earlier years had been devoted to the Labour movement before his election to the Commons in 1903. His experience in office was more extensive than that of any of his colleagues. including the Prime Minister; he had been a Cabinet minister in the wartime coalitions. On MacDonald's resignation as leader of the Parliamentary Labour Party in 1914, Henderson had taken his place. Once Foreign Secretary, he kept in close touch with the Labour Party, spending an hour or so each morning at its headquarters before going on to the Foreign Office.

The Foreign Secretaryship, according to his biographer and admirer, Mrs Mary Hamilton, was "the high-water mark in Henderson's career, and also probably the happiest period of his life".[15] Without doubt he was an experienced negotiator and, although his lack of languages was a disadvantage, he earned the trust of foreign statesmen by his heartfelt commitment to international understanding. "My new chief," wrote Vansittart, "a Wesleyan lay preacher, . . . was a very good man without being a very good Secretary of State. He was a respectable average, respectable indeed in all things, and lovable on his day, which came often . . . He was certainly the next best to Ramsay that the Labour Party could provide".[16] As Permanent Under-Secretary, Vansittart failed to establish the ascendancy over Henderson that he gained over other Foreign Secretaries; there was a mutual reserve, possibly a result of the social and psychological gap between them. On some matters of policy, too, there were differences: Vansittart believed that his chief thought too highly of the Soviets and that he bent foreign policy to the requirements of Socialist electioneering. But, generally speaking, he gained the co-operation and even affection of his officials and was known, as in the Labour Party, as "Uncle Arthur". His political assistants were good choices. Hugh Dalton was the Parliamentary Under-Secretary and to him was delegated much of the detailed working of the Foreign Office. Philip Noel-Baker, who had worked in the secretariat of the League in its early days, was Parliamentary Private Secretary. Unpromising socially, Henderson had little small-talk, was a poor eater, a teetotaller and non-smoker, yet he was accessible and at times positively exuded joviality.

Almost immediately on taking office, Henderson was working for the restoration of active trading and diplomatic relations with Russia. He was under pressure from his party to repair a whole range of outstanding issues but, in spite of Labour indignation, he insisted that a Russian ambassador would not be accredited without the consent and ratification of Parliament. As a further step, he made it clear to the House that he would not "tolerate any form of propaganda that interfered in the internal affairs either of this country or of any part of the British Empire".[17] Relations were restored; although the question of loans to Russia was dropped, ambassadors were exchanged and trade expanded, mainly to the benefit of Russia. It is also worthy of notice that Henderson opposed an application by the exiled Trotsky to reside in Britain.

Henderson's principal objective was European conciliation; the working out of a satisfactory solution to the remaining differences between Britain and Germany and the strengthening of French confidence about their security. The spirit of Locarno was to be carried further and, in more concrete terms, Henderson worked for an extension of the Dawes Plan and an early evacuation of the Rhineland. A conference was held on these matters at The Hague in August, 1929. Since reparations were already under review by the Young Committee,[18] Henderson took Snowden, the Chancellor of the Exchequer, as his negotiating partner. As it turned out, Snowden almost wrecked the conference by his intransigence in opposing a reduction in Britain's share of reparations. Henderson showed remarkable perseverance and stamina in handling his colleague, as well as the Germans, and was principally responsible for restoring a co-operative spirit. Eventually, the Young Plan was adopted, German reparation payments were considerably reduced and Allied forces were to withdraw from the Rhineland five years ahead of time. The British Foreign Secretary emerged with great credit.

From The Hague Henderson moved on to Geneva. Apart from seeking generally to enhance the authority of the League he was concerned specifically to pursue the cause of effective disarmament. At Geneva the good relations already established with the French and German foreign ministers were maintained. Mrs Hamilton had the attractive notion that all three were "men of the people; Briand, son of the little innkeeper of Nantes, and Stresemann, born in the beer-seller's establishment in the Köpenickstrasse". Henderson's teetotalism was clearly no barrier to international bonhomie.

Without showing great gifts of oratory or brilliance of mind, Henderson was the dominant figure at the Assemblies of the League in 1929 and 1930. To a greater extent than almost any other Foreign Secretary between the wars he won the confidence of both France and Germany. By sheer persistence he successfully pushed ahead with a full Disarmament Conference, the preparations for which had hitherto been astonishingly protracted. It was to be summoned for February, 1932, and Henderson was elected president. Before the conference had met, however, Labour had fallen from government in a political crisis which had split their Party. Henderson had broken with MacDonald and, although he took up his presidency, the Foreign Office was in other hands.

Having been called upon by the King to form a National Government, MacDonald decided upon a "Cabinet of individuals" which reflected the groups supporting him. Two Liberal lawyers held the Foreign Office in turn, Rufus Isaacs, Marquess of Reading, and Sir John Simon. Reading was a brilliant advocate who had served in Asquith's Cabinet as Attorney-General and, with greater relevance to the Foreign Secretaryship, had been ambassador in Washington and Viceroy of India. He lasted only until the Cabinet reshuffle following the General Election of October, 1931, when, according to his son and biographer,[20] he was replaced without warning. According to Reading's own testimony, however, it seems that he stepped down willingly. "I liked both the office and the officials, with whom I was in the closest contact, very much indeed. I only gave up because I knew I was at breaking point."[21]

Simon, a former Home Secretary, accepted the Foreign Secretaryship with some reluctance. It was not his métier. "The Home Office, the Exchequer, the Woolsack all suited him better."[22] Simon's detractors would say that he simply clung to office. A more charitable view is that he took it out of a sense of duty and, as leader of the National Liberals, it was essential that he should hold a major post. Vansittart, who remained as Permanent Under-Secretary, said that he was "the snakiest of them all" but the overwhelming impression is that he was a fair-minded, honourable and decent man. Simon's own memoirs reveal surprisingly little about how he regarded himself and his policies; instead he presents a series of clear and well-balanced legal cases. In Cabinet and the Foreign Office, too, he was meticulous in setting out the claims of competing policies. He was certainly distrusted by some, perhaps because he appeared remote and rather cold. An unkind clerihew ran:

> Sir John Simon
> Is not like Timon:
> Timon hated mankind,
> Simon doesn't mind.

Vansittart and Eden, his Parliamentary Under-Secretary, both criticized Simon for being indecisive and lacking in positive action. Eden recorded in his diary: "Vansittart drives him his way but J. S. is reluctant to travel. Yet he clings to the F.O. It is an unhappy situation for us all". There is no doubt that he involved Vansittart and Eden very closely in the discussion and development of policy and he referred to the "comradeship" of the relationship. But Simon gave insufficient ministerial direction to his department and the result was to enhance the position of Vansittart and other senior officials.

Simon was keenly aware of the troubled state of world affairs and the difficulties of the task before him. He recognized that public opinion had a touching faith in international disarmament, and in the authority of the League, but insisted in the forum of the House of Commons that unilateral disarmament would not bring about world peace. Moreover, the League was fatally weakened by the absence of the United States, and during the Manchurian crisis he knew full well that Japanese aggression could not be halted without American co-operation. Again, in the face of the rise of Nazi Germany he found the attitude of the Labour opposition towards armaments obstructive and divisive.

"The central political issue", he said in the House, "is how to reconcile Germany's demand for equality with France's desire about security." When it came to it, the Disarmament Conference failed to achieve this objective. The Treaty of Versailles, which had attempted to lock Germany into the fetters of disarmament, had also looked to the eventual "initiation of a general limitation of the armament of all nations", and the Germans rightly latched on to this. Discussion at the Conference always broke down on the detailed questions of the scale of armaments: the French would not weaken their own forces, the Germans demanded to know why they alone should be restricted. Simon believed that Britain was playing an honourable rôle in the discussions and he tried to be fair to each side; he refused to condone any disregard of the Treaty by the Germans but saw their point on the question of a more general limitation of arms. But Eden took a critical view of Simon's performance at Geneva, complaining that "by temperament he was not suited to drive the Conference. John Simon's brilliant analytical mind hated to take decisions".[25]

Simon inherited the Manchurian crisis from Reading and this was his first great test in office. It is difficult to see how Britain, with depleted resources, could have done anything by way of military or even economic sanctions to prevent determined Japanese expansion. British public opinion would have been sharply divided and no move could have been contemplated without the active involvement of the United States. Simon readily appreciated the complexities of the Manchurian question, and recognized that the Japanese had special rights as well as some genuine grievances there. While condemning the aggression, this was broadly the line taken by the Lytton Report, an investigation which Simon helped to initiate and which he regarded as a "close and impartial study". It was Simon, too, who proposed the resolution adopted by the Assembly of the League that members would not "recognise any situation, treaty, or agreement which might be brought about by means contrary to the Covenant of the League of Nations". In the end, the Assembly condemned Japan as the aggressor and she left the League while retaining her booty. Simon was left to reflect that "Japan, like Germany afterwards, cared nothing for moral restraints".

A further opportunity, or so it seemed at the time, for a general agreement on international armaments presented itself in 1935. After a series of Anglo-French conversations and a joint communiqué, Hitler pressed for an Anglo-German meeting. With some hestitation, it was arranged that Simon and Eden should meet the Führer in Berlin at the end of March. But, even before this meeting could take place, Hitler announced the readoption of conscription and the expansion of his army. After seeing him face to face, Simon at least knew the sort of man with whom he was dealing. He saw that Hitler's views were fraught with danger, the more so for being sincerely held. The dictator made it clear that he would go his own way on rearmament, that unification with Austria was simply a matter of time, and he also announced that Germany had reached parity with Britain in air-power. According to Vansittart, Hitler was unimpressed by Simon and Eden and the visit was characterized by British hesitancy and indecision. "We lost face by our weakness."[26] But on his return Simon did urgently press MacDonald for a full investigation of the nature of German air-power. Meanwhile Eden left Berlin for Moscow, Warsaw and Prague.

The failure of the Berlin conversations made it vital for Britain, France and Italy to draw together and, to this end, MacDonald and Simon met Mussolini and the French at Stresa in April, 1935. They aimed to demonstrate solidarity and to condemn German rearmament while keeping the door open for Germany's return to League membership. Germany was indeed censured and this was confirmed by a unanimous resolution of the League. But events in East Africa showed the solidarity of the former allies to be only skin-deep. Clashes had already occurred on the borders of Abyssinia and Italian colonies, and Italian forces were being prepared for an outbreak of open hostilities. Before the Stresa meeting, it had apparently been agreed by MacDonald and Simon that Mussolini should be confronted on the Abyssinian question. In the event although the matter was raised by the Italians it was not mentioned in the formal sessions. "Here was an unhappy lapse for which the Foreign Secretary, knowing the dangers better, was more responsible than the Prime Minister."[27] An early warning by Britain might have checked Italian aggression. Hugh Dalton regarded the affair as "one of the most criminal blunders in the whole course of British diplomacy in these years". Nevertheless, Mussolini had determined to attack Abyssinia, probably in December, 1934, and it seems doubtful whether a warning from Simon would have deterred him.

With the Cabinet reshuffle in June, 1935, Simon thankfully returned for his second spell at the Home Office. He has had a generally bad press as Foreign Secretary and his own reflections are marked by a tone of weary resignation. "Responsibility ought to call out the best that is in a man, and I never worked harder. But hard work may produce, alas! disappointing results."[28]

More than a few ministers have resigned on principle or been harried from office but not many resignations have been so dramatic as Samuel Hoare's in December, 1935. From its inception the National Government had been dominated by the Conservatives, and by 1935 there was a strong move by them to have one of their own as Foreign Secretary. Although some of the younger Conservatives wanted Eden, Baldwin's choice fell upon Hoare. His tenure lasted for little more than six months. Baldwin's compromise was to appoint Eden Minister for League of Nations Affairs, with a seat in the Cabinet. Neither Hoare nor Eden was happy with the arrangement; Eden argued that "League affairs were foreign affairs and that it would not be possible to separate them".[29] In fact the arrangement worked better than expected. The younger man was generally given his head and was closely consulted, especially over Abyssinia.

Hoare came to foreign affairs from a four-year spell at the India Office where his great achievement had been the passing of a controversial India Act. He had done this with great skill, in the face of furious opposition from Churchill, but it had left him tired and he was unfortunate to have been pitched into a major crisis quite so soon. "His mind was keen, his intentions good, and he might have left a better record if he had not been punched above and below the belt before he found his feet. He reminded one of a diffident boxer, who, stunned by punishment, never regains form."[30] An extension of the metaphor might suggest that Hoare's seconds were unsure how he should approach the fight. The Foreign Office was divided, as was British public opinion. Some agreed with Vansittart that Germany was the principal danger, but most placed faith in reconciliation, disarmament and the authority of the League. But Vansittart, as Permanent Under-Secretary, carried great influence. Volatile, brilliant and ruthless, he was "seldom an official giving cool and disinterested advice based on study and experience. He was himself a sincere, almost fanatical, crusader".[31]

Italy's intentions towards Abyssinia were a cause of serious anxiety well before Hoare took the Foreign Office. It was thought to be a real possibility that Mussolini would act "like a mad dog" in response, for example, to sanctions. As the crisis developed, British naval power in the Mediterranean was increased. At the same time Britain, anxious to preserve the Stresa Front, was concerned not to push Mussolini to extremes. Hoare experienced a further difficulty in working with the French, who saw Britain's recent Naval agreement with Germany as a betrayal of the Versailles settlement. One possible solution to Mussolini's aggressive designs was to interest him in territorial concessions in Abyssinia and to compensate Abyssinia with gains in British Somaliland. Such a plan was agreed by Hoare, Eden and Vansittart. A somewhat reluctant Eden was sent to Rome with this offer, but Mussolini turned it down, thus preserving Eden's reputation as an anti-appeaser.

Hoare then decided to act within the League, first making it clear in the House that there was no question of taking independent action. "As things are, and as long as there is an effective League, we are ready to take our full share of collective responsibility. But when I say collective responsibility, I mean collective responsibility."[32] His address to the Assembly of the League in September, 1935, made much the same point. While at Geneva, however, he gave fresh assurances to the French premier and foreign minister, Laval.

In October the Italians carried out their long-prepared invasion of Abyssinia. The League declared them the aggressors and applied a preliminary set of economic sanctions. But such chances as there were of stopping Mussolini were jeopardized by the continuing mutual distrust of Britain and France. Hoare informed the Cabinet that Laval was intriguing behind the League's back for a deal with Mussolini. Domestic preoccupations made life even more difficult for Hoare. In spite of the Abyssinian crisis, Baldwin had called a General Election and Hoare found himself left very much to his own devices while his colleagues went electioneering. Meanwhile Laval, anxious to arrive at an accommodation before the League further alienated Mussolini by imposing oil sanctions, suggested a plan for ending the Abyssinian war.

At a meeting of the Cabinet in early December, Hoare was authorized to meet Laval in Paris to discuss what turned out to be another version of a plan to partition Abyssinia. Hoare was reluctant, he was over-worked and over-tired, but agreed to go to Paris on his way to an overdue winter-sports holiday in Switzerland. Arriving late and weary, Hoare was plunged into lengthy talks. He finally agreed to Laval's proposal of a formula which British and French officials had been working upon for months. Hoare's stipulation was that the cession of two-thirds of Abyssinian territory to Italy, with some compensation, had to be acceptable to both parties as well as to the League. The plan, the notorious Hoare–Laval Pact, never got that far. In order to ensure that the proposals would stick, Laval leaked them to the French press. But the politicians were thwarted by a storm of public protest. Baldwin's cabinet went into rapid retreat. While Hoare recuperated in Switzerland his colleagues repudiated him. On his return he surrendered his seals and gave his resignation speech from the back benches.

Why did Hoare, normally an astute and shrewdly cautious politician, make the mistake of giving support to something which Laval could so readily present as a binding agreement? His own published explanation was "that nothing short of the proposals would save Abyssinia and prevent Mussolini from joining the Hitler front. This being so, resignation, not recantation, was the only course open to me".[33] It was the Cabinet that recanted, but Hoare blamed himself for not insisting upon clearer instructions from his colleagues on "how far he could go" with Laval. In fact he had been given almost *carte blanche* with the emphasis on taking a "generous view of the Italian attitude", and it could be argued that the mistake was not his but the Government's as a whole. Some such scheme as he had agreed with Laval had, with Cabinet approval, been in active preparation for months before, and was in the logic of general policies which Hoare had inherited. Additional factors in the débâcle were the strains of office combined with ill-health on Hoare's part and, possibly, the influence of Vansittart. But the responsibility was Hoare's; as Secretary of State he accepted it and made the sacrifice. Hans Dieckhoff, the German diplomatist, passed judgement on British cynicism, "You have found a whipping-boy for Mussolini in Hoare. Now that you have relieved your feelings at Hoare's expense you will not feel any impulse to save Ethiopia by having a showdown with Mussolini."

Arthur Henderson, a drawing by I. Opher.          *National Portrait Gallery, London*

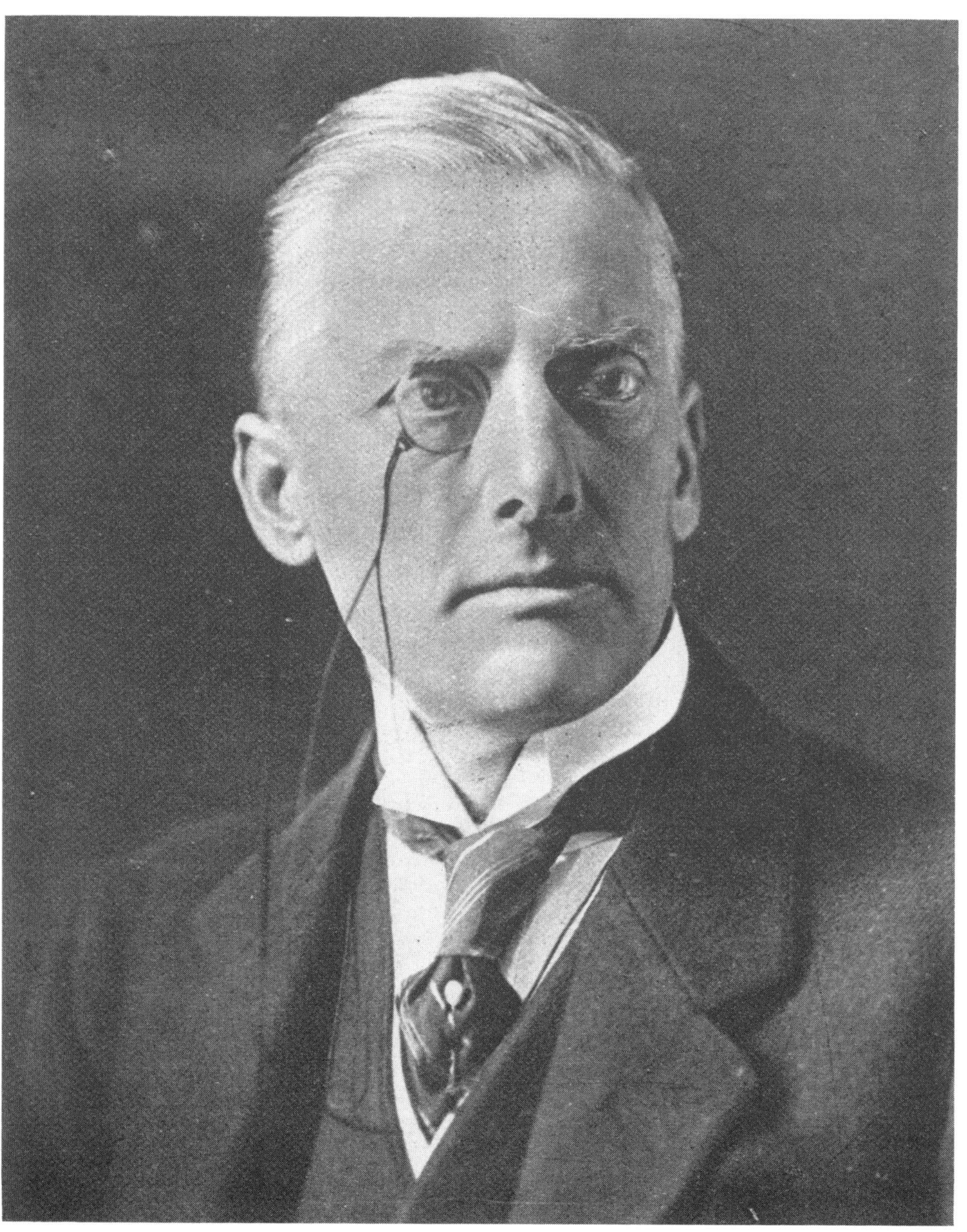

Sir Austen Chamberlain.

*The Mansell Collection*

**NOTES TO CHAPTER SIX**

1  Quoted by Frank Owen, *Tempestuous Journey: Lloyd George, His Life and Times* (London, 1954), p. 501.
2  Union between Austria and Germany. This was eventually accomplished in 1938.
3  Quoted by Mosley, p. 208.
4  Quoted by Mosley, p. 209.
5  Quoted by Mosley, p. 214.
6  Originally drawn up in January 1918 by President Woodrow Wilson of the U.S.A. as a statement of war aims. The principles laid down were accepted (with two reservations) by the Allies as a basis for peace on the signature of the Armistice. In the event some important aspects of the Fourteen Points were overlooked in the eventual peace treaties.
7  David Marquand. *Ramsay MacDonald* (London, 1977), p. 351.
8  A letter allegedly sent to the British Communist Party by Grigory Zinoviev, chairman of the Comintern, encouraging it to incite revolution in Britain. Extracts from the letter were published in the press just before the General Election. In view of Labour's recognition of the U.S.S.R., some considerable body of opinion turned against Labour. The Labour leaders regarded the Letter as a forgery and part of a conspiracy against them by the newspapers. The authenticity of the Letter has by no means been disproved.
9  Earl of Avon. *The Eden Memoirs: Facing the Dictators* (London, 1962), p. 7.
10  Quoted by Keith Middlemas and John Barnes, *Baldwin* (London, 1969), p. 343.
11  Speech to the House of Commons 18 November 1925. Quoted by Martin Gilbert, *Britain and Germany Between the Wars* (London, 1964), p. 44.
12  Quoted by Middlemas and Barnes, p. 356.
13  Sir William Joynson-Hicks. Minister of Health 1922–24; Home Secretary 1924–29.
14  John Henry Thomas. Engine-driver; General Secretary of the National Union of Railwaymen 1917–31; Colonial Secretary 1924, 1935–36; Lord Privy Seal 1929–30; Dominions Secretary 1930–35.
15  Mary Agnes Hamilton. *Arthur Henderson* (London, 1938), p. 283.
16  Lord Vansittart. *The Mist Procession* (London, 1958), p. 397.
17  Hamilton, p. 309.
18  Under the chairmanship of the American businessman Owen D. Young. It drew up the Young Plan, a development of the Dawes Plan.
19  Hamilton, p. 321.
20  Marquess of Reading. *Rufus Isaacs* (London, 1945), p. 365.
21  H. Montgomery Hyde. *Lord Reading* (London, 1967), p. 415.
22  Vansittart, p. 427.
23  Avon, p. 187.
24  Viscount Simon. *Retrospect* (London, 1952), p. 186.
25  Avon, p. 28.
26  Vansittart, p. 512.
27  Avon, p. 179.
28  Simon, p. 177.

29  Avon, pp. 217–218.
30  Vansittart, p. 539.
31  Avon, p. 242.
32  Quoted by J. A. Cross, *Sir Samuel Hoare: A Political Biography* (London, 1977).
33  Quoted by Cross, p. 254.
34  Quoted by Cross, p. 264.

**CHAPTER SEVEN**

SECRETARIES OF STATE
Anthony Eden December 1935–February 1938
Edward Frederick Lindley Wood, third
  Viscount Halifax February 1938–December 1940
Eden December 1940–July 1945
Ernest Bevin July 1945–March 1951

# Facing the Dictators

## Foreign Policy 1935–1951

EDEN'S choice of title[1] for the first volume of his memoirs, which is also chosen as the title of this chapter, is apposite not only to the years immediately preceding the Second World War but to the whole period 1935–51. For ten years, in diplomacy and war, Britain was confronted by the dictatorial régimes of Nazi Germany, Fascist Italy and a militaristic Japan. After 1945 Britain and her wartime ally, Stalin's Soviet Russia, moved along increasingly divergent courses. World War was followed by Cold War. In the whole of this period Britain had three Foreign Secretaries; Eden, twice, Halifax and Bevin.

In the 1930s successive British governments followed a policy of appeasing the dictators. Appeasement, at least in its earlier stages, was not a policy of weakly surrendering to every demand. It was based on the principle that the dictators could be "civilized" and brought into active co-operation in the community of nations. To achieve this objective, legitimate grievances would need to be redressed. As regards Germany in particular, the Versailles settlement was widely regarded in Britain as unjust and unworkable; for example, Germans in Czechoslovakia, Poland and Austria were considered to be entitled to some measure of self-determination. Moreover, Germany was seen as Europe's bulwark against Bolshevism. Having regained her natural place in the world, Germany would co-operate in the great causes of disarmament and economic recovery. Other considerations were the horrifying lessons of modern warfare, the belief that "the bomber will always get through" and pacifist tendencies in British public opinion. Many British politicians were in favour of avoiding war until it was absolutely clear that the country's vital interests were at stake; others feared that to tell the truth about the need for rearmament would lose a General Election. Nevertheless, there was an underlying fear of Hitler and, for this reason, Mussolini was wooed and appeased. He got his own way in Abyssinia, Spain and Albania. The fundamental flaw in appeasement, therefore, was that it misunderstood the character of the Italian and German dictatorships; they were led not by statesmen but by bullies, adventurers and murderers.

Appeasement might have worked if, in the event of the dictators going too far, it had been backed by effective force and a resolute diplomatic front on the part of a united Britain and France. These essentials were lacking. France was rent by internal dissension; London and Paris did not fully trust each other. Britain was slow to rearm, and this very state of military unpreparedness provided an additional argument in favour of appeasement. Germany should be conciliated whilst Britain rearmed. However, British ministers were uncertain whether the electorate would stand for a costly arms programme. Meanwhile, the Labour opposition consistently denounced an increase in arms expenditure.

British rearmament began in 1936 but initially at a slower rate than Germany's. However, perhaps more by good fortune than the judgement of the politicians, the vital radar defences were provided and fighter aircraft production stepped up. During the course of 1939, as the effects of new factory-building and the redeployment of skilled labour came to fruition, Britain overtook Germany in aircraft production. In other ways the picture was less satisfactory. There was no Ministry of Defence, only an ineffective minister for the co-ordination of defence, Inskip, appointed in March, 1936. No Ministry of Supply was set up until July, 1939, and even then its powers were limited.

Chamberlain's accession to the Premiership, in May, 1937, was of the utmost significance. He aimed to arrest what he saw as a policy of drift and to give consistency and vigour to British diplomacy. Determined to have his own way, he appointed men who shared his views and he sought to impose his will on the departments of government, including the Foreign Office. In Cabinet, Chamberlain worked closely with the two former Foreign Secretaries, Simon and Hoare, and with Halifax, the Lord President of the Council. This caused difficulties for the Foreign Secretary, Eden. In addition, impatient of what he believed to be Foreign Office obstruction, the Prime Minister eased out the Permanent Under-Secretary, Vansittart (the leading exponent of an anti-German policy). Vansittart was kicked upstairs to become Chief Diplomatic Adviser to the government. His place at the Foreign Office was taken by Cadogan. Even before this, Chamberlain's distrust of the Foreign Office had led him to rely for advice on foreign policy upon the Government's Chief Industrial Adviser, Sir Horace Wilson. By February, 1938, the differences between Prime Minister and Foreign Secretary led to Eden's resignation. He was replaced by Halifax.

Although Chamberlain detested and feared war, he had supported the need for rearmament and "more than any other man, laid the foundations for British fighting power during the second World War".[2] Hoping that the newly manufactured armaments would never be used, he took upon himself the role of peacemaker. Rejecting Britain's traditional role as the creator of "grand alliances" against those who threatened Europe's equilibrium, he was instead "imbued with a sense of a special and personal mission to come to friendly terms with the Dictators of Italy and Germany".[3]

The failure of the Hoare–Laval plan had left the fate of Abyssinia unsettled. Britain and France had now to depend upon the authority of the League and the use of sanctions against Italy. Sanctions proved ineffective; they were applied half-heartedly by the two democracies for fear of driving Mussolini into the arms of Hitler. Moreover, American oil supplies into Italian East Africa actually increased. The distractions of the democracies over Abyssinia provided Germany with an opportunity. In March, 1936, Hitler reoccupied and then remilitarized the Rhineland, a move originally planned for Spring, 1937. No effort was made to stop him. Germany could rearm in the industrial areas for which the Rhineland now provided a shield. The question of oil sanctions against Italy was postponed and, by early summer 1936, Mussolini was master of Abyssinia. Britain and France had done not enough to stop Mussolini but quite sufficient for him to proclaim the Rome–Berlin Axis in November, 1936. At the same time, the dictators recognized Franco's government in Spain. Not only was the Abyssinian affair and its consequences a grave blow to British and French prestige; it effectively broke the League.

Civil war broke out in Spain in July, 1936. The danger of it spreading was grave: Germany and Italy provided substantial help to the Nationalists; Russia, on a lesser scale, aided the Republican government. Britain's concern was to limit the war by getting the powers to agree to non-intervention. To this end a non-intervention committee, albeit ineffective, was established in London. Needless to say, since Italy was so deeply involved, Britain had to step carefully in order to avoid a complete break with the Duce. In January, 1937, the so-called "gentlemen's agreement" was signed by which Britain and Italy agreed to maintain the status quo in the Mediterranean. Yet Italy still maintained very large forces in Spain. Relations with Italy were not repaired; Mussolini moved even closer to Hitler and, in November, 1937, joined Germany and Japan in the Anti-Comintern Pact. Meanwhile, the preoccupation of Italy, France and Britain with Spain enabled Hitler to pursue his ambitions towards Austria.

Despite everything, Britain continued her attempts to cultivate Italy. In February, 1938, a formula was drawn up whereby, in return for recognition of Mussolini's position in Abyssinia, Italian troops would be withdrawn from Spain. This was the occasion for Eden's resignation. Still hoping that Mussolini might be persuaded to moderate Hitler, in January, 1939, Chamberlain and Halifax visited the Italian dictator. A month later the British government gave its recognition to Franco. None of this prevented a formal alliance between Mussolini and Hitler in May, 1939—the Pact of Steel.

British commitments in these years were not confined to Europe. In the Far East Japan consolidated her hold in Manchuria, and threatened to increase her hold in northern China. Britain's anxieties about her own interests in, for example, Shanghai and Tientsin meant that relations with Japan deteriorated. In addition, Japanese penetration of traditional British markets and unfair competition, as a result of low wages, caused further resentment. Britain's capacity to act was restricted by insufficient naval resources and a failure to engage the co-operation of the United States. Japan's Anti-Comintern Pact with Germany was, from Japan's point of view, largely a way of bringing pressure to bear upon China and containing Russia, but it also represented a threat to British interests. Moreover, the possibility of a division of British forces firmly linked the Far Eastern question with the German problem. Japan's invasion of China proper, in July, 1937, led Eden to contemplate a naval demonstration in the Far East. However, naval resources were already over-stretched, required as they were in the Mediterranean at a critical point in the Spanish Civil War. Britain's policy was therefore a holding operation which aimed to keep Chinese resistance alive. Hong Kong was used to supply China with foreign armaments and, from 1938, the Burma–China frontier was used as a major lifeline. The Japanese took serious offence; as the Western European crisis developed in 1938 and 1939 they moved closer to the Axis powers.

In the early part of 1938 Hitler effectively eliminated the chief critics of his forward policies. Fifteen generals were removed and the Foreign Minister, Von Neurath, was replaced by the anti-British Von Ribbentrop. Hitler was now ready to carry out the *Anschluss* with Austria. The Austrian Chancellor, Von Schuschnigg, was summoned to Berchtesgaden, the Führer's Bavarian retreat, and presented with a set of impossible demands. Schuschnigg accepted all but the most outrageous of these but, on returning home, announced a plebiscite inviting the Austrians to pronounce on the future independence of their country. This provoked Hitler into threatening an invasion and Schuschnigg resigned. His successor, Seyss-Inquart, called in the Germans "to restore order". Hitler himself drove into Vienna on 14th March, 1938. Not a blow was struck. Austria was incorporated into the Reich. Britain and France could only stand by; Mussolini was alarmed but did nothing.

The fall of Austria directed attention towards Czechoslovakia, whose western provinces were now lodged firmly in Germany's jaws. Czechoslovakia, the most successful of the successor states of the Habsburg Empire, was, nevertheless, a mosaic of peoples and languages. Most significant, in the Sudetenland, there were three and a quarter million German speakers. Recruited from among them was an active Nazi Party, subsidized by the German Foreign Office and led by Konrad Henlein.[4] Demands for union with Germany were aroused to fresh enthusiasm by Hitler's triumph in Vienna.

Although Britain had no treaty obligations to defend Czechoslovakia, France did. It was recognized by the British Cabinet, however, that they might be forced to intervene if France, in defending Czechoslovakia, were to be invaded by Germany, or if the seizure of a part or the whole of Czechoslovakia made Germany so powerful as to threaten Britain's vital interests. However, Chamberlain doubted whether France and Britain could do anything militarily to uphold Czechoslovakia. His policy was always to find an accommodation with Hitler, if necessary at Czechoslovakia's expense, and to convince the Czech leaders that this was necessary. The formulation of this policy was removed from the Cabinet as a whole and fell to a quadrumvirate consisting of the Prime Minister, Halifax (the Foreign Secretary) and, discredited though they were, the two ex-Foreign Secretaries, Simon and Hoare.

Hitler opened a virulent propaganda campaign against Czechoslovakia in May, 1938. The Czechs partially mobilized. This crisis was overcome, war was avoided, but Hitler was determined when the moment came to smash Czechoslovakia.[5] Britain attempted to keep the Czechs and Germans talking. In late July, 1938, Chamberlain sent Lord Runciman[6] as a mediator to Prague. His mission failed. Chamberlain turned to personal diplomacy. With Sir Horace Wilson as his only companion he flew to Germany on 15th September and met Hitler at Berchtesgaden. It was agreed there that territories occupied by more than 50% of German inhabitants should be transferred to the Reich. An international body would arrange the adjustment of borders. Having gained the collaboration of the French and the reluctant agreement of the Czechs, Chamberlain met Hitler again, at Bad Godesberg on 22nd September, to clear up final details. Instead, to Chamberlain's astonishment, Hitler increased his demands. He wanted immediate occupation. The Czechs mobilized their army, the British their fleet. France sent out call-up papers. Europe stood on the brink of war. At the eleventh hour, ostensibly as a result of Mussolini's mediation, Chamberlain flew once again to meet Hitler, this time at Munich. There appeasement reached its apogee and Chamberlain believed, for the moment, that he had won his greatest triumph. In complete disregard of the Czechs and Russians, Chamberlain, Hitler, Mussolini and the French Prime Minister, Daladier, resolved "the Czech problem" on terms differing only in detail from Hitler's demands at Bad Godesberg. The Czechs had no alternative but to accept their fate while Chamberlain returned home to a hero's welcome. His triumphal progress was watched by Orme Sargent, the strongest opponent of appeasement in the Foreign Office. "For all the fun and cheers", he recalled "you might think that they were celebrating a major victory over an enemy instead of merely a betrayal of a minor ally."[7] There was only one resignation from the Cabinet; that of Duff Cooper, First Lord of the Admiralty.

Appeasement failed. Not only were the appetites of the dictators unsatisfied but, in terms of military preparedness, the gap between Germany and the Anglo-French partnership widened in the period between Munich and the outbreak of war a year later. Within six months, moreover, Czechoslovakia fell apart as a result of the territorial demands of Hungary and Poland as well as fresh German pressure. Hitler entered Prague in triumph. He then forced Lithuania to give up Memel. Not to be outdone, Mussolini overran Albania at the beginning of April, 1939.

The cynicism and treachery of Germany over Czechoslovakia caused a sharp reversal of British policy. Within days of the occupation of Prague Chamberlain, in a major speech in Birmingham, announced "Any attempt to dominate the world by force was one which the Democracies must resist".[8] The independence of Poland, Hitler's next likely target, was guaranteed. In spite of the risk of driving Mussolini further into the Nazi camp, Italy's annexation of Albania led to similar assurances being given to Rumania and Greece. At home, Britain actively prepared for war.

To prevent a German onslaught on Poland, it was essential for Britain to come to an understanding with Soviet Russia. But the negotiations with Moscow were carried on half-heartedly and in an atmosphere of mutual distrust. The chief stumbling-block was Russia's price for her defence of Poland: a right of intervention in the Baltic States (Latvia, Lithuania and Esthonia) and the facility for moving troops into and across Poland and Rumania. This was a price that these states were not prepared to pay. The only other possibility was a straight military alliance between Britain and Russia. Britain was unable to go this far. As for Hitler, his strategy was to undermine Poland and provoke a quarrel while driving a diplomatic wedge between those who sought to defend her. The Non-Aggression Pact between Nazi Germany and Communist Russia was, therefore, a triumph of incalculable proportions. It was signed by Molotov[9] and Ribbentrop on 23rd August. Russia proclaimed her neutrality and was given a free hand in the Baltic states while Poland was to be partitioned. The destruction of Poland could not be long delayed and German forces moved across her border on 1st September. Britain declared war on German two days later.

Having failed to preserve peace, the thrust of British diplomacy now turned towards achieving the most advantageous conditions for waging war. There were three priorities: to establish a fruitful relationship with Britain's main ally, France; to persuade the neutrals into a benevolent stance, or, at least, to prevent them joining Hitler; to secure the flow of resources from abroad into Britain, chiefly from the United States.

At the outbreak of war the most important neutrals were the United States, the Soviet Union, Japan, Italy and Spain. In the period of the "Phoney War", when there was no serious fighting in Europe, Britain's chief weapon was blockade. As in the First World War, to avoid antagonising the neutrals, watchful diplomacy was required. Italy and the United States were handled with particular care. Despite the Molotov–

Ribbentrop Pact, relations with Russia were reasonable until the Soviet invasion of Finland at the end of November, 1939. This caused a serious breach, but although an Anglo-French expeditionary force was raised for the defence of Finland, it was never despatched. This was fortunate indeed; "for Great Britain and France to provoke war with Soviet Russia when already at war with Germany seems the product of a madhouse".[10]

In Spring, 1940, the Germans turned westwards. Denmark was swiftly occupied and Norway was invaded in April. The Low Countries were bombed and overrun in May and France was forced into surrender by the end of June. In the last days of France's humiliation Italy declared war on her and Britain. Of necessity British foreign policy turned to bolder courses; Britain was alone and the issues were much more clear-cut. Churchill had become Prime Minister in May, 1940, and at once he established a more determined style of leadership. Even when the French surrender seemed inevitable he had offered an Anglo-French Union to keep France and her empire in the struggle. Having failed in this objective, the British crippled the French fleet at Oran in order to prevent it falling into Axis hands. Meanwhile, major political figures were sent as ambassadors to remaining neutrals: Sir Stafford Cripps to Moscow, Sir Samuel Hoare to Madrid, Lord Halifax to Washington. To complete the new policy of "an attacking diplomacy"[11] Eden returned to the Foreign Office in December, 1940.

Churchill had begun his long and remarkable wartime correspondence with Roosevelt as early as September, 1939, when he returned to the Cabinet as First Lord of the Admiralty. With the disasters of 1940 and his own succession to the Premiership, Churchill's relationship with the American President was of the utmost importance. The United States became the "arsenal of democracy", particularly after Roosevelt had been safely elected in November, 1940, for his third term. Britain's first major gain was fifty American destroyers in return for allowing the United States to have bases in the British West Indies and Newfoundland. As for paying for munitions and supplies, Britain was hard pressed since the bills had to be met out of dollar reserves and hard securities. However, the device of Lend–Lease, suggested by the President in December, 1940, and passed by Congress in the following March, enabled Britain to obtain American goods without paying cash. Concerning wider matters, Churchill met Roosevelt in August, 1941, for the first of their wartime personal meetings, at Placentia Bay, Newfoundland. Although the Americans had already decided that, in the event of their being drawn into a war with Japan and Germany, they would make the European theatre their priority, Churchill failed on this occasion to draw Roosevelt into a discussion of future strategy. Instead, the two leaders issued a declaration of principles for the post-war world known as the Atlantic Charter.

By the time of the Newfoundland meeting the war had already been transformed by the Nazi invasion of Soviet territory in June, 1941. Relations between Britain and Russia had been through a particularly cool period and negotiations between them had virtually broken down early in 1941. Nevertheless, within hours of the German invasion Churchill announced an unequivocal British commitment to the Soviets. "We will never parley, we will never negotiate with Hitler or any of his gang—any man or state who marches with Hitler is our foe."[12] A formal agreement of mutual assistance followed. Shortly afterwards, in order to relieve the pressure on Russia, Stalin asked for a "second front"—a British invasion of northern France or the Balkans or of Norway. Such a project was entirely out of the question at this stage of the war but, even when the Allied position improved, Stalin's repeated demands were a major irritant in Anglo-American–Soviet relations.

The second decisive development of 1941 was the Japanese attack on Pearl Harbor, on 7th December. This, together with Hitler's declaration of war against the United States, brought the Americans into a truly global war. Churchill had his Grand Alliance and the defeat of the Axis powers was now eventually certain. The first task of the Allies was to co-ordinate their joint tactics and strategy, but before long, and as the tide of victory turned, discussions increasingly revolved around plans for the post-war world. In December, 1941, Stalin and Molotov, in a meeting with Eden, demanded a full military alliance and a blueprint for the shape of post-war European frontiers. The following March, in what later proved to be only the first step in Russian aggrandizement, Britain agreed informally to recognize the Russian frontiers of 1940, with the exception of claims against Poland. Two months later, in London, Molotov agreed to an alliance for twenty years.

For the rest of the war the Big Three (Churchill, Roosevelt and Stalin) dominated the decision-making. A series of conferences, either *à deux* or *à trois*, were held. Roosevelt met Stalin twice, Churchill and Stalin met five times and the two English-speaking leaders met ten times. The most important conferences were at Casablanca in January, 1943, Teheran at the end of 1943, and Yalta in February, 1945. Stalin met Roosevelt's and Churchill's successors, Truman and Attlee, at Potsdam in July, 1945.

Having failed to take Moscow in the winter of 1941–42 the Axis was decisively checked at the battle of El Alamein in October, 1942. This was followed by a successful Anglo-American landing in North-west Africa a month later leading to the surrender in May, 1943, at Tunis of all the German and Italian forces in North Africa. Meanwhile, with the German surrender at Stalingrad in February, 1943, the final overthrow of Germany and Italy was brought closer. On the diplomatic front, at Casablanca, Roosevelt and Churchill agreed on plans for the invasion of Sicily and to be content with nothing less than the unconditional surrender of the Axis. When the project for the invasion of Italy was revealed to Stalin he reacted angrily and repeated his familiar demands for a second front in France. There were rumours even of talks for a separate peace between the U.S.S.R. and Germany.

Having discussed the shape of the post-war world in Washington in March, 1943, including the possibility of a world security organization, Eden met his fellow foreign ministers, Cordell Hull and Molotov, in Moscow in November. On this occasion it was agreed that Russia would declare war on Japan as soon as Germany had surrendered. Further discussion took place on the question of post-war co-operation. At the Teheran Conference, which quickly followed, the three heads of government, meeting together for the first time, made firm plans for the invasion of France. They then turned their minds to plans for the formation of a world peace-keeping organization.

The success of the Anglo-American landings in Normandy, as well as continued Russian advances on the Eastern Front, gave added urgency to the fate of liberated Europe. It was clear to the British government that, once the war had finished, Stalin sought to dominate the Baltic, Eastern Europe and the Balkans. The chief concern was Poland, in whose defence Britain had entered the war in the first place. When Russia was invaded by Germany, the Polish government in exile in London somewhat reluctantly accepted an alliance with the Soviets. However, when the Poles demanded an investigation by the International Red Cross into the Katyn Massacre,[13] the Russians severed diplomatic relations. In spite of British efforts to reconcile these differences, it was clear well before the end of 1943 that Britain had little alternative but to accede to Russia's demands on Poland. The Polish frontier would, it seemed, have to be pushed westwards to the Curzon Line[14] of 1920, with the Poles being given compensation, at German expense, in East Prussia. In October, 1944, in Moscow, Churchill and Stalin "shared out the political control of Eastern Europe with odd statistical precision: Rumania 90 per cent Russian; Greece 90 per cent British; Hungary and Yugoslavia 50–50".[15] However, difficulties over Poland still remained. Although Churchill was prepared to accept the redrawing of frontiers in Russia's favour he wanted an assurance that there would be free elections in Poland after the war. Stalin, wishing to ensure that any new Polish government would be friendly to Moscow, refused to agree.

Meanwhile, on the other side of the world near Washington, differences arose over the future United Nations Organization. At this meeting, known as the Dumbarton Oaks Conference, representatives of Britain, the U.S.A., the U.S.S.R. and China discussed the institutions of the new organization but were not able to agree on the crucial question of the veto in the Security Council.

Churchill, Roosevelt and Stalin came together for their second joint meeting in February, 1945, this time at Yalta. Stalin was in an exceedingly powerful bargaining position. His armies had already occupied most of Eastern Europe and his entry into the war against Japan was considered vital. He gave a firm understanding that Russia would enter the Far Eastern war after victory in Europe had been gained. Furthermore he pleased Roosevelt by accepting the plan for U.N.O. after a compromise had been reached over the veto. For the rest, he got his own way in almost everything. The Curzon Line was accepted as was the Oder–Neisse Line[16] as Poland's western frontier. The "Declaration on Liberated Europe", by which the three leaders proclaimed their desire for democratic institutions in the lands formerly occupied by Germany, was turned later by Stalin into a hollow farce. The wartime allies were drifting apart and British influence and power were declining.

The German forces finally surrendered on 7th May, 1945. In the weeks following the victory in Europe Britain experienced its first General Election campaign in ten years. "The electors cheered Churchill and voted against him."[17] A Labour government under Attlee was elected. Midway through the last of the great wartime conferences, held at Potsdam, Churchill and Eden were replaced as leaders of the British delegation by the new Prime Minister, Clement Attlee, and his Foreign Secretary, Ernest Bevin. Agreement was reached over the post-war treatment of Germany, including the payment of reparations, and over the vexed question of the Oder–Neisse Line. On virtually every other subject there was deadlock. The Cold War was about to begin. Four days after the ending of the Potsdam Conference Hiroshima was devastated. The nuclear age had opened.

The chief concern of post-war British diplomacy was the handling of relations with her former allies, the two Super Powers. It was the U.S.S.R. which gave more obvious grounds for anxiety but, in the early stages at least, there were considerable difficulties to be overcome in dealing with the U.S.A.

At the Foreign Office Bevin gradually mapped out three basic aims. First, collective security, so inadequately upheld before the war, was pursued with realism and determination. Britain was ready to undertake substantial military commitments, including the retention of conscription, as well as the building of an alliance system. Second, and connected, the interests of the non-Communist West were to be defended wherever they might be threatened, in and outside Europe. Third, a new relationship with the countries of the British Commonwealth was to be developed, while giving independence to, and surrendering strategic control over, the British Indian Empire.

Bevin had hoped that "Left would be able to speak to Left"[18] and Sir Stafford Cripps believed that a Labour Government would "have the broad sympathy of the Russian people". It did not take Bevin long to realize his mistake, although possibly as late as January, 1947, he was not sure whether Germany or Russia contributed the greater threat to the future. For some time he played the part of a disappointed and wounded friend of the Russian leaders, at least until the United States was able to commit herself to an anti-Soviet stance.

It was a seriously weakened Britain which had to face these challenges. The war had exhausted her. Overseas debts amounted to £3,355 million: 28% of merchant shipping had been lost; exports were down to one-third of pre-war levels; houses and factories had been laid waste. "In all Britain had lost about one-quarter (£7,300 million) of its pre-war wealth, and was in the unenviable position of being the world's largest debtor nation."[19] At the same time, in spite of the contribution to the world-wide conflict of Dominion, colonial and Indian forces, the pre-war British Empire was on the verge of dissolution. Britain's weakness as a world power had been ruthlessly exposed, especially by the Japanese. Churchill regarded the fall of Singapore in 1942 as "the greatest disaster in our history". The Super Powers, the U.S.A. and U.S.S.R., dominated the scene by their military and economic superiority. By the late 1940s the gross national product of the U.S.A. was six times that of Britain and Russia's was two to three times greater .[20]

Britain had dropped into the second division. Yet Britain's dilemma was that her responsibilities could not be immediately sloughed off. She was a member of the Security Council of the United Nations; an occupying power in Germany; a defender of Western Europe against possible Soviet encroachment; and, until such time as the Empire was dismantled, still occupied a world role. Meanwhile, for entirely defensible reasons, the new Labour government made domestic reform its chief concern.

Although Britain and the U.S.A. together came to be the mainstay of the Western alliance there was earlier misunderstanding and friction. Immediately after the war there was a very real risk that the Americans would withdraw from Western Europe. Difficulties also arose over the future of the British Empire and Commonwealth, of which the United States was highly critical, especially of British rule in India. This was a result partly of traditional American anti-colonialism, but also of the opportunities envisaged by American business and commercial interests as a result of the weakening of economic relationships within the Commonwealth. In addition, America's "dollar diplomacy" made British economic recovery even more of an up-hill struggle. A major blow was the sudden curtailment of lend–lease aid in August, 1945. Keynes, the government's principal economic adviser, informed the Cabinet that the country faced "a financial Dunkirk". Britain could be sustained only by fresh American aid. It was given, but at a heavy price. A long-term loan of $3,750 million was granted, supplemented by $1,250 million from Canada, but on the condition that sterling should be freely convertible with other currencies by 1947. The British economy was too frail to sustain this and, only five weeks after the introduction of convertibility, the pressure on the pound was so great that exchange controls were introduced. By 1949 sterling had to be devalued from $4.03 to $2.8.

Anthony Eden on his return from a visit to Moscow and Cairo in 1943.
*The Mansell Collection*

Ernest Bevin, painted by T. C. Dugdale.  *National Portrait Gallery, London*

In Eastern Europe the Russians were determined to maintain absolute control of the countries from which, in the closing stages of the war, they had driven the German armies. Such control included the freedom to exact reparations. Soviet occupation had been accepted by the other powers at Yalta, although the Declaration on Liberated Europe might have been held to indicate that this was to be temporary. With the presence of several million soldiers of the Red Army in Eastern and Central Europe the Soviet position was, without another war, unshakable. As a result of this military presence, and by the destruction of non-Communist political parties by force, chicanery and rigged elections, Soviet control was virtually complete by the beginning of 1948. Only Greece, Albania and Tito's Yugoslavia managed to escape control from Moscow.

In the context of the Soviet domination of Eastern Europe, the negotiation of post-war peace treaties was of the utmost significance. It was not only with Germany and Italy that settlements had to be made but also with states that were considered to have been allied to or to have collaborated with Hitler and which were now, in whole or in part, occupied by the Red Army: Rumania, Hungary, Bulgaria, Finland and, in a somewhat different category, Austria. At Potsdam a Council of Foreign Ministers had been set up. In the autumn and winter of 1945–46 it held a series of meetings largely to prepare for the European peace treaties. Divisions quickly arose and were deepened by Soviet intransigence. Early demands were for a share in Italy's former colonies, for Trieste to be handed over to Yugoslavia; Soviet control of the Danube waterway and, more widely, a free hand in the Balkans. These demands were resisted by the Western ministers, Bevin and Byrnes. The Paris peace talks, which opened in July, 1946, provided further opportunities for disagreement. Once the negotiations had been completed and the treaties signed in February, 1947, Russian domination of Eastern Europe and the Balkans was allowed to take place. On the other hand, Italy was saved for the West.

The making of peace with Germany raised the most difficult problems of all, and was left until last. Germany was divided into four zones of occupation (American, British, French and Russian) as was Berlin, although the city actually lay within the Soviet zone. The division of Germany was intended to be temporary but, as a chief cause and then a symbol of the Cold War, became permanent. Since it had been agreed that each occupying power should satisfy its own claims for reparations, the

Russians set about stripping their zone of food, industrial equipment and labour. In addition, a proportion of plant and production from the American and British zones, by agreement, passed into Russian hands. But, when the food surpluses of the agricultural eastern zone were not made available to the western zones, General Clay, the American Commander, in May, 1946, placed an embargo on further reparations deliveries. The Americans and British then amalgamated their zones into one political and economic unit. The Russians reacted angrily.

Although the Americans were alarmed by Russian attitudes and policies towards Germany, it was still their intention to prepare a withdrawal from Europe. That this strategy changed in 1947 was due in no small measure to a series of initiatives by Ernest Bevin, who thus realized his principal aim of getting the United States to commit herself more fully to the defence of Europe. In January, 1947, Bevin negotiated a fifty-year alliance with France, signing the formal treaty at Dunkirk in the following March. This was expanded a year later by the Brussels Treaty which brought in Belgium, the Netherlands and Luxembourg and bound the five allies to take joint military action to resist armed aggression "in Europe".

By February, 1947, Britain's economic crisis had deepened. This reinforced the resolution of Attlee and Bevin to adopt a policy of major disengagement, with the intention of inducing the United States to shoulder additional burdens. In the space of a week it was announced that the Palestine issue was to be referred to the United Nations, that the date for Indian independence was to be advanced and that British assistance to Turkey and Greece, both vulnerable to Communist pressure or takeover, would be curtailed at the end of March, 1947. Truman's response was to pledge American support for "free peoples who are resisting attempted subjugation by armed minorities or by outside pressures". Greece and Turkey were given specific mention, and granted aid of $400 million, but the President's declaration, which became known as the Truman Doctrine, was to have general application and marked the adoption by the United States government of a clear-cut anti-Communist stance.

In June, 1947, the United States Secretary of State, George Marshall, in a speech at Harvard, proposed that "the United States should do whatever it is able to do to assist in the return of normal economic health in the world, without which there can be no political stability and no assured peace".[21] In short, he offered assistance for the reconstruction of Europe, provided that the European countries took the initiative in co-operating and in organizing the aid programme. Bevin, who had been given prior notice of Marshall's speech by Dean Acheson,[22] "seized the offer with both hands". A conference was called in Paris (Bevin and Bidault, the French Foreign Minister, were the leading lights) which led to the formation of the Organization for European Economic Co-operation. Between 1948 and 1952 the sum of $17,000 million was distributed. Molotov rejected the Marshall Plan as a device of capitalist propaganda; Russia and her satellites refused to participate.

During 1948 the wartime allies continued to entrench themselves in opposite camps. In February, having so far failed to subject Czechoslovakia to complete Soviet control, the Communists carried out a coup in Prague. As a result of armed demonstrations President Beneš was compelled to accept a Communist-dominated government and soon forced to resign. Jan Masaryk, the son of Tomas Masaryk, creator of Czechoslovakia, met a violent death. In the West there was shock and alarm at this latest Soviet advance. The Americans gave an enthusiastic welcome to the Brussels Treaty and the Western European Union which grew out of it. In Germany, the Western Powers determined to consolidate their position. By June a constitution had been drafted for a new Federal Republic of West Germany, and currency reform, essential to economic recovery, was announced for the three Western zones. The Soviet riposte was a complete blockade of West Berlin by road, rail and water. In the Kremlin it was anticipated that, unable to supply their zones in Berlin, the Western powers would be forced to abandon the city. Although it was not Russia's intention to start a war, the possibility certainly existed, and was feared, but as Bevin pointed out "none of us can accept surrender". The solution was an airlift which supplied 2¼ million West Berliners for 324 days before the Russians lifted the blockade. Not only were food, clothing, medical supplies and fuel flown in, but raw materials for industry. Britain's contribution was between a quarter and a third of the supplies and flights.

While the blockade continued the West went ahead with its plan to establish a Federal Republic, which was inaugurated in May, 1949. Even more important, and the surest sign of Anglo-American cohesion, the North Atlantic Treaty was signed in April, 1949. The members of the Brussels Treaty were joined by the U.S.A., Canada, Denmark, Iceland, Italy and Portugal. "The biggest step of collective security in the history of the world", was Bevin's triumphant verdict.[23] "This was not only the climax of his career as Foreign Secretary but—with a German settlement at last secured and the prospect of a Berlin blockade being lifted—the greatest ten days of his life."[24]

In the Middle East, by constrast, the question of Palestine caused major disagreements between Britain and the United States. Bevin was subjected to a bewildering variety of pressures and counter-pressures. Against the Balfour Declaration, which had promised a national home in Palestine for the Jews, the British wre bound to balance the claims of the Arabs. In the early days of Hitler's persecution Britain had allowed the number of Jewish immigrants to increase but had cut back again in the face of Arab opposition. This was at a time when Nazi atrocities were plumbing new depths. In 1937 the Peel Commission had recommended the partition of Palestine but this was opposed by Jew and Arab alike. On the eve of war fresh controls were placed on Jewish immigration. While Hitler and Mussolini presented a danger to the Middle East and the desert war raged, Britain could not afford to alienate the Arabs. Meanwhile, in 1942, Zionists in the United States produced the Biltmore Programme which called for the establishment of a Jewish state immediately after the war. This Programme was supported by Truman, well aware of the importance of five million Jewish-American voters, who called for the immediate admission into Palestine of 100,000 Jewish immigrants.

For his part, Bevin announced to the House of Commons that he would stake his political reputation on resolving the Palestine question. It was an unwise statement. Bevin was operating from a position of fundamental weakness. The pressures exerted by the United States have been noted. Successive Labour Party conferences pledged support for a Jewish National Home; in government, Labour could not afford to jeopardise Britain's Middle Eastern oil interests by antagonizing the Arabs. Public sympathy went out to the victims of Nazi persecution; the British administration could cope neither with the flood of would-be immigrants nor the Arab resistance it provoked. The War Office wanted to maintain a presence in Palestine as a back-up to the Canal Zone; the Treasury, in the midst of Britain's economic crisis, would have welcomed a British withdrawal. Against this background, an Anglo-American committee, appointed in November, 1945, condemned violence, recommended the admission of 100,000 Jewish immigrants and rejected the solution of partitioning Palestine. Bevin's approach was that the British government would "accept entry of 100,000 Jews as part of a comprehensive plan to solve the two problems of Palestine and the Jews in Europe, but will not tolerate having their hand forced by terroristic methods".[25] But violence continued to flourish and in July, 1946, the Irgun, a Jewish terrorist group, blew up the King David Hotel in Jerusalem with large loss of life. Until the private armies in Palestine were disbanded Bevin refused to give the go-ahead to the proposed scale of immigration.

Therefore, all attempts by the British and American governments to find a political and administrative solution failed. With increasing weariness and frustration politicians on both sides of the Atlantic rehearsed the alternatives of partition, a bi-national state, provincial autonomy. All attempts eventually foundered. Truman was under intense Zionist pressure. At one point in Cabinet he said of the Jews: "Jesus Christ couldn't please them when he was here on earth, so how could anyone expect that I would have any luck?"[26] At last, in February, 1947, unable to find a solution to the Arab-Jewish impasse, Bevin referred the problem of Palestine to the United Nations.

In September the British government announced its surrender of the mandate. The Palestine question has been set down as Bevin's greatest failure and he has, unjustly, been accused of anti-Semitism. A much more serious criticism concerns the nature of Britain's withdrawal. It might have been possible to have created a Jewish state under British influence, but the irreconcilable interests of Arab and Jew and the pressures of American public opinion prevented it.

In India, although faced with similar problems, albeit on a larger scale, of conflicting claims and communal violence the British government disentangled itself with relatively greater ease and with honour largely intact. The Labour government at least knew what it wanted to do—to grant independence to India. Greater urgency was added to this plan by American anti-colonialist pressures and Britain's own financial and military inability to maintain the commitment. The great problem was that of the clashing demands of the Congress Party for an undivided India and of the Muslim League for partition. Labour's solution was to announce an early date for the transfer of power, in order to bring Hindu and Muslim together by concentrating their minds. The first transfer date to be announced was June, 1948, but in May, 1947, with violence in India raging unabated, this was brought forward to August, 1947. A plan of partition was agreed upon and both India and Pakistan accepted Dominion status within the British Commonwealth. The Labour leaders believed, with good reason, and in spite of the violence and massacre that accompanied partition, that their achievement had indeed been remarkable. A great imperial power, victorious in a world war, had voluntarily surrendered vast dominions and had, at the same time, launched a multi-racial Commonwealth of Nations. Ceylon, like India and Pakistan, passed into independence and Commonwealth membership in 1947. Burma, in the following year, became a republic outside the Commonwealth.

Britain and her American ally were concerned to contain Communism in Asia as well as in Europe. Thus, in Malaya, Britain proclaimed a state of emergency as a result of the activities of Communist guerillas and deployed large forces and an imaginative strategy to prevent a Communist takeover. In a very positive way, and due in large measure to Bevin's imagination, a plan was developed to provide economic assistance to the underdeveloped countries of southern and south-eastern Asia. The plan was launched at a meeting of the Commonwealth foreign ministers in Colombo, Ceylon, in January, 1950. Out of these discussions came the Colombo Plan, an eastern equivalent of the Marshall Plan.

That the advance of Communism was indeed a world phenomenon was demonstrated to the West by the triumph of Mao Tse-tung in China in 1949 and, especially dramatically, by events in Korea. In June, 1950, the Russian-sponsored state of North Korea mounted a surprise attack on the American-nurtured South. Under the aegis of the United Nations, the United States made an immediate response and committed very substantial forces to the defence of the South Koreans. Britain followed suit but her response was, significantly, small.

By the time of the outbreak of the Korean War Attlee's administration was past its best and reduced to a small overall majority in the Commons. Bevin was a very sick man. In the post-war years the Labour government faced a formidable accumulation of problems: grave economic difficulties; an apparent early indifference on the part of the United States; a rapid breakdown of relations with the wartime ally Russia; virtually insoluble issues in Palestine; mounting Communist pressure across the world; a devasted and weakened Europe; India sliding into internecine strife. Nevertheless, by the time Labour surrendered office in October, 1951, many of these problems had been tackled successfully or, at least, ameliorated. In the perspective of the whole period since the creation of the Foreign Secretaryship, Britain was not often weaker than she was in those post-war years. Yet rarely has there been a more successful period in the history of British foreign policy.

## The Foreign Secretaries

Anthony Eden held the Foreign Secretaryship in three contrasting periods. During his first spell, under Baldwin and Chamberlain, although Britain moved towards the climax of her appeasement policies, Eden gained the reputation of being determinedly opposed to the dictators. His resignation in 1938 appeared to hinge on this very issue. He returned in 1940 as Churchill's Foreign Secretary in the most perilous war which the country had ever faced. After the war, in Churchill's peace-time ministry, he conducted the foreign policy of a visibly declining power. Meanwhile, in domestic politics, he waited with growing impatience to inherit Churchill's mantle.

Eden was born in 1897, the third son of Sir William Eden, baronet. The Edens had been a prominent family in County Durham for centuries and the baronetcy had been granted by Charles II. Antony's mother was related to Lord Grey of the Reform Bill and, more distantly, to Sir Edward Grey.

When the Great War broke out Eden was at Eton. He volunteered in 1915 and served for most of the war on the Western Front, reaching the rank of brigade major, the youngest in the army. Two of his brothers lost their lives in action, the youngest aged sixteen, at Jutland. Eden, like every other member of his generation, was influenced and marked by the war. "The Cabinets which governed Britain in the 1930s were composed of men who believed that almost no price was too high to pay to avoid another war. The exceptions, curiously enough, were those who had first-hand experience of war. Anthony Eden and Alfred Duff Cooper: who knew that, vile as the experience was, it was not utterly intolerable, and there might be others yet worse."[27]

The war over, Eden, rather than follow a professional military career, went up to Christ Church, Oxford. He read Oriental Languages, specializing in Turkish and Persian, and took a First. His entry into politics was not long delayed. In 1923 he was returned as a Conservative for

Warwick and Leamington, a constituency he represented until his retirement in 1957. Almost all of Eden's time in office was, in some capacity, connected with foreign affairs. His first opportunity came in 1926 when he was made Parliamentary Private Secretary to Austen Chamberlain, then Foreign Secretary, whom Eden later proclaimed his mentor.

With the formation of the National Government in August, 1931, Eden, aged thirty-four, gained his first ministerial appointment—Parliamentary Under-Secretary at the Foreign Office. His first chief, for three brief months, was Reading and his second was Simon. Further promotion followed in January, 1934; while continuing with the same work he was made Lord Privy Seal, although without a seat in the Cabinet. In these years he came to be seen as a strong supporter of the League of Nations. He also met the dictators. On meeting Hitler, in February, 1934, he found the Führer "in conversation quiet, almost shy with a pleasant smile. Without doubt the man has charm".[28] Later he wrote—"Hitler impressed me during these discussions as much more than a demagogue. He knew what he was speaking about and, as the long interviews proceeded, showed himself completely master of his subject".[29] Mussolini was "lively, friendly, vigorous and entertaining" and the discussion was "crisp and easy".[30] In Moscow, in March, 1935, Eden was conscious that it was "the first occasion when Stalin received a political representative from the West" and although Eden "knew the man to be without mercy, I respected the quality of his mind and even felt a sympathy which I have never been able entirely to analyse".[31]

Eden's final step before the Foreign Office itself was in June, 1935, when Baldwin offered him a specially created post, Minister for League of Nations Affairs, with a seat in the Cabinet. Eden expressed strong reservations to the Prime Minister, in particular that two ministers in Cabinet each with responsibility for foreign affairs would prove unworkable. Nevertheless, he accepted.[32]

Eden did not have long to wait for the Foreign Secretaryship: the ill-fated Hoare resigned in December, 1935. In the midst of this political crisis Eden was travelling home by train from Geneva. He was in the company of Stanley Bruce, the leader of the Australian delegation at Geneva. Their conversation turned to the question of Hoare's successor. They agreed that "this was the moment for a respected statesman at the Foreign Office" and "considered that Austen Chamberlain would be the best choice". On arrival in Calais, Eden received a message that he was to report to Downing Street with all possible speed. Arrived there, Eden was asked by Baldwin to give his views on candidates for the Foreign Secretaryship. Eden put forward Austen Chamberlain and then Halifax. Both were rejected. At last the Prime Minister turned to Eden and said, "It looks as if it will have to be you". Just before Christmas Eden travelled to Sandringham to receive the seals from George V. The King advised Eden of his own interest in foreign affairs and in the appointment of ambassadors. He offered help when required as well as asking to be kept fully informed. Finally he added: "I said to your predecessor: 'You know what they are all saying, no more coals to Newcastle, no more Hoares to Paris.' The fellow didn't even laugh."[33]

Eden, aged thirty-eight, was the youngest Foreign Secretary since Granville. Already he enjoyed considerable prestige. He was the Golden Boy of British politics—elegantly dressed, handsome and charming. His style was a considerable asset to the government in domestic as well as foreign politics. He had immersed himself in foreign affairs at an important level for some ten years. For Gilbert Winant, the wartime United States ambassador in London, he was "one of the best trained diplomats I have ever met".[34] However, there were some who saw him as arrogant and apt to take offence. In November, 1937, Hankey wrote that "at bottom he is vain and doesn't like anyone else to get any credit in Foreign Affairs".[35] Neville Chamberlain believed that he would "always agree in theory but disagree in practice".[36]

Eden felt that he had succeeded to a "wretchedly disordered heritage". Most certainly, the Abyssinian affair had revealed the pitiable weaknesses of the League; Britain and France were anxious to cause the least possible offence to Mussolini while applying sanctions against him. In short, they were on the verge of a considerable reverse. While attempting to steer a steady course, Eden sat in a Cabinet all of whose members were his seniors. Two of his colleagues, Simon and MacDonald, were former Foreign Secretaries. In June, 1936, with Hoare's return to the Cabinet as First Lord of the Admiralty, a third was added. As for the Prime Minister, Eden believed that Baldwin's support "would be fitful and lethargic".[37] In point of fact, Eden seems to have had his way on most matters as well as the backing of his chief when required.

The position of Halifax in the Cabinet, as a minister without portfolio but with a special brief in foreign affairs, might have caused trouble. However, Eden did not seem to have felt threatened. "We have long been friends and I was grateful for an arrangement which never caused me any anxiety, even when we did not agree about the decisions to be taken, as happened later."[38] One issue of disagreement was over Halifax's visit to Berchtesgaden to see Hitler, in November, 1937. Halifax believed that Eden had no objections. Indeed the two men had, with Churchill, dined together at the Foreign Office before Halifax's departure. "The facts thus differed", wrote Halifax, "from the story that tends to become established of the decision being made by a Prime Minister, bent on appeasement, against the wishes and advice of a robust Foreign Secretary."[39] The Eden memoirs show the Foreign Secretary to have had doubts about the wisdom of the visit and to have been concerned that Halifax gave insufficiently strong warnings to Hitler about possible ambitions against Austria and Czechoslovakia.[40] Halifax's impression of Hitler is revealing. "He struck me as being very sincere and believing everything he said."[41] For Eden, one effect of the visit "was to weaken my own position and I was mistaken in ever tolerating it".[42] However, there was comparatively little friction between Eden and Halifax and when Eden announced his resignation, in February, 1938, Halifax made strenuous and sincere attempts to reconcile the Foreign Secretary to the Prime Minister.

Until 1938 Eden seems to have been more strongly opposed to Italy than to Germany. This was because he thought that Hitler might to some extent be relied upon but that Mussolini certainly would not. In 1936 Eden saw the Duce as "a tough and clever opportunist who would rate concessions as weakness and who cared nothing for the principles of the League or the Stresa Front".[43] A year later he wrote: "Mussolini has the mentality of a gangster"[44]—and that "Italy's attitude towards us was based on the dream of a revival of the Roman Empire at the Zenith of its power and glory". For Eden Mussolini represented anti-Christ. *In extremis* he preferred Stalin to Mussolini and, until Munich, Hitler too.[46] For years the Foreign Office had favoured an understanding with Germany, and Eden thought this worth pursuing as a basis for a general settlement. In a sense, then, Eden favoured appeasement,[47] but parted company with other appeasers as a result of his strong support for the need to rearm. Nevertheless he was prepared to countenance changes, by negotiation, in the Versailles and Locarno settlements. For example, in an interview with the German ambassador he condemned the remilitarization of the Rhineland as a *"unilateral* repudiation of a treaty freely negotiated and freely signed". On this issue too, he urged the French to show restraint. This policy had the full support of the Cabinet which hoped to move towards, in Eden's words, "as far-reaching and enduring a settlement as possible whilst Herr Hitler is still in the mood to do so".[48] While using strong words in public, Eden persuaded the French that negotiation over the Rhineland was essential and they backed down from military action.

With regard to the Spanish Civil War, Eden made non-intervention the lynch-pin of his policy. He recognized that this could never fully succeed, however, and even the direct arrangement with Italy, known as the Gentlemen's Agreement and signed in January, 1937, was of limited scope. Nevertheless, Italian intervention was kept within bounds and, as an additional safeguard for British interests in the Mediterranean, Eden improved relations with Egypt and Turkey. This was to be of the utmost importance in the Second World War.

By the time Baldwin retired, Eden had very little to show for his diplomacy. Even so Taylor's judgement may be too harsh: "He had provided the idealistic smoke-screen with which to save Baldwin after the outcry against the Hoare–Laval plan. He had acquiesced in the Italian conquest of Abyssinia and had deterred the French, so far as they needed it, from action in the Rhineland. He sponsored the pretences of the Spanish non-intervention committee. He relied on moral disapproval: strong words and no acts".[29]

The replacement in May, 1937, of Baldwin by Chamberlain was welcomed by Eden. He looked forward to a Prime Minister who "would give his Foreign Secretary energetic backing".[50] Although there were policy differences—Chamberlain was prepared to go further than Eden in conciliating the dictators—they were largely a matter of emphasis. Personal relationships were cordial. Eden's memoirs imply that Chamberlain lacked knowledge of foreign affairs. But, although the Foreign Secretary surpassed the Prime Minister in the more specialized areas of foreign policy, Chamberlain, as a Cabinet minister of long standing, far outstripped Eden in his grasp of the interrelationship between foreign, military, and economic policies.

Prime Minister and Foreign Secretary were in agreement about the removal of Vansittart from the Foreign Office. Eden had discussed this with Chamberlain as early as May, 1937, even before Chamberlain became Prime Minister, and they made the final decision in the following autumn. Vansittart's new appointment was announced in January, 1938. The Foreign Secretary believed he was strengthening the office by promoting Sir Alexander Cadogan to Permanent Under-Secretary. Chamberlain had his own reasons for easing Vansittart out.

Within weeks of his appointment as Chief Diplomatic Adviser, Vansittart reported to Eden that he had heard it from a Cabinet minister not only that he himself had been "kicked upstairs" but that foreign affairs were to be conducted in future by the Prime Minister with a small committee. When Eden repeated this to Chamberlain the Prime Minister showed astonishment but Eden was "not reassured".[51]

The chief policy issue dividing Eden and Chamberlain arose over Italy. Although the Foreign Secretary was prepared to recognize the position Italy had gained in Abyssinia, he was far more suspicious of Italy's wider intentions than was Chamberlain. The way in which relations with Italy were handled led to a widening rift and the Foreign Secretary's resignation. In July, 1937, in order to improve relations with Mussolini, Chamberlain wrote him a personal message. This was done, with every appearance of spontaneity, in the presence of Grandi, the Italian ambassador. "I did not show my letter to the Foreign Secretary," wrote Chamberlain later, "for I had the feeling that he would object to it."[52]

By November, 1937, Eden was having second thoughts about the merits of recognizing the Italian position in Abyssinia, and the question of Halifax's visit to Berchtesgaden served to do further damage to the relationship between himself and Chamberlain. Nevertheless, in early January, 1938, and only six weeks before his resignation, Eden was able to write to Chamberlain: "I do hope that you will never for an instant feel that any interest you take in foreign affairs, however close, could ever be resented by me. I know, of course, that there will always be some who will seek to pretend that the Foreign Secretary has had his nose put out of joint, but this is of no account beside the very real gain of close collaboration between Foreign Secretary and Prime Minister which, I am sure, is the only way that foreign affairs can be run in our country".[53]

However, within a few days of this letter, and while Eden was out of the country, Chamberlain was turning down a proposal from Roosevelt for an initiative to improve international relations. The Prime Minister consulted

Wilson and Cadogan, but not the Foreign Secretary, even though he returned some days before Roosevelt's deadline for a reply.

By the end of January, Eden's stated position on Italy was that he could only agree to a *de jure* recognition of Italy's conquest of Abyssinia as part of a wider settlement which would include Spain, the Red Sea and the Italian garrison in Libya. The final break with Chamberlain came over the scope of any deal to be negotiated with Italy and, perhaps more important, the manner in which relations were conducted.

According to Chamberlain,[54] he and Eden agreed to meet Grandi together on 17th February, 1938, for important discussions. Eden then asked Chamberlain whether he could meet Grandi alone and when this was refused begged the Prime Minister, when they met Grandi, not to commit Britain to talks. Chamberlain was determined "to stand firm, even though it meant losing my Foreign Secretary".[55]

The behaviour of Prime Minister and Foreign Secretary at the meeting led Grandi to write in his despatch that they were like "two enemies confronting each other, like two cocks in true fighting posture".[56] After the meeting, Chamberlain was in favour of immediate conversations with Italy. Eden was against. In Cabinet, Eden found himself in a minority and although a group of ministers, including Halifax, sought to persuade him to stay, he resigned on 20th February. Eden objected not only to the objectives of British foreign policy but to Chamberlain's personal dealing with Grandi and his unofficial contact with Mussolini through his sister-in-law Lady Chamberlain, who read the Prime Minister's letters to the Duce. Apart from the issue of whether British foreign policy should be run from Downing Street or the Foreign Office, there were other factors which may have contributed to Eden's resignation. Ambition almost certainly played its part; he no longer wished to associate himself with a policy which might be unpopular. Should the policy fail and war follow he might then return to office untarnished. In addition, Eden had a very special view of his role: "I thought that Foreign Secretaries ought to be as far as possible above the battle; I always had it in mind that one day I might have to go down to the House of Commons and tell the nation that it was at war". Quite differently, Simon and Malcolm MacDonald, who were both in Eden's company at the time of his resignation, thought him physically and mentally ill.

Eden returned to the back benches. When he delivered up his seals to

George VI, according to Eden, the King remarked that he had sympathy with Eden's point of view and thought it would not be long before he saw him again. He had to wait a year and a half. On the day he declared war on Germany, Chamberlain brought into his Cabinet the two men most closely associated with resistance to the Axis dictators, Churchill to the Admiralty and Eden as Dominions Secretary. With the formation of Churchill's own ministry in May, 1940, Eden was given the War Office, although without a seat in the War Cabinet.

Eden's second term at the Foreign Office began in December, 1940. At the same time Churchill brought him into the War Cabinet. He was, in Churchill's words, "like a man going home".[58] Eden said that his responsibility was "greater as Churchill's colleague at the Foreign Office, than as his subordinate with the army. In wartime diplomacy is strategy's twin."[59] The long-accepted view of the relationship between Eden and Churchill is that it was a powerful partnership based on intimate consultation and, on a personal level, free of serious friction. The Foreign Secretary provided the professional diplomacy which balanced the Prime Minister's bold approach.[60] Contemporary public opinion saw the two men in an almost father and son relationship, with Eden the chosen political heir. On Eden's resignation in 1938 Churchill confessed that his heart sank and the dark waters of despair overwhelmed him.[61] On Eden's reappointment Churchill recalled that they had dwelt in close agreement for the past four years; they had been united in thought and sentiment at the outbreak of war; they thought alike even without consultation.[62] Eden's memoirs tell a similar story. During the wartime partnership Churchill never sent an international message without Eden's approval. "Complete confidence and candour between Prime Minister and Foreign Secretary are indispensable conditions for the conduct of a successful foreign policy under our parliamentary system."[63]

In reality their personal and political relationships were somewhat different. Before the war they were equals and rivals. In 1935 Churchill had written that he had no confidence in Eden's appointment as Foreign Secretary. Unlike Eden's, Churchill's chief anxiety had always been Hitler rather than Mussolini. In 1938, Eden did not consult Churchill over his resignation.

During the war they disagreed over a wide range of issues including recognition of the Free French, India, the Balkans and the future of

Germany. Eden was not above manoeuvring against his chief in Cabinet and outside. Churchill responded with counter-manoeuvres. Both men recognized that given a particular set of circumstances, illness on the part of Churchill or a run of defeats in the war, Eden would make a bid for the Premiership itself. The major policy difference was probably over Soviet Russia. Until 1944 at least the Foreign Secretary saw the Russians as allies of liberal democracy. Churchill was more doubtful of Russian intentions. It was Eden who persuaded the Polish government-in-exile to re-establish diplomatic relations with the Soviets. In order to please Stalin he was able to get the War Cabinet to agree to a declaration of war on Finland. After meeting Stalin in December, 1941, Eden tried to persuade Churchill to recognize the Russian frontiers of June, 1941. Churchill refused on the grounds that they had been obtained "by acts of aggression in shameful collusion with Hitler". (Nevertheless, these were the frontiers eventually granted.) By the early part of 1944, when Russian ambitions were clearer, Eden had changed his view. So had Churchill. In October, 1944, when Eden and Churchill were in Moscow together, the Foreign Secretary was in favour of resisting Stalin, especially over Poland. Churchill remarked that Eden "must be told that there was only one course open to us—to make friends with Stalin".[64]

During the wartime administration there were real tensions between the two men. Churchill's eccentric habits of work and particularly his late hours, which others were expected to keep, exhausted Eden and drove him almost to distraction. There were times when a serious break seemed inevitable. Underneath, however, there was a mutual regard and affection. In international affairs Eden was the only Cabinet colleague to have significant influence on the Prime Minister. Nevertheless, throughout the war, Churchill carried on a private correspondence with Roosevelt. At Casablanca Prime Minister and President met *à deux*, excluding their respective foreign ministers. There were also times when Churchill's correspondence with Stalin was direct and by-passed the Foreign Office.

On more than one occasion, Eden's burden of work led him to consider giving up the Foreign Office. In November, 1942, he added the Leadership of the House to the Foreign Secretaryship. For reasons of domestic politics this was an important step and it fortified his position as Churchill's likely successor. But the necessity of spending large amounts of time in the Commons weakened his grip on foreign policy. As a direct and intended consequence, Churchill took a more independent role for himself in shaping diplomacy and strategy, particularly with Britain's major allies.

In the early months of 1943 Eden was seriously considering becoming Viceroy of India. By June he had finally decided against. To have accepted would certainly have weakened his chances of the Premiership. But less than a year later, in March, 1944, "the physical effort of combining the Foreign Office with the leadership of the House of Commons, to say nothing of the Defence Committee and the War Cabinet, was beginning to tell".[65] After discussions with Churchill he decided to carry on but, on Churchill's insistence, took three weeks' rest. Again political ambitions played their part. There were doubts about Churchill's health and Eden did not want to put himself out of the running should a vacancy occur.

Whenever he could, Eden escaped to the country for refreshment but in London lived on the job. He had a flat on the top floor of the Foreign Office which was twice blasted by bombs. Winant knew no one who "carried a heavier load in the war".[66] In spite of the pressures upon him he was still able to undertake important reforms, including the amalgamation of the Consular Service with the Foreign Office and Diplomatic Service.[67]

Eden may be considered the first of the modern Foreign Secretaries in terms of the scale, frequency and importance of his diplomatic missions abroad. Before his time, and especially in the nineteenth century, Foreign Secretaries tended to stay at home, not meeting their counterparts face to face. To a large extent Eden's mobility was made possible by air travel, although for his visit to Moscow in 1941 he travelled to Murmansk by destroyer and cruiser. Among his more important journeys the following itinerary may be noted. As an indication of the importance of the Balkans, the Middle East and North Africa, Eden made an extensive tour of the area in the early months of 1941 with particularly weighty discussions in Cairo, Athens and Ankara. In December, 1941, he met Stalin and Molotov in Moscow. His visit to the United States and Canada in the spring of 1943 was a great personal success, although there were disagreements with Roosevelt. Later the same year, in August, he and Churchill met Roosevelt, Harry Hopkins, the President's adviser, and Cordell Hull, the American Secretary of State, in Quebec. Among other matters, plans for the Normandy landings were discussed. The last months of 1943 were busy: Moscow, via Cairo and Teheran, for the Foreign Ministers' Conference in October; Cairo with Churchill, Roosevelt, the United States Chiefs of Staff and Chiang Kai-shek in November; Teheran for the first summit of the Big Three. In September, 1944, he was again in Quebec with Churchill and Roosevelt. It was there that Morgenthau, the United States Secretary of the Treasury, presented his Plan for the pastoralization of Germany after the war. A few weeks later Eden accompanied Churchill to Moscow where the "percentage proposals" were discussed with Stalin. He was present at Yalta in February, 1945, but was very much in Churchill's shadow while the Prime Minister himself represented the weakest of the three major allies.

Potsdam, in July, 1945, was Eden's last conference as wartime Foreign Secretary. There he laboured under great personal and private anxieties. He was drained and ill and was still recovering from a duodenal ulcer. There was the additional burden of the news that his eldest son, an R.A.F. officer, had been reported missing in Burma. At home a General Election was taking place.

On hearing the news that the Conservatives had been voted out of office, Eden's mind turned to his successor. There was considerable uncertainty about who was to hold the major offices in the new Labour Government. Eden recorded: "I resolved to do anything I could to slant events, for I was sure that Bevin was the man for the job".[68]

Considering Eden's relationship with Chamberlain, Halifax's acceptance of the Foreign Secretaryship in February, 1938, implied a more compliant role for him than for his predecessor. Halifax liked and admired Chamberlain and was unswervingly loyal. Given the Prime Minister's lively interest in foreign affairs, and his suspicion of the Foreign Office, the Foreign Secretaryship under Halifax underwent a partial eclipse. It is noteworthy that Halifax did not accompany Chamberlain to Berchtesgaden, Bad Godesberg or Munich, nor did he appear to have objected to being excluded. Although assiduous and devoted to the public service, the new incumbent accepted the seals without enthusiasm. He was "not fitted by nature to preside over the Foreign Office at such a moment of history".[69]

Edward Frederick Lindley Wood, son of the second Viscount Halifax, was born in 1881. On appointment to the Viceroyalty of India in 1925 he was created Lord Irwin, he succeeded to his father's title in 1934 and was granted an earldom ten years later. Educated at Eton and Christ Church, he took a first in history and was elected a Fellow of All Souls before entering the Commons in 1910 as M.P. for Ripon. In spite of his physical handicap, an atrophied left arm with no hand, he served in the Great War on the Western Front as a yeomanry officer in the Yorkshire Dragoons. He was recalled in January, 1917, to be assistant secretary at the Ministry of National Service. After the war he was Churchill's Under-Secretary at the Colonial Office and in 1923 entered Bonar Law's Cabinet as President of the Board of Education.

As Viceroy of India for more than five years, he sought to prepare the way for the granting of dominion status to India and to quieten its racial disharmony. He negotiated with Gandhi, showed great administrative skill, sympathy and vision but, in the end, failed to achieve his objectives.

Having returned home he was offered, in autumn, 1931, the Foreign Secretaryship in MacDonald's National Government. He refused, partly for family reasons and partly because of tensions with the right of the Conservative Party. Within a year, however, he returned to the Board of Education and the Cabinet. When Baldwin became Prime Minister, in 1935, Halifax transferred to the War Office, but within five months he was made Lord Privy Seal. In this office and as Lord President of the Council, under Chamberlain, Halifax had no departmental responsibilities. His attention was directed more and more towards foreign affairs: he spoke for the Government in the Lords on this subject; accompanied Eden to Paris for discussions on Hitler's remilitarization of the Rhineland; and, in controversial circumstances, met Hitler at Berchtesgaden.

When Halifax took Eden's place he brought with him wide and relevant experience. Like Aberdeen before him, his life and outlook were guided by a strong Christian faith. He was a devout Anglo-Catholic and the solace he found in prayer and contemplation may have insulated him from the realities of a Europe dominated by the dictators. On the other hand his character has been described as one of "baffling opaqueness".[70] He chose his words with inordinate care, his speeches were ambiguous. It may be that beneath his other-wordly exterior there was concealed a shrewd and pragmatic politician. To William Strang, at that time Head of the Central Department of the Foreign Office, he was "inscrutable".

His chief physical attribute was his remarkable height. One of his private secretaries, Valentine Lawford, records that "when Halifax moved, he could be graceful and grave and shy simultaneously, like a tall water-bird wading in the shallows".[71] His biographer noted the "recognizable marks of the Squire and the Colonel of Yeomanry in the forward tilt of his bowler hat and the way he carried his umbrella, less frequently in the crook of his elbow than horizontally in the hand, as it might have been a riding-crop or a woodman's tool."[72] He was so well regarded by George VI that he was given a key to the gardens of Buckingham Palace.[73] This provided him with a short cut from his home to the Foreign Office.

In spite of his wide experience Halifax was not a specialist in foreign affairs like Eden. Unlike all the great Foreign Secretaries, he was not absorbed and fascinated by foreign policy. The Foreign Secretaryship was a duty and a rather disagreeable one. Like Chamberlain he seems to have believed that the Nazis were reasonable men who could be persuaded, by patient negotiation, to moderate their demands. In 1936, in a speech at Bristol, he maintained: "We want no encirclement of Germany. We want to build a partnership in European society in which Germany can play the part of good Europeans for European welfare".[74] Although his eyes were opened by his staff at the Foreign Office he was unable to grasp the warnings of Sir Horace Rumbold, a former Ambassador to Berlin, about the true nature of Nazi Germany. As late as 5th August, 1938, Halifax informed Sir Nevile Henderson, the British Ambassador in Berlin, that Germany did not want a general war, especially over Czechoslovakia, and that German policy might well be determined by bluff or fear. As for Mussolini, whom he met in Rome in January, 1939, he "spoke quite quietly, very reasonably, and so far as I could judge, with sincerity". Nevertheless, by the time of Munich he was anxious and worried, unable to sleep with the burdens of office pressing cruelly upon him.

In the Foreign Office itself Halifax made a good start. Cadogan wanted to sack the whole of the cipher department. Not only was it poorly and inefficiently staffed but one of its members was later proved to be a traitor. Halifax, in support of Cadogan, took it upon himself to interview the whole department and explain the reasons for dismissal and replacement by a more professional group. In other ways, however, he damaged the Foreign Office by allowing Chamberlain a free hand in the use of personal advisers, notably Wilson. Such advisers encroached on the role of Foreign Office trained staff. Strang believed that this would not have been countenanced by Grey or Eden.

Halifax himself was influenced to a considerable extent by his officials. For example, Cadogan was outraged by the Godesberg terms and by

Halifax's acceptance of them in Cabinet. Believing that Chamberlain had "hypnotised" Halifax, Cadogan, in his own words, "gave him a bit of my mind". Next day the Foreign Secretary informed the Prime Minister that he had changed his view and that Hitler's terms should be rejected.

In the immediate aftermath of Munich, Halifax missed what might have been a crucial political initiative. He suggested to Chamberlain that he should reconstruct his Government, along truly national lines and committed to rearmament, "bringing in Labour if they would join, and Churchill and Eden. He seemed surprised, but said he would think it over. Nothing however happened, and I have often wondered whether or how the course of history might have changed if he had acted in the sense I suggested".[77] Halifax might have forced such a decision on the Prime Minister had he threatened his own resignation. Loyalty to Chamberlain prevailed once again, however.

The occupation of Prague marked a turning-point for Halifax as well as for British foreign policy. His attitude stiffened markedly and it was his influence that led Chamberlain to come out as strongly as he did in his Birmingham speech. But, although Halifax supported the guarantee to Poland, he failed to seize the opportunity of winning the co-operation of Russia. Such an understanding was fraught with difficulties, but Halifax's approach was tardy and when he was invited to Moscow by Molotov in May, 1939, he declined. Strang was sent instead.

Halifax survived Chamberlain's resignation and, since he was not as closely associated with Munich as the Prime Minister, escaped most of the blame for the failures of appeasement. Indeed, he was a serious candidate for the Prime Ministership itself. George VI would have preferred him to Churchill. Halifax himself was thankful that constitutional and political imperatives prevented him from being chosen. He remained Foreign Secretary and a member of the War Cabinet until in December, 1940, he was persuaded by Churchill to go as Ambassador to Washington. This post was not necessarily a demotion; Anglo-American relations were reaching a crucial stage and the choice of Ambassador was a vital one. Even so, although he eventually accepted, Halifax was characteristically reluctant and tried to persuade Eden to take it in his stead.

It has been said of Halifax that he sometimes doubted his fitness for a particular task but that he did not question his right to be called to high office.

Ernest Bevin became Foreign Secretary in July, 1945. His exceptional background, his special abilities, the magnitude of the problems facing him and his success in handling them, mark him out as one of the most remarkable of British Foreign Secretaries. An ex-labourer with no formal education after the age of eleven, his grasp of public affairs had been gathered "from the 'edgerows of experience". He was neither the first working-class man nor the first Labour politician to hold the office. Ramsay MacDonald and Arthur Henderson preceded him, but in almost every way he surpassed them. Like Churchill he was a "big" man, a larger-than-life figure.

In the first Labour government ever to hold an overall majority, Bevin had wanted to be Chancellor of the Exchequer. The Foreign Office had expected Hugh Dalton to be Eden's successor. When Bevin and Dalton arrived at Buckingham Palace to receive their seals, Bevin said, "I wanted your job". "And I wanted yours", replied Dalton.[78] On that same afternoon, 28th July, 1945, Bevin and Attlee were on a plane to Potsdam. In the morning the new Foreign Secretary had had audience with the King–Emperor George VI; by the evening he was in the presence of Joseph Stalin.

Not surprisingly, the Foreign Office regarded Bevin's appointment with some trepidation, "fearing that it had been given into the hands of a clumsy Visigoth incapable of comprehending the niceties and delicacies of diplomacy", but "he soon won from its members a wholehearted admiration and loyalty".[79] One of his greatest advantages was that his experience was so different from that of the permanent staff of the Foreign Office. His skills as a patient and shrewd negotiator had been learned as a trade unionist and wartime Minister of Labour. In this ministry, and as a member of the War Cabinet, he had been at the very centre of things but it was a different centre of the world from that seen by the Foreign Office. He was no stranger to foreign affairs, however. Before the war he had exercised a decisive influence over the shaping of Labour's foreign policy, especially by his efforts in developing relations with European trade unionists. He had also travelled extensively: to Australia, India, Africa, the United States and, in particular, Europe. Orme Sargent,[80] who had served under practically every twentieth-century Foreign Secretary before becoming Permanent Under-Secretary in 1946, believed that Bevin had a more extensive range of contacts in the United States and Europe than any foreign minister since Salisbury.[81] The contacts were made largely through the trade union movement. In Potsdam he took Pierson Dixon and Nicholas Henderson (at that time members of his Private Office) into his confidence about negotiating with foreigners. "You see I've had a good deal of experience with foreigners: before the last war I had to do a good deal of negotiation with ships' captains of all nationalities. These people, Stalin and Truman, are just the same as all Russians and Americans; and dealing with them over foreign affairs is just the same as trying to come to a settlement about unloading a ship. Oh yes, I can handle them".[82] His first impact on foreign statesmen was, however, rather alarming. At Potsdam the American Secretary of State, James Byrnes, found him "so aggressive that both the President and I wondered how we would get along with this new Foreign Secretary". Byrnes quickly changed his view and came to "respect highly his fine mind, his forthrightness, his candour and his scrupulous regard for a promise".[83]

Bevin's obvious ability and self-confidence, as well as his loyalty to and consideration for his officials, soon won over the Foreign Office itself. They were also relieved by his bi-partisan approach—he remained in close contact with Eden—and the continuity with the policies of the wartime coalition. "Hasn't Anthony Eden grown fat?" remarked R. A. Butler.[84]

Bevin was born in 1881 in Winsford, Somerset, on the edge of Exmoor. He was the seventh child of Diana, the village midwife, and was illegitimate. His mother died when he was aged eight, he never knew his father and he experienced real poverty. Having left school at eleven he was employed as a farm-boy until, two years later, he went to Bristol where he worked in a great variety of jobs, many of them menial. For the rest of his life, it seems, he cleaned his own footwear. In 1944, during the D-Day preparations, Churchill was astonished that a member of the War Cabinet should be doing this, and offered to find a batman. "I wouldn't like you to do that, Prime Minister," protested Bevin, "I get such splendid ideas when I'm cleaning my boots." As Foreign Secretary, at a Foreign Ministers' Conference, he confided in Molotov that the idea for breaking a particular deadlock had occurred to him whilst cleaning his boots that morning.[85]

In 1901 Bevin became a van-driver delivering mineral water in and around Bristol. It was while in this job that he became involved in labour and trade union affairs. This led to one of the great turning-points in his life. In 1910, during a dock strike in Bristol, the van-drivers were not organized. As a result he became the Chairman of the Carmen's Branch of the Dockers' Union. By the outbreak of the Great War he was one of his union's three national organizers. Even from this early stage he demonstrated great self-confidence, even egotism, and considerable negotiating ability.

In these years the great formative influences of his life were established. First, he developed an unshakable sense of identification with the working class, "my people" as he called them. He was an ardent Socialist although he always saw his people as individuals rather than a class. In contrast to the intellectuals of the Socialist movement, of whom he had a generally low opinion, his aims were practical: decent living standards, fair wages, and improved conditions of work. This close identification with ordinary men and women formed the guiding principle of his career and was strongly reflected in his foreign policy. Second, as for many others, the nursery of his Socialism was the chapel. His mother had been a staunch Nonconformist; Bevin was baptized in 1902 and, in later years, he described himself to Truman as "a bush Baptist". In 1907 he had written in his Bible: "This evening Sept 18th 1907 I have resolved By the Grace of God to serve him where ever he may call me. May God keep me and guard me till he shall call me home".[86] Third, he came to benefit from a stable and happy family life, for it was in this period that he married Florence (Flo) Townley.

Bevin's trade union career was immensely distinguished: he travelled widely; he developed remarkable skills in negotiation and advocacy; he moved among the powerful. Largely as a result of his efforts, not least in the financial field, the *Daily Herald* became a significant and influential daily paper.

In November, 1919, he wrote: "The first and most important thing is to stir, enlighten, organize the minds of the people. Physical poverty will remain as long as there is mental poverty".[86] Characteristically, he referred to the *Herald* as "my paper". It was Bevin who created the Transport and General Workers' Union by merging, in the first instance, fourteen unions and 300,000 workers. He became its first General Secretary in January, 1922. By 1939 he had made it the largest union in the world. His role in the General Strike was highly significant and he himself learned the lesson that future advance lay in negotiating from strength rather than by public confrontation and conflict. In 1930 he was appointed to the Macmillan Committee on finance and industry. Thenceforward, although in the same year he declined a peerage, his role became more actively political. As for international affairs, he very quickly saw the dangers of Nazism and, as he had in the Great War, strongly opposed pacifism. His election in 1936 as President of the Trades Union Congress was, for him, the zenith of his career. He looked forward to retirement at sixty and to family life in the country. Yet his greatest days still lay ahead.

In May, 1940, Churchill appointed Bevin Minister of Labour and National Service. A parliamentary seat was found for him at Central Wandsworth. In the following October he joined the War Cabinet. Only three other men (Churchill himself, Attlee and Sir John Anderson) held continuous membership from this time until the end of the wartime coalition. Bevin's achievement was to organize the nation for total war. "The work he did in mobilizing the manpower and the industrial resources of the country could have been done with equal efficiency, sane judgement and resolute purpose by no other man."[87] When he took over there were still one million unemployed; by September, 1943, nearly twenty-three million men and women were serving in the armed forces, civil defence and industry. With energy, imagination and, once again, superb negotiating skills, he wrought a complete transformation unmatched by the dictatorships. There was very little industrial unrest; stoppages were reduced to less than one hour per worker per year. "His role in the organization of victory was second only to that of Churchill."[88]

In appearance, manner and voice Bevin did not abandon his working-class roots. This was never more clear than when he was called upon to speak at a conference or public meeting. His progress to the platform, with rolling gait and thick-soled boots, was a prelude to a speech in a low, somewhat harsh voice, with a West Country burr. He had scant regard for aitches or for the difference between singular and plural. His big shoulders and broad hands bore testimony to his years of manual labour. To the delight of his fellow-countrymen and Foreign Office staff he stubbornly misprounounced foreign names: the Italian foreign minister, Count Sforza, was "that man Storzer"; Bidault, his French colleague, was rendered as Bidet or Biddle; Molotov, to the Russian's anger and irritation, became Mowlotov. Nevertheless, Bevin's lack of formal education gave him distinct advantages; he shunned the intellectual game of playing with ideas and was able to go straight to the heart of things and establish main principles. His use of anecdote and real-life experience was always illuminating. In explaining the importance of a psychological understanding of people, he told the following story. "For instance, if I wanted to get the busmen to agree to something, I'd never approach them when they were tired and hungry. You'd only get turned down. I'd just wait till they'd had their dinner and were feeling better. Then nine times out of ten they'd listen."[89] Bevin is the subject of innumerable anecdotes as well as a source of them. It would be a mistake, however, to see him as just an earthy, rather simple man. He was subtle, complicated, highly creative and a very serious politician. Oliver Franks[90] said that Bevin "was a big man doing a big job which he took with great seriousness and thought about all the time".[91] Attlee said that he had "never met a man in politics with as much imagination as he had, with the exception of Winston".[92] This judgement is exemplified by Bevin's brilliant initiative in seizing the opportunity presented by Marshall's Harvard speech in June, 1947. Hardly less imaginative was his contribution to the Colombo Plan.

Bevin excelled chiefly as a careful and patient negotiator. Even when he became resigned to failure in maintaining the wartime co-operation with Russia, he continued to talk and to hope. One reason for his support of Marshall Aid was the possibility that he might be able to include the Russians and their satellites. His optimism had a special cheerfulness, as when departing from the Foreign Office for yet another session with the Russians he would say: "If peace breaks out anywhere, I'll give you a ring".[93] His bargaining skill was all the more remarkable when it is realized that the cards he held were often poor. It was a position he had been in before, in his trade union days. A major reason for his success in his dealings with foreign countries was his integrity and reliability. Having given his word he never went back on it. In February, 1946, Secretary of State Byrnes "gave it as his opinion that we could not be in the position of doubting the good faith of Britain . . . he said that Bevin had lived up completely to his agreements—he had debated vigorously and sometimes harshly before entering into them, but having once committed himself he would carry out his contracts to the full".[94] His courage and doggedness were also admired. In January, 1950, although very ill, he insisted upon flying to Colombo for the crucial meeting of the Commonwealth Foreign Ministers. The risk to his life was very serious and he knew it.

As a result of his trade union experience Bevin rated loyalty above almost any other quality. He gave it and expected it. On the other hand he possessed a highly developed suspiciousness, when, for example, dealing with his own Labour left-wingers. At a Labour Party celebration of its 1945 election victory Bevin fixed Kingsley Martin[95] with a piercing look. "'Ullo gloomy," he said loudly, "I'll give you about three weeks before you stab us all in the back."[96] He tended to believe that those who were not for him were against him, but although Bevin might trample opponents he did not stick a knife in their backs.

Like all the great Foreign Secretaries, Bevin worked prodigiously hard. Not only did he face as serious and complex a set of problems as any of his predecessors but he also suffered from the pressures and disadvantages of modern communications. When Eden took over from Morrison in October, 1951, he said that the work had doubled since pre-war days.[97] Bevin was also a key member of the Cabinet and of the Labour Party.

As a member of the War Cabinet Bevin was already well informed in the field of foreign affairs. Once arrived in the Foreign Office he impressed his officials by his ability to soak up information and by his diligence in dealing with his boxes. He took time to make up his mind and would not be rushed. There were some ideas which emerged only after weeks, months, or even years, of rumination. A poor sleeper, Bevin was often up by five. He then did three hours' work on papers, annotating them with brief observations or instructions. By the time he arrived at the Office, at about 10 a.m., he had a clear view of the day ahead. In departmental conferences he provoked argument and debate; Dean Acheson[98] observed that he could "lead and learn at the same time".[99]

Although a physically strong man, Bevin's exacting métier and lifestyle seriously undermined his health. He was overweight (at one time he was urged to lose three stone), overate, slept badly and smoked and drank heavily. His preferences were whisky, brandy and champagne. According to one of his secretaries he used alcohol like a car uses petrol, to keep himself running. His doctor, Alexander McCall, whom Bevin rightly suspected of watering his whisky, was in constant attendance during the last phase of Bevin's Foreign Secretaryship. When McCall first examined Bevin in 1943 he diagnosed angina pectoris, cardiac failure, arterio-sclerosis, sinusitis, enlarged liver, damaged kidneys and high blood pressure. McCall was introduced to George VI as follows: "This is Alec. 'E treats me be'ind like a dartboard".[100]

Bevin was at something of a disadvantage in the Commons since he came to it late. He had unsuccessfully contested Central Bristol in 1918 and Gateshead in 1931. It was not until 1940, aged sixty, that he was first elected. He had served no apprenticeship as a bankbencher; he came straight to the government front bench. From the Labour Party's point of view it was regarded as a disadvantage that he had not experienced the baptismal fire of opposition. Henderson had been in the Commons for twenty-six years before he became Foreign Secretary. But Bevin's "transparent integrity and dogged determination were so manifest that he never lost the attention of the House".[101]

Bevin's principal difficulties came from the left of his own party—Michael Foot,[102] Richard Crossman[103] and Konni Zilliacus[104] from inside the House, Harold Laski[105] and Kingsley Martin outside. The Labour Left expected a radical change in foreign policy—a "socialist policy"—and were disappointed. They were in a minority but were nevertheless significant in numbers, determined and vociferous. There was a constant barrage of criticism of foreign policy and defence policies. Bevin was the main target. It was not only policy that was criticized. There was also a demand for a purge of the Foreign Office, which for many Labour supporters was dominated by upper-class guardians of a highly conservative set of policies. One Labour back bencher asked: "Are the present diplomats with their present outlook to carry on the policy in Europe, or are we going to have diplomats with a Labour and Socialist outlook?"[106] Bevin refused to make changes along party political lines and appointed career diplomats. Cadogan, the son of an earl and Permanent Under-Secretary since 1938, expected to be asked to retire. Instead, Bevin specifically asked him to stay on. The Left's attacks on Bevin were particularly intense in his first two years as Foreign Secretary and came to a head with the publication of *Keep Left* in April, 1947. After this, especially as the menace of Russia became clearer, Labour Party and public opinion ran more strongly in the Foreign Secretary's favour. Nevertheless, the Left never entirely gave up.

Throughout these trials Bevin was sustained by his Prime Minister, Attlee. The contrasts between them were striking. Attlee was impeccably middle-class, public school and Oxford; small in stature, modest and self-effacing. Bevin was working-class, physically big and rough-hewn, egotistical and passionate. Cadogan noticed that "at Big 3 meetings (Bevin) does all the talking while Attlee nods his head convulsively and smokes his pipe".[107]

Although originally Attlee had considered Bevin for the Treasury and Dalton for the Foreign Office, in the end he reversed his choice. He had already decided that Morrison would be Lord President with an overall responsibility for domestic affairs. Since there was personal antagonism between Morrison and Bevin they were kept apart. Moreover, Attlee feared that the Russians would be unco-operative and that Bevin was, temperamentally, the better man to deal with them. Encouraged by George VI, Attlee appointed a heavy tank rather than a sniper.[108]

Bevin was intensely loyal to Attlee. He regarded him as one of the few men in politics who could be depended upon to keep his word. In the challenges to Attlee's leadership in 1945 and 1947, Bevin's loyalty and unshakable position as the embodiment of British trade unionism won the day. On a personal level there was mutual respect and affection between the two men. On the political side, in regularly keeping Bevin behind after Cabinet meetings, Attlee almost created an inner Cabinet of two. In return for his loyalty, "Attlee gave Bevin more of a free hand in foreign policy—even when he disagreed with him, as over the Middle East—than any other Prime Minister this century".[109]

Bevin's relations with his Prime Minister were paralleled in the spirit of loyalty and co-operation which reigned in his own department. With his trade union and negotiating experience it is not surprising that Bevin's man-management in the Foreign Office was excellent. He showed an interest in and concern for his staff at all levels. It was he, for example, who provided glass partitions at the Park Door entrance to the Foreign Office so that the office-keepers and messengers might be protected from the rigours of winter.[110] To celebrate his seventieth birthday the staff of the office, regardless of rank or salary, contributed 6d per head for a tea-party and presentation of a desk and dinner-service. Compared with Eden, whose staff found him touchy, Bevin was patient and considerate. Although capable of fits of anger, he soon got over them. It was almost as though the Foreign Office had a General Secretary rather than a Secretary of State. Indeed, in some ways Bevin treated the department rather like a union. When Bevin informed Sir Archibald Clark Kerr that he was to be appointed to Washington, the new ambassador was unable to conceal his pleasure. "Ah, Archie," said Bevin, "I know you want the job, but you needn't think you're the best man for it. What you are is a member of the Union and I'm the General Secretary. So you're going to get it".[111]

Bevin's team at the Foreign Office was immensely strong. Besides Cadogan and Sargent he had William Strang, Ivone Kirkpatrick,[112] Oliver Franks, Edmund Hall-Patch,[113] Roger Makins[114] and Gladwyn Jebb.[115] Jebb very quickly gained the confidence of the Foreign Secretary. On being summoned into Bevin's office Jebb was greeted with the remark: "Must be kinda queer for a chap like you to see a chap like me sitting in a chair like this?" When Jebb did not reply Bevin, scowling, went on: "Ain't never 'appened before in 'istory". Jebb thought that he could not let this go and, on the spur of the moment, replied: "Secretary of State, I am sorry that for the first time I open my mouth in your presence it is to contradict you. But you're wrong. It has." "What do you mean, young man?" answered Bevin. "Well," said Jebb "it was a long time ago—rather more than four hundred years I think. But there was then a butcher's boy in Ipswich whose origins, I suspect, were just as humble as your own, and he became Foreign Secretary to one of our greatest kings. And for that matter, a Cardinal too. His name was Tom Wolsey. And incidentally, now I come to think of it, he was not unlike you physically." Bevin was visibly impressed and pleased.

Bevin himself had a sense of history, especially concerning the Foreign Office itself. He made frequent references to "Old Palmerston" and "Old Salisbury" and the fact the he was familiar with their papers helps to confound the myth that he read very little. In November, 1946, when under attack from the Labour Left, he complained: "Ain't nothing like this been heard of since the days of Castlereagh". On more than one occasion he pondered: "I wonder what Lord Curzon would do if he was in my shoes".[116]

One fear felt by the Left, especially in the early days of the Labour government, was that ministers, including Bevin, would be run by their departmental professionals. To counter such influence it was held that ministers should direct their departments in all things, even if it meant making new, political, appointments. Bevin was neither cipher nor dictator. Nor should he be seen as simply the representative of his department in Cabinet, acting as a means by which the advice of civil servants is made known to the Cabinet. Yet another model is the one which "makes the Foreign Secretary the originator of policy and the principal spokesman on foreign affairs in both Cabinet and Parliament. There is no doubt that this was the case with Bevin, and he stands as the last of the line of foreign secretaries in the tradition created by Castlereagh, Canning and Palmerston in the first half of the 19th century, with Salisbury, Grey and Austen Chamberlain as his predecessors in the 20th century and (thanks to the reduction in British power) with no successors".[117] As with most successful Foreign Secretaries in the twentieth century there was a fruitful interaction between Bevin and his department. He sought advice from officials; he allowed it to influence him but he made his own decisions and formulated his own policy. If the Foreign Office did not run its Secretary of State, it at least had the inestimable benefit of a chief who was a powerful member of the Cabinet, in close working harmony with the Prime Minister and with enormous political influence.

Bevin's most difficult period as Foreign Secretary was from his taking up of the office until Spring, 1947. Try as he might, he was frustrated by the increasing intransigence of the Russians and the uncertain stance of the Americans. Britain itself faced grave, even crippling, economic problems which hamstrung her role in international affairs. Bevin himself was castigated by the Left. Most of his great achievements were crowded into the next three years: eliciting the response known as the Truman Doctrine; seizing the opportunity of Marshall Aid; negotiating the Brussels Treaty and NATO; beating the Berlin Blockade; attending and inspiring the Colombo Conference. This period also contained his greatest failure, Palestine. After the general election of February, 1950, the Labour government, with a drastically reduced majority and running out of steam, had to fight for its life. Bevin himself, although, his mental powers were largely unaffected, was very ill. The most important international test, the Korean War, was less subject to his influence than those European and transatlantic events in which he had triumphed.

Bevin's basic aims were relatively simple. When a foreign diplomat asked him his chief objective, he replied: "Just to be able to go down to Victoria Station and take a ticket to where the hell I like without a passport".[118] In this fashion he declared his commitment to the interests of the common man on the one hand and of internationalism on the other. He saw his foreign policy as being concerned with the interests of working people throughout the world; he aimed to support "peasants not pashas".[119] The North Atlantic Treaty would enable ordinary people "to sleep safely in their beds".[120]

His distrust of Communists was of long standing; he had had to deal with them and fellow-travellers in his own trade union movement. Even at an early stage of the Soviet experiment he had not liked what he saw; Stalin's régime was a cruel tyranny and as damaging to human rights and dignity as any Right-wing dictatorship. In October, 1945, he spoke of a spiritual hunger in Europe but "if every country could get free parliaments and free expression without dictatorship or orders, and if people could express themselves freely on these problems, we might get a better world for the future than we have experienced in the last 25 years".[121]

As a result of his trade union background, and especially his work with the International Labour Office and the International Workers' Federation, Bevin had wide experience of international co-operation. His faith in the merits of such co-operation remained with him as Foreign Secretary. At the same time, he knew that it would be unrealistic to expect the new world organization of the United Nations, with the wide range of interests within it, to cope successfully with all the economic, social and political problems of the post-war world. Therefore he worked for the development of more regionalised international bodies such as OEEC and NATO. Learning from the failures of the League of Nations, he also appreciated that collective security could not be upheld unless Britain was prepared to play the role of a policeman. Such an approach did little to endear him to his own Left Wing.

Yet for all his internationalism Bevin, like Palmerston and Canning before him, was principally the upholder of the national interests of his own country. Although, perhaps for the first time, Britain had no territorial demands to make at the peace conferences, she still had wide concerns: in Europe; in the Mediterranean and Middle East; in her Empire and Commonwealth. Despite Britain's diminished power Bevin was determined that she should not surrender her world role or, at least, not until she had succeeded in involving the aid of the United States or in developing the necessary security organizations.

The verdict on Bevin of the Labour Home Secretary, James Chuter-Ede, was simple: "Was he the biggest man I met in the Labour Movement? He was the biggest man I met in any movement".[122] As Foreign Secretary he "played as decisive a part in shaping policy as any Foreign Minister in modern times".[123] His greatest achievements were connected with Marshall Aid and NATO. There were times when he "seemed to hold the Western world itself on his shoulders"[124] and the European stability which he helped to achieve has long survived his death. Far from burdening Britain with a world role which she could no longer support (a major criticism levelled against him), Bevin led the country into a new role, with realistic objectives and making a significant contribution to a new balance of power. By his refusal to retreat in the face of Soviet pressure he gained time for American eyes to be opened. With the economic and political involvement of the United States, in Europe particularly, he was able to develop the kind of positive foreign policy for which so much of his life's work had prepared him—the enhancement of prosperity and the human condition across the world.

Bevin had wanted to die in the Foreign Office.[125] It was not to be; his deteriorating health convinced Attlee that he should resign. In the course of his seventieth birthday celebrations in March, 1951, at the Foreign Office, he was called away to take a telephone call from the Prime Minister. Unaware of the occasion which the Foreign Secretary was enjoying, Attlee announced that a forthcoming Cabinet reshuffle would require Bevin's resignation. Bevin returned to the party to tell his wife, "I've got the sack".

There followed for Bevin a brief spell as Lord Privy Seal.[126] He died on 14th April while working on official papers. The key to his despatch box was clutched in his hand.

But it was on the day of his dismissal from the Foreign Office that his career really ended.[127] One of his staff said that he was the only person she had seen with a broken heart.


**NOTES TO CHAPTER SEVEN**

1  Avon. *Facing the Dictators.*

2  A. J. P. Taylor. *English History 1914–1945* (Oxford, 1965), p. 414.

3  W. S. Churchill. *The Second World War: The Gathering Storm* (London, 1948), p. 218.

4  Henlein's policy may be summarized as follows: "We must always demand so much that we can never be satisfied. The Führer approved this view". Alan Bullock, *Hitler: A Study in Tyranny* (Penguin, 1962), p. 443.

5  In a directive to the service chiefs on 3rd May, 1938, Hitler wrote: "It is my unalterable decision to smash Czechoslovakia by military action in the near future. It is the business of the political leadership to await or bring about the suitable moment from a political and military point of view". Quoted by Bullock, *Hitler*, p. 447.

6 Viscount Runciman. Liberal and, after 1931, Liberal National; President of Board of Trade 1914–16 and 1931–37; Lord President of the Council, 1939–39.

7 Quoted by M. Gilbert and R. Gott, *The Appeasers* (London, 1963), p. 180.

8 Quoted by Taylor, p. 441.

9 Vyacheslav Mikhailovich Molotov, Soviet Foreign Minister from May 1939 to March 1949 and again from Stalin's death in 1953 until 1956. In May 1939 he succeeded Maximilian Litvinov. It is significant that Litvinov was a Jew who would have been far less ready to make terms with the Nazis.

10 Taylor, p. 469.

11 W. N. Medlicott. *British Foreign Policy Since Versailles* (London, 1968), p. 240.

12 W. S. Churchill. *The Second World War: The Grand Alliance* (London, 1950), p. 332.

13 A report by the Nazi Ministry of Propaganda, in April 1943, that the bodies of thousands of Polish officers murdered by the Russians in 1940 had been buried at Katyn near Smolensk led the Polish government-in-exile to ask for an International Red Cross enquiry. Stalin broke relations with the Polish government-in-exile and blamed the Germans for the massacre.

14 Suggested in 1920 by Lloyd George (and subsequently handled by Curzon) as a settlement of the Russo-Polish frontier. It ran from Grodno through Brest-Litovsk and Przemysl to the Carpathians. It was rejected by the Poles but in 1939 was the basis of the Nazi–Soviet division of Poland.

15 Taylor, p. 588.

16 This formed the frontier between Poland and Germany being provisionally agreed at Yalta and conceded at Potsdam. The line followed the River Oder southwards from the Baltic to the River Neisse and then the Western Neisse to the Czechoslovakian frontier.

17 Taylor, p. 596.

18 Francis Williams. *Ernest Bevin* (London, 1952), p. 242.

19 Paul Kennedy. *The Realities Behind Diplomacy* (Fontana, 1981), p. 318.

20 See Kennedy, pp. 341–342.

21 Quoted by David Thomson, *Europe Since Napoleon* (Penguin, 1966), p. 823.

22 Dean Acheson was at that time Under-Secretary of State. He was later Secretary of State (1949–53). He was on close terms with Bevin who always called Acheson "me lad".

23 Quoted by Mark Stephens, *Ernest Bevin* (Transport and General Workers' Union, London, 1981), p. 116.

24 Alan Bullock. *Ernest Bevin: Foreign Secretary* (London, 1983), p. 672.

25 Bullock, p. 292.

26 Bullock, p. 295.

27 Quoted by David Carlton, *Anthony Eden* (London, 1981), p. 13; Michael Howard, *The Continental Commitment: The Dilemma of British Defence Policy In the Era of the Two World Wars* (London, 1972), p. 100. Eden and Duff Cooper both enjoy reputations as anti-appeasers. Duff Cooper resigned as First Lord of the Admiralty in October 1938 over Munich. He was the only Cabinet Minister to do so. Eden had departed in the previous February.

28 In a letter to Baldwin. Quoted by Carlton, p. 45.

29 *Facing the Dictators*, p. 61.

30  *Facing the Dictators*, pp. 76–77.

31  *Facing the Dictators*, p. 153.

32  Eden records that before his interview with Baldwin, offering him the post, he had been telephoned by Sir Maurice Hankey, Secretary to the Cabinet, to tell him that he was to be Foreign Secretary in the new Cabinet. In the meantime, however, Chamberlain had intervened and pressed the claims of Hoare. *Facing the Dictators*, p. 217.

33  Eden's account of his appointment is given in *Facing the Dictators*, pp. 315–317.

34  Alan Campbell-Jones. *Sir Anthony Eden: A Biography* (London, 1955), p. 175.

35  Quoted by Carlton, p. 109.

36  Carlton, p. 109.

37  *Facing the Dictators*, p. 318.

38  *Facing the Dictators*, p. 319.

39  The Earl of Halifax. *Fulness of Days* (London, 1957), p. 184.

40  *Facing the Dictators*, pp. 508–516.

41  Quoted by the Earl of Birkenhead, *The Life of Lord Halifax* (London, 1965), p. 371.

42  *Facing the Dictators*, p. 516.

43  *Facing the Dictators*, p. 421.

44  *Facing the Dictators*, p. 451.

45  Quoted by Carlton, p. 102.

46  Carlton, p. 124.

47  Eden wrote in his memoirs: "I had by this time (January 1936) occasionally used the word 'appeasement' in a speech or a minute for the Foreign Office in the sense of the first meaning given in the *Oxford English Dictionary*, 'to bring to peace, settle (strife, etc.)'. It was not until some years later, when the results of the foreign policy pursued by Mr Chamberlain became apparent, that the word was more strongly associated with the last meaning given in the dictionary, 'to pacify by satisfying demands'."—*Facing the Dictators*, p. 324.

48  Carlton, p. 79.

49  Taylor, p. 421.

50  *Facing the Dictators*, p. 445.

51  *Facing the Dictators*, p. 576.

52  Quoted by Carlton, p. 108.

53  Carlton, p. 119.

54  See Carlton, p. 127.

55  Chamberlain's diary. See Carlton, p. 127.

56  Quoted by Carlton, pp. 127–128.

57  *Facing the Dictators*, p. 486.

58  W. S. Churchill. *The Second World War: Their Finest Hour* (London, 1949), p. 505.

59  Earl of Avon. *The Eden Memoirs: The Reckoning* (London, 1965), p. 183.

60  See Medlicott, p. 240.

61  Churchill, *The Gathering Storm*, p. 231.

62  Churchill, *Their Finest Hour*, p. 505.

63  *Facing the Dictators*, p. 453.

64  Carlton, p. 243.

65 *The Reckoning*, p. 449.

66 Campbell Johnson, pp. 175.

67 See *The Reckoning*, pp. 257–258.

68 *The Reckoning*, p. 550.

69 Birkenhead, p. 607.

70 *D.N.B.*

71 Quoted by Birkenhead, p. 417.

72 Birkenhead, p. 417.

73 Halifax, p. 216.

74 Quoted by Birkenhead, p. 354.

75 Sir Horace Rumbold. Among a number of senior diplomatic posts he held the ambassadorship in Berlin 1928–33. An outspoken opponent of appeasement.

76 Quoted by Birkenhead, p. 429.

77 Halifax, p. 200.

78 Nicholas Henderson. *The Private Office* (London, 1984), p. 21.

79 Francis Williams, p. 244.

80 Sir Orme Sargent (1884–1962). Entered Diplomatic Service 1906; 1919–25 in Paris attached to Ambassadors' Conference; 1925 transferred to Foreign Office. Assistant Under-Secretary 1933; Deputy Under-Secretary 1939; Permanent Under-Secretary 1946–49. Known as "Moley".

81 Bullock, pp. 75, 108.

82 Henderson, p. 22.

83 *D.N.B.*

84 Stephens, p. 127–128.

85 Stephens, p. 15.

86 Stephens, p. 34.

87 *The Manchester Guardian*, quoted in *D.N.B.*

88 Alan Bullock. "Ernest Bevin, Foreign Secretary" *in The Listener*, 14th October 1982, p. 10.

89 Henderson, p. 24.

90 Oliver Franks (Baron, 1962). After an academic career became a temporary civil servant in the Ministry of Supply 1939–46. Ambassador to Washington 1948–52.

91 Bullock, p. 109.

92 Bullock, p. 85.

93 Stephens, p. 121.

94 Bullock, pp. 94–95.

95 Basil Kingsley Martin. Conscientious objector in the First World War. Assistant Lecturer in politics at the London School of Economics 1924. Friend of Harold Laski. Leader Writer on *Manchester Guardian*, 1927; Editor of *New Statesman* 1931–60.

96 Bullock, p. 92.

97 Herbert Morrison. *An Autobiography* (London, 1960), p. 273.

98 Dean Acheson said of Bevin: "His indomitable courage, his simplicity and directness, his love of his country and his understanding of the grandeur of its contribution to the cause of human liberty, his humanity and knowledge of the struggles and aspiration of his

fellow-men, his own warm affectionate good humour made him both loved and trusted. All of us to whom freedom and liberty are the foundation of our lives will stand in gratitude and joy that in these times such a man has lived". (Quoted by Stephens, pp. 135–136).

99  Quoted by Bullock, p. 99.

100  Bullock, p. 288.

101  Lord Kilmuir. *Political Adventure* (London, 1964), p. 146.

102  Michael Foot: MP for Devonport 1945–55; Editor of *Tribune* 1948–52; political columnist for the *Daily Herald* 1944–64; Secretary of State for Employment 1974–76; Leader of the House of Commons 1976–79; Deputy Leader of the Labour Party 1976–80; and Leader 1980–83.

103  Richard Crossman: Assistant Editor of the *New Statesman* 1938–55; elected M.P. for Coventry East 1945; Minister for Housing and Local Government 1964–66; Leader of the House of Commons 1966–68; Secretary of State for Social Services 1968–70; Editor of the *New Statesman* 1970–72.

104  Konni Zilliacus: Royal Flying Corps in First World War; wrote extensively on League of Nations affairs: M.P. for Gateshead 1945–50; expelled from the Labour Party in May 1949 for presistent opposition to the Government's foreign policy.

105  Harold Laski: worked briefly on the *Daily Herald*, 1914; appointed lecturer at the London School of Economics 1920; and Professor of Political Science in 1926 (until his death in 1950); associated with Victor Gollancz in Left Book Club; Chairman of the Labour Party in 1945.

106  Quoted by Bullock, p. 73.

107  Quoted by Henderson, p. 23.

108  Stephens, p. 108.

109  *The Listener* 14th October 1982, p. 10.

110  See Henderson, p. 25.

111  See Bullock, p. 100.

112  Sir Ivone Kirkpatrick: entered the Diplomatic Service 1919; transferred to Foreign Office 1920; various posts in Rome, the Vatican and Berlin in the 1930s; appointed Director of the Foreign Division of the Ministry of Information 1940; Controller (European Services) B.B.C. 1941; Assistant Under-Secretary at the Foreign Office 1945; Deputy Under-Secretary 1948; Permanent Under-Secretary (German Section), 1949; United Kingdom High Commissioner for Germany 1950–53; Permanent Under-Secretary at the Foreign Office 1953–57.

113  Sir Edmund Hall-Patch: Assistant Secretary to the Treasury 1935–44; Assistant Under-Secretary at the Foreign Office 1944–46; Deputy Under-Secretary, 1946–48; Chairman of the Executive Committee of the Organization for European Economic Co-operation with rank of ambassador, then Permanent United Kingdom Representative on OEEC.

114  Sir Roger Makins: Assistant Under-Secretary at the Foreign Office 1947; Deputy Under-Secretary 1948; appointed Ambassador to Washington 1952. It was he who coined the term "The Caber" for Bevin's outsize fountain pen.

115  Gladwyn Jebb, created Baron Gladwyn, was at that time a senior Deputy Under-Secretary at the Foreign Office and was later United Kingdom Permanent Representative to the United Nations. The anecdote quoted here may be found in Lord Gladwyn, *The Memoirs of Lord Gladwyn* (London, 1972), p. 175.

116  Bullock, pp. 88–89.

117  Bullock, p. 75.

118  Francis Williams, p. 245.

119  Stephens, p. 127.

120  Stephens, p. 117.

121  House of Commons, 26th October 1945, quoted by Bullock, p. 10.

122  Quoted by Bullock, p. 93.

123  Bullock, p. 102.

124  Lord George Brown. *In My Way, Political Memoirs* (London, 1971), p. 237.

125  See Hugh Dalton, *High Tide and After* (London, 1962), p. 359.

126  On being appointed, Bevin remarked: "I am neither a Lord, nor a privy, nor a seal". See Stephens, p. 123.

127  Giving up the Foreign Office was made even harder for Bevin by Morrison being appointed to succeed him. "He's enjoying himself now", said Bevin, "but let him wait a month or two. It'll be different then". See Bullock, p. 834.

# Postscript

IT IS fitting that this study should close with the resignation of Bevin. As Castlereagh's acceptance of the Foreign Office represented a milestone in the rise of the Foreign Secretaryship, so Bevin's departure marked a stage in its decline. With the partial exception of Eden no Foreign Secretary since Bevin has approached him in stature or influence. Three factors help to explain this: Britain's diminished authority and power; the Foreign Secretaries themselves and their generally short periods in office; and the role and methods of their Prime Ministers.

The economic ruin inflicted upon Britain by the Second World War made it impossible for her to regain her former status or to compete with the Super Powers of the United States and Soviet Russia. Since the war the United States has been the chief bulwark of Europe's military defence, while the most significant economic and political framework has been provided by the Treaty of Rome. Britain no longer provides the balance of power on the Continent. More widely, Britain has divested herself of vast territories, chiefly in Asia and Africa. In post-war conflict, it is significant that in Korea Britain provided but two infantry brigades, one armoured division, two R.A.F. squadrons and her Far Eastern fleet. Her casualties were 4,286 compared with the Americans' 142,000. "For the first time since the Thirty Years War, a major international conflict had arisen in which Britain was too weak to play any significant part."* The Suez débâcle demonstrated a further stage in her decline as a world power.

The Foreign Office has had fifteen different incumbents in the thirty-five years since Bevin's resignation. Few have held the office for long enough to have made a real mark. With the exception of Eden, Selwyn Lloyd and Home, no one since Bevin has been Foreign Secretary for more than three consecutive years. Even these periods of office seem brief in comparison with those of Castlereagh, Palmerston and Grey. Although Eden and Home enjoyed substantial tenures, others who later became Prime Ministers were at the Foreign Office only briefly: Macmillan for a few months, Callaghan for little more than a year. It is interesting, too, to reflect on the watershed of Eden's being the only post-Bevin Foreign

*See L. C. B. Seaman, *Post-Victorian Britain* (London, 1966), p. 486–488.

Secretary to have sat in a wartime or pre-war Cabinet. Besides Eden and Home, Michael Stewart is the only man since the war to have returned to the Foreign Office. Other Foreign Secretaries have had their period of office cut short by electoral defeat for their parties (Morrison, Butler and Owen), by political or personal differences with their Prime Ministers (Brown and Pym) or by premature death (Crosland). Lord Carrington resigned, it might be said, at the height of his powers.Meanwhile, the Foreign Office has lost its monopoly of dealing with foreign governments. As a result of Britain's membership of international organizations such as N.A.T.O., E.E.C. and I.M.F., other Departments of State have significant international responsibilities.

Eden complained of Chamberlain's and Churchill's interference in Foreign Office affairs but as Prime Minister he too interfered. Over the past thirty years, as Prime Ministers have cultivated a presidential role and basked in the glare of international publicity, so the office of Foreign Secretary has been further weakened. In their particular ways Macmillan, Wilson and Mrs Thatcher have all sought to influence foreign policy in a way that Liverpool, Melbourne, Asquith, Baldwin and Attlee never attempted. Thus Castlereagh, Palmerston, Grey, Austen Chamberlain and Bevin flourished while their modern successors in the office have been diminished.

# Bibliography

Paul Adelmann. *Gladstone, Disraeli and later Victorian Politics* (London, 1970).

L. S. Amery. *My Political Life,* 3 Vols. (London, 1953–57).

M. S. Anderson. *The Eastern Question, 1774–1923* (London, 1966).

C. M. Andrew. *The Entente Cordiale from its Origins to 1914* in Neville Waites (ed.), *Troubled Neighbours: Franco British Relations in the Twentieth Century* (London, 1971).

Earl of Avon. *The Eden Memoirs: Full Circle* (London, 1960).

Earl of Avon. *The Eden Memoirs: Facing the Dictators* (London, 1962).

Earl of Avon. *The Eden Memoirs: The Reckoning* (London, 1965).

Sir Roderick Barclay. *Ernest Bevin and the Foreign Office* (London, 1975).

C. J. Bartlett. *Castlereagh* (London, 1966).

Earl of Birkenhead. *The Life of Lord Halifax* (London, 1965).

Kenneth Bourne. *The Foreign Policy of Victorian England, 1830–1902* (Oxford, 1970).

Lord George Brown. *In my Way, Political Memoirs* (London, 1971).

Alan Bullock. *Hitler: A Study in Tyranny* (Penguin edition, London, 1962).

Alan Bullock. *Ernest Bevin: Foreign Secretary* (London, 1983).

Alan Campbell-Johnson. *Viscount Halifax* (London, 1941).

Alan Campbell-Johnson. *Sir Anthony Eden* (London, 1955).

David Carlton. *Anthony Eden* (London, 1981).

Algergon Cecil. *British Foreign Secretaries, 1807—1916* (Edinburgh, 1927).

Lady Gwendolen Cecil. *Life of Robert Marquis of Salisbury,* 4 Vols. (London, 1921–32).

M. E. Chamberlain. *British Foreign Policy in the Age of Palmerston* (London, 1980).

Winston S. Churchill. *The Second World War,* 6 Vols. (London, 1948–1954).

G. D. Clayton. *Britain and the Eastern Question: Missolonghi to Gallipoli* (London, 1971).

Valerie Cromwell. *The Foreign and Commonwealth Office* in Zara Steiner (ed.), *Times Survey of Foreign Ministries of the World* (Times Books, 1983).

J. A. Cross. *Sir Samuel Hoare: A Political Biography* (London, 1977).

Hugh Dalton. *The Fateful Years: Memoirs* (London, 1957).

Hugh Dalton. *High Tide and After* (London, 1962).

J. W. Derry. *Charles James Fox* (London, 1972).

J. W. Derry. *Castlereagh* (London, 1976).

*Dictionary of National Biography.*

B. E. C. Dugdale. *A. J. Balfour* (London, 1936).

Max Egremont. *Balfour* (London, 1980).

R. C. K. Ensor. *England 1870–1914* (Oxford, 1936).

M. D. R. Foot. *British Foreign Policy Since 1898* (London, 1956).

Lord Edmund Fitzmaurice. *Life of Granville* (London, 1905).

Martin Gilbert. *Britain and Germany Between the Wars* (London, 1964).

Martin Gilbert and Richard Gott. *The Appeasers* (London, 1963).

Lord Gladwyn. *The Memoirs of Lord Gladwyn* (London, 1972).

J. A. S. Grenville. *Lord Salisbury and Foreign Policy* (London, 1964).

Viscount Grey of Falloden. *Twenty-Five Years, 1982–1916* (London, 1925).

P. Guedalla. *Palmerston* (London, 1926).

Lord Halifax. *Fullness of Days* (London, 1957).

Mary Agnes Hamilton. *Arthur Henderson* (London, 1938).

Paul Hayes. *Modern British Foreign Policy: The Nineteenth Century 1814–80* (London, 1975).

Paul Hayes. *Modern British Foreign Policy: The Twentieth Century 1880–1939* (London, 1978).

Nicholas Henderson. *The Private Office* (London, 1984).

Sir E. Hertslet. *Recollections of the Old Foreign Office* (London, 1901).

Wendy Hinde. *George Canning* (London, 1973).

Wendy Hinde. *Castlereagh* (London, 1981).

F. H. Hinsley, ed. *British Foreign Policy under Sir Edward Grey* (Cambridge, 1977).

D. B. Horn. *The British Diplomatic Service, 1689–1789* (Oxford, 1961).

D. B. Horn. *Great Britain and Europe in the Eighteenth Century* (Oxford, 1967).

H. Montgomery Hyde. *Lord Reading* (London, 1967).

Robert Rhodes James. *Rosebery* (London, 1963).

Robert Rhodes James. *The British Revolution Vol. II.* (London, 1977).

Ray Jones. *The Nineteenth Century Foreign Office* (London, 1971).

Denis Judd. *Palmerston* (London, 1975).

Paul Kennedy. *The Realities Behind Diplomacy: Background Influences on British External Policy, 1865–1980* (London, 1981).

Lord Kilmuir. *Political Adventure* (London, 1964).

Paul Langford. *Modern British Foreign Policy: the Eighteenth Century, 1688–1815* (London, 1976).

David Lloyd George. *The War Memoirs of David Lloyd George* (London, 1938).

John P. Mackintosh. *The British Cabinet* (London, 1976).

John P. Mackintosh, ed. *The British Prime Ministers* (London, 1977).

A. J. Marcham. *Foreign Policy* (London, 1973).

David Marquand. *Ramsay MacDonald* (London, 1977).

W. N. Medlicott. *British Foreign Policy Since Versailles 1919–1963* (London, 1968).

Keith Middlemas and John Barnes. *Baldwin* (London, 1969).

C. R. Middleton. *The Administration of British Foreign Policy, 1782–1846* (Duke University Press, 1977).

G. W. Monger. *The End of Isolation: British Foreign Policy, 1900–1907* (London, 1963).

Kenneth O. Morgan. *Lloyd George* (London, 1963).

M. C. Morgan. *Foreign Affairs 1886–1914* (London, 1973).

Lord Morrison. *An Autobiography* (London, 1950).

Leonard Mosley. *Curzon: The End of an Epoch* (London, 1960).

C. L. Mowat. *Britain Between the Wars* (London, 1955).

Lord Newton. *Lord Lansdowne* (London, 1929).

Harold Nicholson. *Curzon: The Last Phase* (London, 1934).

Frank Owen. *Tempestuous Journey: Lloyd George His Life and Times* (London, 1954).

L. Penson. *Foreign Affairs under the Third Marquess of Salisbury* (London, 1962).

Sir Charles Petrie. *The Life and Letters of Sir Austen Chamberlain* (London, 1940).

Sir Charles Petrie. *Canning* (London, 1946).

Marquess of Reading. *Rufus Isaacs* (London, 1945).

Jasper Ridley. *Lord Palmerston* (Panther edition, London, 1972).

Keith Robbins. *Sir Edward Grey* (London, 1971).

P. V J. Rolo. *George Canning* (London, 1965).

Norman Rose. *Vansittart: Story of a Diplomat* (London, 1978).

Howard Morley Sachar. *The Course of Modern Jewish History* (New York, 1958).

Viscount Simon. *Retrospect* (London, 1952).

Donald Southgate. *The Passing of the Whigs* (London, 1962).

Zara Steiner. *The Foreign Office and Foreign Policy* (Cambridge 1969).

Mark Stephens. *Unskilled Labourer and World Statesman: A Portrait of Ernest Bevin 1881–1951* (London, 1981).

Lord Strang. *The Foreign Office* (London, 1955).

A. J. P. Taylor. *English History 1914–1945* (Oxford, 1965).

A. J. P. Taylor. *The Struggle for Mastery in Europe* (Oxford, 1954).

Robert Taylor. *Lord Salisbury* (London, 1975).

H. M. V. Temperley and L. M. Penson, eds. *Foundations of British Foreign Policy from Pitt to Salisbury* (Cambridge, 1938).

H. M. V. Temperley. *The Foreign Policy of Canning* (London, 1966).

Viscount Templewood. *Nine Troubled Years* (London, 1954).

David Thomson. *Europe Since Napoleon* (Penguin edition, London 1966).

Sir John Tilley and Stephen Gaselee. *The Foreign Office* (London, 1933).

G. M. Trevelyan. *Grey of Falloden* (London, 1937).

Lord Vansittart. *The Mist Procession* (London, 1958).

S. Walpole. *Life of Lord John Russell* (London, 1889).

D. R. Ward. *Foreign Affairs 1815–1865* (London, 1972).

A. W. Ward and G. P. Gooch, eds. *The Cambridge History of Foreign Policy* (Cambridge, 1922).

R. W. Seton Watson. *Britain in Europe, 1789–1914* (Cambridge, 1937).

J. Steven Watson. *The Reign of George III, 1769–1815* (Oxford, 1960).

Sir C. Webster. *The Foreign Policy of Castlereagh, 1815—22* (London, 1934).

Sir C. Webster. *The Foreign Policy of Lord Palmerston* (London, 1951).

Sir C. Webster. *The Art and Practice of Diplomacy* (London, 1961).
Francis Williams. *Ernest Bevin* (London, 1952).
Kenneth Young. *Arthur James Balfour* (London, 1963).
Sydney H. Zebel. *Balfour* (Cambridge, 1973).

# Index